BALLIOL COLLEGE
OXFORD

In memory of

Lord Thomas Bingham

(1933 - 2010)

PRESENTED BY
LADY ELIZABETH BINGHAM

TRADITION AND EUROPEANIZATION IN ITALIAN LAW

TRADITION AND EUROPEANIZATION IN ITALIAN LAW

GUIDO ALPA

BIICL
British Institute of
International and
Comparative Law
www.biicl.org

Published and Distributed by
The British Institute of International and Comparative Law
Charles Clore House, 17 Russell Square, London WC1B 5JP

British Library Cataloguing in Publication Data
A Catalogue record of this book is available from the British Library

ISBN 0–903067–48–X

Typeset by Cambrian Typesetters
Camberley, Surrey
Printed in Great Britain by Biddles Ltd
King's Lynn

FOREWORD

Professor Guido Alpa is well known and highly regarded in the United Kingdom as is evidenced by his election as a corresponding Fellow of the British Academy and as an Honorary Bencher of Gray's Inn. He supported the initiatives concerning the drafting of a model of a European Civil Code, on the law of contract and tort; he made a substantial contribution to the XXth Congress of the International Federation of European Law (FIDE) in London in 2002 as one of the General Rapporteurs. It is good therefore that his 'Tradition and Europeanization in Italian Law' has been made available in English since even if the principal concern of the book is Italian law, it goes into many matters of high relevance to the concepts underlying other national laws including English law and 'European law' in its widest sense.

He begins with an analysis of the underlying principles which have emerged in national law—particularly Italian law—and the way in which they, as found in the Napoleonic Code, the German Code and the Common Law, have found their way into European Community Law and he asks what are the respective roles of the legislature, 'the interpreter' and the judge in the development of these principles. In doing so he cites copiously from the philosophy and conclusions of jurists from Roman law through Pothier and Kant to Ronald Dworkin and he concludes that in the Italian experience 'the history of general principles is one of phases, and these phases normally occur in periods of crisis and renewal'.

From this scholarly beginning he moves into a detailed analysis of many aspects of the law which are of great contemporary importance—the concept of personal rights and in particular the right of privacy; the concept of tort and the scope of liability for nervous shock. He consider whether the embryo is a person, with reference to the Warnock Report, and whether a person 'has the right to be born healthy'.

But there is also much valuable discussion of commercially orientated matters—the underlying principle of contract law, Unidroit, arbitration, the notion of good faith in pre-contract negotiations, the impact of European Community Law through legislation. He deals with the EC Directive 93/13 on unfair contract terms in consumer contracts and proposals for the European Civil Code.

Then comes the way forward. Professor Alpa is much concerned with the development of an integrated legal system in Europe—a modern maybe different *ius commune*—and with the arguments for and against codification of the law. In detecting a change in the attitude of common lawyers to codification he says with apparent sympathy 'In his conclusion on future development of commercial law in the United Kingdom one of the most prestigious scholars of the subject, Professor Roy Goode looks forward to the arrival of internal codification of the rules in force today relating to economic transactions.' He adds that 'at the same time in the European countries with civil codes it would be naïve to pretend that there has been no case law which enlivens the written text, adds to it and corrects it' (p 172).

The book is thus a remarkable amalgam of comments on abstract concepts, a description or analysis of many very practical aspects of the law and a consideration of the methods by which European law should be developed. Law students will want to read it all. Fortunately there is a detailed table of contents for those with less time for wider contemplation but who need guidance on particular topics.

SLYNN OF HADLEY

CONTENTS

INTRODUCTION

The chapters of this book—some previously published in other books or journals—examine some of the most discussed aspects of the Italian legal system. They concern the sources and interpretation of law, the use of general clauses by judges, the circulation and legal transplants of rules, institutions, contractual models, the direct or indirect application of constitutional rules on the relationship between private parties and of European Community Law on the domestic member states' law, the projects on a European model code of contract law, the evolution of the values on which the Italian society is based and the challenges of globalization.

These subjects refer mainly to 'private law', a field that in Italy includes both civil and commercial law.

They register the tensions of all national systems, trying to adapt to the new demands dictated by the economy and the social and cultural changes. These changes are sometimes promoted or supported by jurists, other times they are imposed by the political process.

In the tradition and mentality of my country ideas of the law, as an autonomous system of technical rules, or as an expression of the political will of the majority, have lived together for at least two centuries. In the 17th and 18th centuries the principles of natural law spread, together with the Roman law heritage; during the 19th century codifications were introduced, but at the end of the 19th century the practical dimension of law broke off from the theoretical one and legal dogmatism and formalism established itself, and then in the 'short century' the system went through the fascist dictatorship, the new codification (of 1942), the advent of the Republic (in 1946), the new Constitution (in 1948), the entry in the European Community (in 1957) and then the penetration of European law into our national law.

The present book is a representation of Italian law as interlaced with other national laws and with the emerging principles of the European legal culture, proposed by highlights, as a cross-section of reality, problems of general nature and solution of particular questions. The book offers a representation without a general systematic approach, but a thematic one. The aim of the book is to inform the reader, who comes from a different legal culture and tradition, of some key-passages of the formation and present evolution of the Italian legal system which has still not parted with its past. Considered in its entirety, our system looks a very original one: many foreign jurists think that our system is a 'bad copy' of the French model, because the first Italian Civil Code had literally translated many articles of the *Code Napoléon*. But much before the introduction of the present Civil Code in 1942, the Italian model took a different course: on the text of the code, of French roots, a conceptual framework of Roman and German origin had been built. Pandectism with its rational qualities and its great burden of pure conceptualization had an extraordinary success in Italy and dominated the Italian legal culture even in the second half of the 20th century.

The Italian Civil Code of 1942—having been cleansed of all references to the old political regime which had implemented it—presents innovations that, even today, surprise with its modernity, its clarity and its precision. It would take too long to explain here how many solutions to practical problems, that French case law still has to identify and resolve, are solved by the provisions of the 'new' Italian Civil Code. Also the unification of the former Civil and Commercial Codes in one code—a solution followed in Europe by the Dutch Civil Code half a century later—has improved the coordination of the institutes and rules which govern the relationship between individuals.

Many foreign jurists think that Italian law is all codified. To the contrary, many areas of civil and commercial law are regulated outside the code, in special statutes and one here finds in the code only faint references or a frame of principles. This is particularly obvious in the areas relating to property and to certain contracts (as the lease, agrarian contracts, insurance, banking and financial law, employment law, competition law, etc.). The space left to the Civil Code had been so reduced that 30 years ago the idea that private law had undergone a process dismantling the codification was proposed.

Looking at its surface, Italian law could appear as a fundamentally written law, so in some sense inelastic, 'petrified', slow in its evolution, static in the construction of its rules. In reality there are entire areas of private law in which the rules are created by case law, as it happens in tort law.

The legal culture, what we call *dottrina*, has an enormous importance for the interpretation, the adaptation and the evolution of the system. It is difficult to imagine from abroad the immense production of the academics, who ceaselessly write books, commentaries, treaties, essays, notes of cases, and legal journals springing up in the market, filling library stacks in law firms and courts.

The impact of European law has been remarkable. New terms have been created in private law, institutes not previously provided for, complicated rules, general clauses difficult to adapt to the original fabric. But the reaction of the jurists has been positive. Consumer protection is mainly a product of European law and also banking, financial and competition law. In this respect we can say that the Italian private law has benefited by the membership of the European Union.

In trade practice many contractual models of American and English origin have been acquired; many financial operations are dealt by English law firms operating in Italy; very often the applicable law chosen by the parties is English law. This can explain the spreading of the English language and the interest for the English legal system. This is an interest which I also try to promote further in my courses of Civil law at the University of Rome 'La Sapienza' and of Anglo-American law at the University of Genoa, but also in my capacity as member of the Italian Bar Council since 1995 and President since 2004.

The evolution of the Italian private law bear witness to the 'gradual convergence' theory of Sir Basil Markesinis, the great scholar of comparative law and an old friend of mine I hold in the highest esteem. He created a new and original method which he called 'packaging'. In his last book *Comparative Law in the Courtroom and the Classroom*, which I have translated into Italian with Vanna Levi and Nello Pasquini (*Il metodo della comparazione. Il retaggio del passato e le sfide del futuro*, Giuffré Milan 2004) he splendidly clarified this method. I have also been able to test his method—and his patient intelligence—in a book that we, together with Michael Coester and Augustus Ullstein have just written (and under Sir Basil's guidance) called *Compensation for Personal Injury in English, German and Italian Law*.

For this book I thought more appropriate, instead of adapting to the mentality of the English jurist the ideas and information that I wanted to give on Italian law, to give the foreign reader the typically Italian taste of the way of thinking and using the law.

I should like to express my deep gratitude to Dr Mads Andenas for having encouraged me to publish this work, for having hosted it in the series of the British Institute of International and Comparative Law and for the generous, intelligent, and attentive help in revising this book. And I am very grateful to Nello Pasquini and Anne Thompson for their translations into English, the *lingua franca* which I hope will be a useful channel in order to show better our hidden 'treasures'.

The dialogue with illustrious English and American colleagues helped me to understand my own legal system. In particular I should like to thank Sir Basil Markesinis and Sir Roy Goode, Mark Freedland, Hugh Beale, John Spencer, Tony Weir, Hugh Collins, Ross Cranston, and Simon Whittaker. And finally Dominick Vetri of the University of Oregon who in 1977 was the first to invite me to Eugene to give a course on comparative law. An experience which I have repeated—for Italian law—at the Institute of European and Comparative Law of the University of Oxford and at the Institute of Global Law at University College London, in both institutions at the invitation of Sir Basil Markesinis. This dialogue systematically developed in the courses on contract and banking law that—together with Mads Andenas and Francesco Capriglione—had been given for eight years at the University of Malta and then in Italy with the support of the Italian Bar Council.

In his foreword Lord Slynn of Hadley has expressed very kind and generous words to me: these words are due to his kindness and could create in the reader expectations which I hope will not be too disappointed. My effort has been richly rewarded.

Rome, 6 January 2005

1. THE SYSTEM OF SOURCES OF LAW AND THE METHODS OF INTERPRETATION

1.1. GENERAL PRINCIPLES, OR HOW TO CREATE RULES USING WRITTEN PROVISIONS

1.1.1. The uses of the term 'general principle'

The term 'principle' is perceived in clearly different ways, however close they may be to one another. One can identify these different meanings of the term by taking into account the profession of the person interpreting the term: the scholar (doctrinal use), the judge (jurisprudential use), and the legislator (legislative use). In colloquial Italian, although less frequently today, '*principio*' is used as a synonym for 'beginning' ('*In principio era il verbo*'—'In the beginning was the word'). Otherwise, principle is used as a synonym for fundamental value ('It is a question of principle'), for basic notion (the principles of ethics, of mathematics, of physics, etc), or as a progressive abstraction generalized from a series of data and particular cases. Jurists use the expression 'principle' in different contexts: as an element of a discipline (principles of private rights), as a value (principle of correctness), as an instrument (principle of contradiction), but above all as an abstract rule applicable to particular concrete instances.

In his treatment of the interpretation of law, Emilio Betti, multifaceted jurist, lawyer, scholar of Roman Law and International Law, philosopher of hermeneutics, used an etymological argument to demonstrate that principle (understood in the technical juridical meaning which we will discuss) alludes to the 'beginning of a standard or of all the standards and criteria in a country at a historic moment'. This defines principle as above and outside the system, but he concluded that 'principles' are at the same time an external and internal source of the legal system.

We will dedicate some time to 'principle', because of the significant role assigned to principles in the theory of rights. In every case, principles exert a strong fascination: they evoke and allude to values. This calls for caution and careful discrimination. If the principle is handed down, from one source to another, and from one system to another, flowing from one century to another, it gains such an aura of prestige and authority to become indisputable and ineluctable. The principle achieves a legitimacy on its own or as such. Its existence, its validity, and its force are at the same time a means of persuasion and a means of standardization. And indeed because it is often joined to or confused with an ethical rule (one thinks of 'The Principle of Responsibility' by Hans Jonas), it may appear as a bulwark of and prelude to civilization. But one must be careful; not all the formulas that present themselves as principles are 'truly' principles; neither are all principles of the same relevance; nor are all principles used the same way.

Jurists normally understand 'principle' colloquially as a synonym for 'fundamental notion'. In this case, however, one is not dealing with simple notions but with notions somewhat artificially complex that allude to the quintessence, to the distillation of the system or to a sector of the system. Giuseppe Chiovenda understands it this way in his successful manual on civil procedure. Also, George Edward Moore used it this way in his *Principles of Ethics* as did Bertrand Russell in *Principles of Mathematics*. But philosophers, sociologists, economists and disciples of the exact sciences during the last century all erected an architecture of knowledge in a systematic way based scrupulously on a foundation of principles.

Going back by this path, the principles of a system are understood also as the essential characteristics of the system, its way of being and appearing, its physiognomy, its soul or spirit. Locré first uses them in this sense in his *Espirit du Code Civil*, of 1804, and then Rúdolf Von Jhering uses them in describing the 'spirit' of Roman rights. Jhering sees Roman law as 'a whole in and of itself', as a phenomenon of the history of law, and as a whole ensemble of techniques still useful in his day. In his introduction, principles are at the same time the points from which the formation and evolution of Roman law depart (the original principles), and the propulsive force of the mechanism of rights in the system (the unifying criteria). Jhering sees in that analysis, the principle of the subjective will (the system of private defence), the principle of family (the origin of social aggregation), and the religious principle (from the indistinction to the distinction between the sacred and the illicit, *fas et jus*).

Other illustrious jurists such as Gustav Radbruch and Roscoe Pound, in their work to illustrate the spirit of common law, understand this use of 'principle' as a expression of the spirit of the system. Fritz Schultz, a historian closer to us in time and culture, refers to Jhering in the individuation of principles. He lived in Germany until the Nazis came to power, and then moved to England where he continued to study the style of the Roman jurists with acumen. Even Schultz places himself within the proud tradition of those who connect principles to the spirit of the 'system'.

1.1.2. The collections of general principles

As we see, principles are used to accomplish many interpretative operations and manoeuvres. Paraphrasing an assumption of Damaska, the world of principles 'seems to be a collection of contrasting arguments waiting to be used for a controversy'. We will discuss this further with regard to the penetration of values behind the motivation of a decision, with regard to the ideology of the interpreter, and with regard to the weight of tradition.

If the craft of the jurist is 'to do things with rules', then one can do many things with rules. Because one can do many things with principles, jurists have fortified themselves and have proceeded to gather principles into non-peremptory lists, ordering them according to different criteria. However, we are dealing with unofficial lists. In Italy, lists were proposed at the moment the codification entered into force (1942), but the idea was rightly abandoned. There are several reasons for this. On the one hand, the fear was that an omission would result in an imprecise work. On the other hand, the fear was that a more complete list (that could not have been anything but peremptory) would have wound up burying the interpreter under a mass of written rules denying him any active function.

In other epochs, the attempts at official systemization were not rejected. Justinian, as recorded, dedicated a book of his Digest (the 50th) to the gathering of principles (*de regulis juris antiqui*). But that collection had another function. Justinian wanted to restore authority to the maxims expressed by the greatest jurists (ie that is by the 'official' jurists), and give some order to material that, not being codified, could result in confused, if not contradictory, solutions to the same question. The same exigency was also felt in canon law, as the 'Sixth Sextum' demonstrates (that is, the decrees of Boniface VIII, L. V., tit. XII, to which 88 *regulae juris* are added).

In the experience of every country, there have been lawyers, professors, students and scholars of law in general that have devoted themselves to collecting principles. Some examples are easily found. In Italy, the collection of 2000 maxims compiled by L De Mauri in the first years of the 20th century has had some success and is still reprinted today. In France, during the same era and in years before, Boulanger refers to the success that such collections had encountered. He points to the collections of Daguin and Jouanneau. In fact, recently a new collection has appeared edited by Roland and Boyer, where principles expressed in the form of a 'brocard' or maxim is considered 'adages of French law'. In Spain, the catalogue put in order by a historian, James Mans Puigarnau, was particularly painstaking. He has classified rules, maxims and aphorisms, refering to judgments of the Supreme Court of Justice. But the maxims collected by Broom in the 19th century had, and were still having, a notable success in the 1940s in the UK and the USA.

To gather maxims, principles and aphorisms is not difficult; it is enough to have some patience and a little luck. It is more difficult to understand what is effectively served by the quotation of the maxim, and if the maxim acts as a rule. To understand how often they are used, one can read the principles cited in the jurisprudential maxims collected by the editors of legal journals.

1.1.3. The 'common values of the West'

The Congress in Hamburg in 1962, the research that followed in the next 30 years, and the deeper study of the similar characteristics of the diverse systems, have brought us to a very relevant conclusion—there are values that constitute a common foundation among Western systems, and these values are currently expressed by principles. Principles not only go beyond historic phases and cultural traditions, but they yield to transplantation, osmosis, connection, and overlapping points in common.

For the moment let us limit ourselves to the use of theoretical models without consulting legislative texts or the decisions of judges. Peter Stein and John Shand have attempted to illustrate a panorama of these common values and believe to have individualized them: the exclusion of violence and the values of security; the limits of discretion on the part of the interpreter and of the administration; the responsibility for contractual fulfilment and for illicit deeds; personal liberties; the right to life and privacy; propriety and protection of reasonable expectations; and the cooperation and limitation of economic initiative for reasons of public interest.

For his part, Karl Larenz, discussing the notion of 'fair law' and the foundation of juridical ethics, enumerates among the principles of the individual sphere, self-determination and contractual autonomy, the principle of equivalence in synallagmatic contracts, and the principle of trust and good faith. Among the principles inherent to the communal sphere, he cites: participation, equality and proportionality, to which he then adds the principles that govern political representation and legal procedure (impartiality of the judge and of the proceedings).

How can we avoid to share this classification, and how can we not retrace it in our own tradition?

(a) In the fresco of general value principles, the first among all is the principle of 'reciprocal respect' (a part of the neighbour principle). This is at the base of every form of cohabitation that is founded on a democratic basis inasmuch as it expresses the fundamental Kantian juridical relationship. It is precisely in his *Metaphysics of Morals*, that Kant poses the rule of the free exercise of one's own rights, and the limits of the rights of others. It is easy to recall the antecedent to this rule, the evangelical precept, 'Do unto others as you would have them do unto you.' The Kantian rule however, is not dictated by love and the overcoming of egoism, but by corresponding rational rules. It remains therefore much further from the other evangelical precept, connected to the first, 'Love thy neighbour as thyself'.

The vein of natural law is interwoven with these Christian values, that translated into rational formulas, define the free exercise of rights on the part of the individual in such a way as to render them compatible with the exercise of rights by the other members of society.

But let us return to what we were saying at the beginning: he who starts from the Kantian categorical imperative—like Karl Larenz—cannot then abandon the philosophic camp. He must then take into account the development, or better, the successive critical constructions derived from this principle. Religiously, only if one recognizes in the other a being similar to oneself can we say that the 'recognizer is a person, as is the recognized'. In other words, one is a person, a being free to express his own will, only inasmuch as other beings are respected as persons.

From this principle we derive: the injustice of slavery, the illegality of 'corporal' servitude, the illegality of forced labour inflicted without the necessity of sanctions, and in the positive sense, the legal capacity recognized for all men. This principle Larenz sees as imminent in paragraph 1.1 of the German Basic Law, according to which the *dignity* of man is intangible. It is indeed from this norm that the jurisprudential construction of fundamental rights of the individual is derived. A derivation of the same principle with respect to the person is the liberty of conscience and worship. The general view in German doctrine is that the principle of respect for the person and therefore of reciprocal respect, while not absolute, eternal or unalterable, is a 'natural right of the modern epoch'.

The liberty of the will is reduced to the freedom to do anything that is not prohibited and anything that does not obstruct the equal liberty on the part of others.

(b) The general rights of personhood, in its image, honour, and privacy, is a value principle in all Western systems. Connected to this principle are corollaries that deal with the freedom to exercise a profession and the prohibition to conclude contracts that result in the total dependence of one subject to another. Stein and Shand, who place the protection of privacy within the range of fundamental values, also agree on this conclusion.

(c) The principle of individual responsibility is found in the material for civil responsibility.

(d) The prohibition on acts of rivalry (foreseen in Article 833 of the Italian Civil Code) the good-neighbour rules (Article 872 e ss), and the prohibition on pollutants (Article 844 e ss), are other examples of the principles of 'respects for the other'. Reciprocal respect entails limitations on the right that by its nature is the most self-centered (the most '*terrible*' as the French revolutionaries used to say): the right of property. But we find examples of the application of this principle in the literature on contracts, in which the model of commutative contracts, according to which the parties exchange reciprocal advantages and divide among themselves the risks and burdens, is the scheme normally followed in the discipline of special contracts. In the literature dealing with tort liability, he who causes damage is charged with the obligation of damages. He who does not respect the person, the goods or other protected interests of which an individual is entitled, must pay the consequences, compensating for the damage caused.

(e) The principle of the 'abuse of rights' is, by contrast, controversial. In other systems this is accepted in doctrine and in case law. In Italy, it has a rather difficult life. But it seems to be like the Arabian phoenix that rises from its ashes as many times as it is expunged by the system. We will return to this point, and beyond, where the 'hidden' principles are described.

(f) Further value principles are those concerning the non-retroactivity of the law and those which concern the presumption of knowledge of the law (*numquam legem ignorare censetur; ignorantia legis non excusat*). The first, as well as the second, is, however, derogated from and is derogable. The second, in reality, codifies the presumption that everyone is in a position to know the law. Originating in a historic period in which there were few laws, made known by town criers and directed towards a rather restricted circle of persons, the presumption gradually became a less realistic consideration and more of a fiction, but no less binding for this.

Laws became ever more numerous, new ones being superimposed over the old; those of the dominators over those of the dominated. It was customary to write laws in the cultured language (Latin), though the majority of the population knew only the local dialect, and was often illiterate, incapable of reading even the vulgar or demotic language. Today this world has disappeared, and we have remaining an immense number of norms not easily retrieved. But it is not for that reason that these norms, which at one time emanated from regular procedures, remain subject to the condition of 'publication' for the benefit of those to whom it is directed. These norms are promulgated in legislation and the fundamental principle cited above (Constitutional Court, 24 March 1988 n 364). We have already dealt with their effectiveness by convention.

(g) The principle of contractual autonomy and freedom of contract is also considered one of the fundamental values.

Larenz observes that in all systems, the principle of *pacta sunt servanda* is recognized, even if in each individual case it may be realized differently. Everyone can freely make contracts, and in binding oneself, realize an act of self-determination. Someone holds that self-determination is an expression of personhood. In a contract, one party recognizes the personhood of the other. Others (such as Ghestin) point out however that autonomy cannot be exercised without recognizing the principle of social solidarity.

1.1.4. The value of the 'person'

In the Declaration of the Rights of Man we find a series of positions that reflect the aspirations and values of the West. These unite the individual situation with that of the collective, conforming in part to the tradition of natural law. This is evident in the area of private law for the right to life and security (Article 3), the prevention of slavery (Article 4), legal capacity (Article 6), equality and non-discrimination (Article 7), the right to defence (Article 8), to property (Article 17), and to association (Article 20).

Obviously, the use of these terms and their teleological interpretation is more developed than those of the 19th century; the social dimension has developed. But in the national constitutions, these dimensions, individual and collective, are still more precise.

In summary, one can retrace the construction of a table of values common to Western systems. A sort of progression or ramification proceeds from persons, to groups, and then to the activities pursued within a society in an orderly fashion, the goal being to mitigate the private interests between persons and the interests of the collective. These are as set out below.

(a) At the base of this configuration is the principle of protection of the person's fundamental liberties.
(b) Among persons so protected, a relationship of equality in treatment is instituted that carries with it the respect for differences (equality in diversity).
(c) Towards the aim of survival, the individual is in need of goods and must be able to exercise the right of property with such goods. In some systems the right of property is directly tied to the protection of the person and appears as almost a 'natural' right. In many systems the right of property is tempered in its egoistic–individual dimension by the social function, more generally by the limits that derive from collective exigencies. Individual economic interests, as well as general interests in the dynamics of the market, always require that goods circulate freely, or at least with as few obstacles as possible. By this, the protection of

property is maintained, and in certain legal systems (German), the circulation of goods is by way of abstract transactions. In other systems, with the simple consent of the transfer of property (as in the French, and Italian systems), the freedom to leave an inheritance, tempered by the protection of the heirs, is guaranteed as the corollary of protection of property and the free circulation of goods.

(d) The principle of worker protection in all its social and economic aspects.

(e) The principle of economic freedom, the freedom to exercise a profession and the freedom of competition; in some systems a corollary of contractual freedom is individuated that however does not seem to have constitutional coverage in the Italian constitution.

(f) The protection of the individual extends to members of the family of which he is a part. Within the family, the following principles apply: the principle of equality between husband and wife that is expressed in the principle of spiritual and material communion, characteristic of married life, the equal power to administer goods, the equal responsibility for and authority over their offspring, and the principle of equal treatment of children, legitimate or illegitimate (with regard to this, differences still exist in the different systems with respect to specific successor rights of illegitimate children).

(g) The principle of the freedom of association, whose corollary is the principle of free economic association, and the free exercise of collective enterprises.

As for the principle of contractual freedom, it has the following correlations: the principle of mutual consent; the principle of *iusta causa*, for which any change in patrimony or inheritance must have a legal and justifiable reason that merits protection; and the principle of contractual balance, giving relevance to corresponding services, their fulfilment or non-fulfilment, to occurrence of unforeseen circumstances, or to foreseeable circumstances that may upset the economic transaction. This principle, formulated in diverse techniques in Germany (*Geschäftsgrundlage*), in France (*imprévision*), in England (frustration of contract) and in Italy (*teoria della presupposizione*), aims to conserve the original equilibrium of the contract and to keep the economic programme of the parties involved in harmony with contemporary events.

(h) The principle of responsibility, on the basis of which he who is engaged in an activity, commercial or non-commercial, must provide compensation for damages caused, has the following corollaries or coordinates: the principle of causality, the principle of fault and the principle of assumption of risk.

1.1.5. The principles of EC Law

A recent reflection on the common values of the West has been formulated in European terms by André-Jean Arnaud. He submits a thorough historical examination of the development of the fundamental themes of 'European' juridical culture. He sustains that however ambiguous the term 'European' may be, it is still possible to outline a common thread or connection among them. Historic memory is thus the foundation of a 'promise' to realize a complete European integration. Historic memory has its roots in the Middle Ages in the canonical tradition. Modern juridical thought draws sustenance from the rationalism of the juridical naturalists, thanks to which, doctrines of will, legalistic positivism and subjectivism are rooted. These values promote a discipline of international relations and are at the base of the declarations of the rights of man as well as the first codifications. The surfacing of national rights and the social dimension of rights introduces caesuras in this homogeneous and unitary development. But according to Arnaud, this does not have to mean an impediment to European unification as much as a process of growth stimulating useful discussion for the evolution of the systems.

The process of European unification, promoted by means of the two techniques—'integration' and 'harmonization'—is based on the logic of flexibility recognizing pluralism, the plurality of the systems, and the concentration and application of the rights of the person. This complexity of the legal systems can be governed with logic; through consultation with scholars and with development of a system of compromise and resolution of internal conflicts.

Statutory references to principles may be found in European Community (EC) texts. For example, Article 215, paragraph 2, of the Treaty of Rome says: 'in cases of extra-contractual responsibility, the Community must indemnify, in conformity with the general common principles of the Member States, damage caused by its institutions or by its agents in the exercise of their functions.' Here the expression 'general principles' is employed in the sense of a norm obtainable through dispositions contained in the internal systems that are 'common', that is, that correspond. In other words, they are in force and observed in the internal systems of the Member States.

As far as the Community principles of law, Italian literature operates in the same way in which interpreters in other sectors of law operate. Principle is understood from time to time as notion, institute or a rule of a general character. Here we consider it in its meaning as a norm having a general content, obtainable by way of induction from the complex of other norms or as the object of explicit enunciations of formal texts. In this sense they are extracted from the diverse affirmations of principle of EC law: individual liberties, rights of an economic nature, the right of defence, the principle of certainty of law and legitimate expectations, the principle of equality, the principle of proportionality, the principle of exemption from responsibility due to an act of God, the principle of good administration, the principle of extra-contractual responsibility and hermeneutic principles. In a recent attempt to review case law, Toriello leaves one to understand that even the European Court of Justice employs general principles in the same way in which these are used in Italian courts: an integrative, corrective and explanatory usage of the dispositions in force that appear unclear, incomplete or generic.

Among the principles collected in the Community system, one in particular, often overlooked by internationalist and EC law scholars, appears within private law: the principle of consumer protection.

The existence and utility of general principles of law is still today the object of some perplexity, notwithstanding that in 1964 Paul Reuter had attempted to establish that the European Community Court of Justice, has recourse to general principles. Recently, Robert Kovar has confirmed that the Court utilizes principles from unwritten sources of Community law. The doubt exhibited today in France is in regard to not so much the existence as the 'necessity' of general principles of law.

Above all, we shed light on the fact that general principles are tied to the laws of the different Member States, although one could object immediately that for some families, the Romanic–Germanic, there are undeniable identities or affinities in the cultural and historic 'humus' of the legal systems of which they are a part. And some principles, together with many maxims, are also common to English law.

It is evident, however, that the principles of Community law that receive from time to time different denominations have pragmatic origin and, therefore, a great eclecticism pervades them. Besides, one must point out that the absence of a more complete set of fundamental norms in place at the base of the Community system deprives the judge of a point of reference for the construction of principles. On the other hand, having its specific and limited focus, the Community system cannot be considered a system closed, there being osmosis among the diverse systems and a notable circulation of juridical models.

The sources of Community principles must therefore be sought in international law, in the laws of the individual Member States, and in particular in the constitutional laws of the Member States. Beyond these sources one must take into account Community law in itself, and therefore the complex of economic–juridical values that are at the base of the Community. More precisely we single out those principles having a structural nature that includes the principles of free circulation, non discrimination, free competition and promoting the Community or the unity of the Common Market.

What are added, more than structural principles, are 'supreme' principles founded on all the other principles, the rule of law, that is the right to live in a community founded on a rule of law and access to justice. From the rule of law, follows the principles on legal certainty, that is the obligation of institutions to observe a reasonable period of time for notification or for controls, the respect for publicity, motivation, non-retroactiveness, the clarity and precision of reliance juridical rules, good faith (including the brocard *patere legem quam fecisti*), and legitimate trust. Then there is the principle of equality, non-discrimination for reasons of nationality of the Community nations or for reasons of sex, and so on. Also included is the principle of proportionality with reference to sanctions. The birth of a community of law (*Rechsgemeinschaft*) completed by the 'access to justice,' that is, to a procedure consistent with Community law. In adherence to the characteristics of this Community, it is necessary that the general principles are clear, expressed in a precise form, and are accessible.

The Community method of creating principles is not different from that of the individual Member States. It follows the inductive method. It makes use of principles drawing upon international law and the internal law of the Member States. This selection allows for the deletion of principles that, in accentuating the autonomy or the individuality of the individual systems, would lead to incompatible Community law. This is the case, for example, with the principle of reciprocity. This selection has not always been possible. In fact, it has happened at times that the Community has not taken into account the fundamental rights of the person guaranteed by individual constitutions. It found itself in difficulty because internal judges, even national constitutional courts, made internal constitutional rights prevail over Community rights. Here was the issue of the development of Community product liability, which had made the common principles its own, to the internal constitutional rights.

Even comparative rights have contributed their share to the construction of Community rights and thus to the principles of these rights. The method followed has from time to time been to actuate, on the basis of value judgments, the selection of models considered worthy even if they are expressed by only a single Member State. The introduction of a system of responsibility, founded on the risk of enterprise for the circulation of defective product law, bears witness to this. As it has been noted, it could not be assimilated either into Italian law, where it prevailed, at least formally, over the responsibility founded on fault (or the presumption of fault), or into English law (no liability without fault).

1.1.6. *The Italian model: the general provisions of the Civil Code of 1942*

General principles are mentioned in the general provisions which precede the Civil Code and in numerous other normative texts of the Italian legal system (special laws, regional statutes, regional laws, city and provincial statutes). In the Community system, explicit reference is made to the general principles common to the laws of the Member States on the subject of extra-contractual responsibility (Article 215, paragraph 2 of the EC Treaty). In the international system, reference is made to the recognized principles of the civilized nations (Article 38, paragraph 1 of the Statute of the ICJ). The compilers of the texts have not always employed the same formulas; sometimes one speaks of principles of the system, sometimes of fundamental principles, and at other times of the principles of the civilized nations.

Article 12 of the prelaws (prel) as the general provisions of the Civil Code are referred to, merits more thorough comment for a variety of reasons. It contains the most well-known, diffuse and tormented text in Italian discipline. It is a disposition that fulfils the task of dictating the criteria for the interpretation and application of normative texts. Thus, it is placed on a different plane with respect to the other dispositions which refer to specific concrete instances. It is a norm about norms and for that reason it precedes all the others from both the interpretative and prescriptive points of view.

Article 12 prel presents a particularity with respect to the other provisions. It regulates the interpretative process, it dictates (or claims to dictate) the behaviour of the interpreter and the limits of interpretation. Article 12 has a complex history whose developments are necessary to know in order to understand it fully. It contains similarities with rules of other systems which we need to study in order to understand the peculiarity. Moreover, it represents one of the possible models to trace the boundaries of the authority of the interpreter and therefore it poses problems of the general theory of law.

The heading of Article 12 is titled 'the Interpretation of the Law' and the text is comprised of two paragraphs. The first regulates the literal and teleological interpretation. The second adds: 'If the controversy cannot be decided with a precise disposition, one can turn to dispositions that regulate similar cases or analogous subjects, if the case still remains doubtful, it is decided according to the principles of the legal system of the State.'

Above all, it is necessary to consider the existence of Article 12, the exigency, of which the compilers of the codification of 1942 cautioned in a written norm ordering the principles.

Let us pose the question with a different tenor. If the final paragraph of Article 12 had not been inserted into the preliminary dispositions, would the interpreters have been equally able to have recourse to principles, and with what limits and with what methods?

Not all systems of written laws are provided with such a provision. It has already been brought to light that nothing like it can be found in the 'Father' code, that is the Napoleonic Code, in the German code, nor in the common law. This does not mean that the principles, or some interpretive technique, have not been noted or applied in France or that they have not been noted or applied in Germany or in the common law. We can go beyond the first elementary question, responding therefore that the provision in Article 12 is useful but not necessary. In an interpretive and systematic way one arrives at the recognition and the application of general principles. Some hold that the provision is superfluous because the interpretation of texts is exhausted in their analogical application. But this extreme thesis has no basis, as is revealed in the following investigation.

The provision was introduced in the prelaws for many reasons; for historic reasons (inasmuch as a provision of a similar nature had already existed in the publication, interpretation, and application of laws in general (Article 3)) in the code previously in force since 1865; for political reasons (inasmuch as it was felt important: to reaffirm through law, the unity and completeness of the system, to render more precise, through law, discussion on the efficacy of natural law); for ideological reasons (inasmuch as it was desired to assign only to those norms of the system 'established' by the state (law in force) the task of governing Italian society in an exclusive way).

The location of Article 12 within the prelaws is also due to logical reasons. The world of principles brought back into interpretation has dimensions a specific and circumscribed role is assigned to principles through laws which aid the interpreter in ascertaining the meaning of the provisions of the Code and their application.

The legislator is not content to recall principles and to determine their function; he is also given the responsibility to establish when one may have recourse to them.

Article 12 is formulated in the impersonal; commands are directed toward the third person ('one cannot', 'one has regards to', 'one decides'). They therefore concern all interpreters: the judge, the administration or whoever in general has the task of applying the law. Principles are norms in the true sense and thus must be respected by everyone and in particular by those who must interpret the laws institutionally. But the normative area of Article 12, paragraph 2, has boundaries which are more circumscribed because it is directed not to the moment of the interpretation, but indeed to the moment of the decision of a controversy.

From this it is deduced that the 'judging' interpreter must make recourse to the principles in the cases and within the limits indicated in the same disposition. It deals with the 'judge', and thus not only the judge concerned with the controversy, but also the arbitrator that must decide in a procedure. In all other cases in which one does not have to decide (that is, in the work of the same judge that pronounces (either requested or allowed) according to equity, in the case of the arbiter of equity or of a contractual arbiter, such as in the case of an interpreter) there would be freedom to use principles in the most opportune way. Obviously, the fair judge, the regular arbitrator, or a contractual arbitrator is not allowed to decide in an illogical or unjust fashion; the interpreter assisted by scientific rigour cannot operate in fantasy, but must concern himself with the rules of doctrinal interpretation.

The letter of Article 12 seems to credit an order of criteria: the literal criteria (the true meaning of the words), the psychological criteria (the intention of the legislator, the teleological criteria (the aim of the legislator and of the law), and the analogical criteria (similar cases or analogous materials: *analogia legis*; the recourse to principles *analogia juris*).

One notes that in this succession, principles can be applied to resolve the doubtful cases, only as a residual and final route; the integration is only residual and subordinate to the interpretation. The interpreter (the judge and related figures) is therefore the arbiter of whether or not to turn to principles; the choice is up to him because it is he who decides if the case is doubtful. If it is not, then it is not necessary to turn to the application of principles, as the application of the written disposition would be sufficient.

The apparent crystalline and pyramidal structure of the criteria of interpretation of the law becomes, however, more opaque with regard to the praxis that belies the legislative dictate. This same technique of interpretation (which for logical reasons) presupposes that the singling out of principles comes before any other criteria.

In jurisdictional practice, principles receive a much extended application, not subordinate to hierarchical criteria, and wider than the role that the legislator had foreseen and prescribed a bit ingenuously. In the belief that gaps can be filled and that these can be found directly in the text rather than being the fruit of an interpretative process is still more ingenuous. In the interpretative technique, the fruit of the verification of the meaning of the disposition determined by the interpreter and filtered through his cultural baggage, is always framed and flammable in a principle.

But even the rule presupposed by Article 12, *in claris non fit interpretatio*, can be denied. The decision whether a formula is doubtful belongs to the same interpretative process. Whenever the interpreter prepares himself to fulfil his role, he realizes an operation that is not (and could not be) mechanical. The fact itself of distinguishing the clear particular cases from those that are unclear, is already that fruit of a pre-comprehension that leaves no doubt as to the active role he performs.

Interpreted literally, Article 12 thus reveals all the ingenuousness of a legislator fearful of the betrayals of the interpreters. On the other hand this is not new. Napoleon never liked commentary on the rules of his code. In fact, it is said that when they brought him the first work of interpretation and comment he is said to have murmured, 'mon Dieu, mon code est perdu!'

In conclusion, even if we wanted to conform strictly to the dictates of Article 12 prel, we would not be able to do so without turning to principles. This is because the use of principles is innate to the interpretive process.

1.1.7. The identification of principles

Because principles are mentioned within the scope of the criteria for the interpretation and application of laws, their normative nature can be founded on this textual argument: principles are also laws, they are norms with characteristics different from those that are written. We can verify the assumptions consolidated by the light of the orientations of Italian doctrine. The following characteristics are assigned to principles: they are vague and imprecise, but it is not for this that the written dispositions are to the contrary always clear and precise; they entail the use of an interpreter, but it is not for this that the other dispositions do not require interpretive choices; they encompass a wider range in their normative content than the other dispositions, but it is not for this that equally broad dispositions are not found in the legal system.

There are discussions as to whether principles obtained by the inductive method from written dispositions are directly applicable to concrete specific cases. The affirmative response descends from textual reasons (the formula of Article 12, paragraph 2), as well as logical reasons; if they are norms, then as with all norms, they are directly applicable to concrete specific cases.

With some authoritative exceptions as with Betti, scholars agree that principles are 'norms'.

On the other hand, if principles are extracted from norms by way of a process of generalization and of subsequent abstraction, nothing but a norm is born from a norm. This, with greater reason, applies to the fundamental principles expressed. It is a jurist–positive canon. But modern supporters of natural law also agree on the normative nature of principles. He who holds that principles are founded on the ethics and therefore have a metajuridical origin, that inspires and shapes rights and thus their epiphany (that is the whole complex of rules which comprise the system), cannot but consider the observance of principles as binding. Otherwise, the judge who ignores them or directly violates them would emit a decision contrary to law.

The legal-realists, instead, express doubts about the normative nature of principles: a principle would be observed not because it is binding in itself, but because it is held to be such in the collective imagination. A principle is a ductile instrument that serves to cover, legitimately, the operations of the interpreter.

The impersonal formulation of Article 12, that would limit the task of applying principles to the judge, clashes however with another logical exigency. Even before it is practical, the legislator has not enumerated the principles that one can or must apply. One wonders then whether principles are a 'source' of law with characteristics similar to common law, as this would not be a written norm, but a norm referred to and observed in the interpretative and applicative practice. In contrast to the common law, that in modern systems does not precede but follows the written norm and is subordinate to it, principles come before the other norms (if one wants to go beyond the rigid scheme of Article 12) because the other norms presuppose the principles. However, while the customary law is observed, inasmuch as it is held binding (*opinio iuris ac necessitas*), principles are observed because in the mitigating of interests, these offer solution most consonant with law (that is to the culture and sensibilities of the interpreter).

Here then is the second illusion of the legislator: principles would be a closed number, circulating within well-defined boundaries. This is because principles are inferred from the norms, and thus cannot exist (juridically) if they do not have a foundation in them.

Also here the legislator has forgotten, or has pretended to forget, the role of the interpreter who is able to create principles and to anchor them to norms.

There are not a closed number of principles, and therefore they cannot be inventoried. This is an ancient consideration that finds ample confirmation in practice.

The introduction of principles has three origins: by the same legislator, by the judge, and by the legal scholars.

Examples of the first origin are in Italy, Article 1 of the law on abortion, according to which abortion cannot be utilized as a means of birth control; Article 7 of the law on administrative procedures, according to which the administration must operate effectively and efficiently; the dispositions on military discipline; the dispositions of the statutes on workers and those contained in the laws on parity.

The greater part of the decisions that decide a case applying a principle are examples of the second origin. It is enough to think of the application of the principle *pacta sunt servanda*, *rebus sic stantibus*, and of the employment theory of supposition; of enrichment without cause; of the acquisitive occupation; of the protection of minors in custody cases connected to the separation of parents; and of all the other cases which are the object of analysis in the second part of this work.

The legal scholar identifies principles attaining them from case law, from the policy followed by the legislator, and from legal culture, proposing principles that organize diverse and scattered norms in a systematic way or introducing new principles to adapt the system to new requirements (eg consumer protection, protection of savings, transparency of contracts, etc).

Today, the normative nature of principles is universally recognized. It could appear contradictory to deny doctrine a role as a source and assign to doctrine the task of in fact describing principles. The legal-positivists escape the contradiction sustaining that the principles in force are those extracted from norms.

Can we place boundaries on the will of the interpreter that insure that principles are not transformed into an authentic Trojan horse that would make interpretative subjectivity re-enter into areas where it had been previously banished and thus transforming the judge into a legislator? Even those sceptical of bridling interpretation spare some limitation: logical consistency, and the reducibility of the topic.

Principles can be classified, ordered hierarchically, and analysed historically. Since the fundamental values of a system are contained in its fundamental laws, these serve to render the constitution compatible with the norms in force. In their way of being, they can have a more general importance, if found in the constitution, in the civil code, or in the devolved regional statutes, and a more circumscribed importance, if expressed in special legislation that gives rise to 'microsystems'.

1.1.8. The origins of the Italian Code model

A history of positivist data means researching the formulas antecedent to those codified in the Article 12 prelaws. But it also means analysis of the questions elaborated by the doctrine and by the jurisprudence or case law that surround that positivist data.

A textual comparison apparently yields meager results. As has been revealed, a disposition which makes reference to general principles as such, understood as a technique of enunciating values and directions to which the interpreter must refer in given situations, is not found in the Napoleonic Code, the father code of the systems belonging to the Roman–French family. Single general principles are codified (like the principle *alterum non laedere*, the principle of the binding power of contracts, and so on).

A most important fact in political history and in the history of law must not be forgotten. It is the space of time that separates the end of the 18th century and the beginning of 21st century, which we can define as the epoch of codifications, that the 'positivization of general principles' occurred.

In the Napoleonic codification as well as in the Austrian codification, the imprints of natural laws can be traced. In the latter they are more distinct because they correspond to rules in the code that make explicit reference to values of the rights of nature. However, such rights are 'encapsulated' in the code, and are thus rendered as positivist rights in force and translated into either explicit norms or general principles. Pre-dating the code because they permeate juridical science, the general principles in the new epoch that express a new way of conceiving legality, are applicable inasmuch as they are recalled by the code. In short, the general principles take inspiration from natural rights, pre-date the system and enter and take part in it only when they are recalled by the system.

In the *Code Civil*, where it is repeated many times, principles are not spoken of explicitly. The preoccupation of Napoleon is to give clear rules that the judge '*bouche de la loi*' must apply in a literal way; not even comment is permitted for fear that the legislative intent would be diminished or distorted.

The doctrine hesitates to elaborate general principles but not for the survival of Roman studies. One notes also that the Italian translation of the Civil Code, that is, the Civil Code of the Kingdom of Italy concerning Italian provinces conquered by Napoleon, enter into force in 1806 with the obligation of university professors to comment in their courses on the Civil Code with the aid of Roman law. Even the typically French tendency towards classification and abstraction, is a potent spur towards individuation, coordination, criticism, and the application of principles. In the manuals of private law of Laurent, Toullier, and Zacharie, an ample use of principles is made, in contrast to the original legislative will, but in conformity with the doctrinal needs and logic of every juridical experience.

On the other hand, an explicit mention of the expression 'general principles' is contained in the Austrian Civil Code of 1811, in force in Italy by 1816 in the Italian provinces under Austrian control. Section 7 is formulated in this way: whenever a case can neither be decided according to the words nor the natural sense of the law, one will have recourse to other cases decided under the laws and to other analogous laws.

If, nonetheless, the case remains doubtful, one will have to decide according to the principles of natural law, having weighed all the pertinent circumstances with diligence and consideration. Few references can be found in the systems of the other Italian states prior to the Napoleonic conquest. In some states, as in the Kingdom of Sardinia, the situation after the fall of Napoleon and the Restoration was still more complicated.

In 1837, in the moment of the unification of the civil discipline of the States of Piedmont (Piedmont and Savoy, where the Savoiard constitutions were in force; Liguria, where the Napoleonic Code remained in force; and Sardinia, where particular laws were in force) the compilers of the code were beset by a problem: to use or not to use the expression 'general principles?' And in the positive case, whether to copy the Austrian expression which refers to natural rights? The solution is singular and at the same time illuminating: a thin wording contained in the 'principles of rights' is preferred.

And it is this expression that passes in Article 3 of the prelaws to the civil code that in 1865 unified the legal systems in the new Kingdom of Italy. From that moment the history of positivist data becomes the history of the techniques of the doctrine and of the case law the purpose of which is to escape the literal and restrictive application of dispositions, to enrich positive rules and above all to satisfy the exigencies of reality and find a response in positive rules.

This direction is sustained primarily by the scholars of commercial law that, before any of the other sectors of the system, are affected by the latest developments of the market beyond those that come from abroad and circulate in international relations. Here, principles besides being the skeletal framework of the sector, are seen as instruments that permit the rapid adaptation of the system to the new reality. It is in the 'nature of things' that requires the rejuvenation of the commercial code of 1865; but the code of 1882 also leaves the door open to principles and therefore to new interpretation.

After the First World War the jurists warned that a turning point had been reached; the centuries'-old empires had fallen and the world of the 19th century had vanished with exaltation of the individual and private property. The growing industrialization, the intervention of the state in the economy, and the new social circumstances rendered the code, already grown old, inadequate for the new realities.

1.1.9. The general principles under the Italian Civil Code of 1865: the statist thesis

The historians of Italian law have not yet deepened the analysis of the jurisprudence or case law of the 19th century so that we do not know how principles were utilized in the motivations behind decisions. Moreover, a work such as Broom's which allows us to understand the role of principles of the law in action, does not exist in the Italian literature. But from the analysis of the scholars of law in force who have investigated single sectors or single institutions of private law, one can comprehend that these were not applied in a manner very much different from the way they are applied today. Even the problems of general theory of a practical nature that these pose to the interpreter are very similar to those that we pose today. Retracing history then has a dual purpose: it serves to reconstruct the origin of texts, but also to avoid repeating the errors of the past.

In an Italy divided by cultures and traditions so different from one another, the legislative unification that cemented the political unification, had to be integrated by the uniform application of laws. What is more, the victory of positivism (the modern technique of the organization of knowledge) in all the natural sciences and in the philosophic and social sciences, led to the marginalization, by the science and of practice of law, of those values not explicitly recognized by the laws. Political reasons associated with scientific reasons (beyond, obviously the observance of Article 3 of the prelaws) thus militated in favour of a positivist conception of law and therefore of general principles of law traceable in the dispositions of the code.

Vittorio Scialoja was the interpreter of this conception. In his inaugural speech for the academic year of 1879/80 at the University of Camerino, Vittorio Scialoja, who had just won the Chair of Roman law and Civil Law, enunciated a sort of manifesto of Italian jurists that would remain vital and persuasive for more than half a century. The speech bears the title 'of positive law and equity'; but its content is much broader (according to the Italian legal culture and tradition equity is in itself a system of values which should be compatible with codified law). In fact, the order of the speech is as follows: the role of moral and physical forces in the creation of law; the consensual nature of law (that could be also expressed in terms of the original 'social contract'); the necessity of the juridical forms; common law, written law and case law; the restrictions of written law (*strictum jus*) on case law; and how judicial law gives effect to equity.

Following this itinerary, Scialoja focuses on the points of intersection in the speech, that become the development of his thesis: nothing outside of the law, everything within the legal system. Equity is not an 'alternative system'; equity is a source (material) of law. In this prospective general principles (eg principle of equality, the principle of citizenship, the principle of protection for foreigners) are constructed within the range of rights. These do not derive from natural rights as if they were in a latent or unconscious state, but they are the fruit of convention and will.

The idea of equity, understood as a natural foundation of the sense of justice, is to be refuted because it falls into subjectivity. It can be justified only as a response to formalism and to the crude, thin and insidious application of codified written law, but not because it proposes an alternative system of rules with respect to the law in force. According to this illustrious jurist, this idea is dangerous because it incites the judge to not apply the positivist law considered unjust, and to choose the solution no longer adherent to positive data but more adherent to his own sense of justice. Since the sense of justice is subjective, the risk of falling into arbitrary interpretation is too easy.

In this same way he refutes the idea of equity as a 'support and correction of positivist law'.

The judge, unless authorized by the same legislator, may not substitute his own will for that of legislation. Equity, since it compels the judge to attend to the concrete circumstances of the case and to combine the norms with one another, is not 'equity' in the true sense, but expresses the same task of the interpreter. In other words, the judge is not free to interpret the norm but must seek out the intent of the legislator. He can modify his application only when he finds himself—using expressions that the article defines as having a relative meaning (and that we would define as general clauses) such as public order, good faith, or correctness. In these hypotheses, the legislative intent is that these norms be interpreted according to the ideas, the sentiments and the conditions of the diverse cases and times. But also here we are not dealing with a free choice entrusted to the interpreter; the legislator is the one who explicitly authorizes and avails himself of the general clause destined to survive for a century.

Here he arrives at the conclusion of the speech that now points to general principles. Principles are not mathematical formulas nor are they elastic formulas, 'such as to allow them to stray from the laws: a law does not propose principles, it dictates commands; . . . from these commands one may extract principles, but the supreme difficulty consists in formulating them'.

The juris-positivist and statist credo regarding general principles is contained in these few lines. Rights are understood as an ensemble of commands. Consequently, the general principle is understood as a secondary norm that is extracted by way of abstraction from the written norm or from custom.

How then must we interpret the Article 3 prelaws to the Civil Code of 1865, where it makes reference to 'general principles of law?' Currently, with what he has sustained to this point, Scialoja excludes that such an expression alludes directly to Roman law, to natural law, or to equity, as some of his contemporaries had held. Such formulas are suitable for those systems where they are utilized in an explicit way and are directly recalled as happens in the Ticino Code (Article 5) that referred back to 'principles of law' or in the Austrian Code that referred to 'principles of natural rights.' The formula of equity as an expression consolidating general principles is to be recalled, inasmuch as it is applicable by the judge, only when the law in force permits it: the judge has the duty 'not to exceed his powers'.

Scialoja (in a note to the text) returns to the problem and gives his instructions to the interpreter. These instructions are directed more towards describing what we call today the technique of qualification than to describing the technique of abstraction of general principles from norms ('don't believe that every element of a fact is a juridical element, don't forget to give a just value to those elements of a fact that at first sight do not appear to be juridical elements'). Taking nothing away from a moral imperative in life, he concludes with the assumption, 'to bend the private will and private judgment to the will of the State, whatever it may be, is the work of a good citizen'.

The liberty of the interpreter, the uniformity of the legal system, and the conformity of the application of rights to the law, are the main points of this reading of the norms and of the message of this jurist to other jurists.

1.1.10. The natural-law thesis

The Italian Civil Code of 1865 was beginning to show its first cracks after half a century. The growing industrialization, modifications in the social structure, and special legislation along with the advent of the period of belligerency was becoming ever wider, colliding with work relations, local relations, and urban and agrarian relations. All these were provoking a rethinking of the role of the code and therefore of the interpreter. Moreover, the brief period of juridical socialism at the end of the 19th century had denounced the ideological options of a civil code on property that was overturned in the same way that the commercial code on the micro-economy of exchange was overturned. The new times required a modernization that could happen without traumas.

Projections for a new codification were not lacking but most of these dealt with internal procedures, with progressive adaptations that above all bent existing norms to the new exigencies. Even without reaching the maximum degree of autonomy entrusted to the judge, good results could be obtained. Swiss legislators, in the same years had resolved the question in another way, allowing the judge who cannot find a specific rule in the system with which to resolve a case before him, to make himself a 'legislator of a single case'. Others, a few years before had centred interpretative liberty in analogies. The rules of logic, in the case of analogic interpretation as well as in the application of principles, would naturally serve as a restraint on discretion, thus tempering the creative power of jurisprudence.

In this climate of reform, waiting and dissatisfaction, the models, currents and directions that would eventually take root in our juridical culture began to take shape. This included subsequent re-elabourations in the 1940s, again at the end of the 1960s, and finally in the present moment. In our experience, the history of general principles is one of phases, and these phases normally occur in periods of crisis or renewal.

In the 1920s, in the first effervescent post-war climate, characterized by the desire to instal a new order, the positivist jurist began to doubt the granite-like certainties that the 19th century had sculptured. Alongside of those who still wanted an interpreter devoted to the letter of the law and deprived of any fantasy, a mere executor of a *voluntas legis* obtainable without hesitation from a text that permitted neither nuances nor deviations, there were those who believed it possible to introduce meta-juridical values into the system, entering by way of the general clauses like equity, good faith and public order, availing themselves of the general principles of rights.

In this climate, the beginning of a new phase and therefore of a new discussion, provoked first by the writings of Donati with his book on analogies in 1910, and then by Brugi with a work in 1916, is given by Giorgio Del Vecchio's broad essay, informed by a moderate and modern idea of natural law (1921).

In this essay, destined to become a pillar of the theory of interpretation, Del Vecchio departs from the consideration of the inevitable incompleteness of the law in force and thus from the necessity of recourse to reason, or better, to 'natural reason that governs the creation and interpretation of norms' so as to be able to resolve juridical questions in a just way. Some principles are of a logical nature (*nemo transferre*; *cuius commoda*, etc.); others derive from 'the nature-of things' that is, from the evaluation of the circumstances of single cases; others are postulated by the same Civil Code that refers back to equity, or to natural equity (Articles 463, 578, 1124, 1652, 1718, Civil Code previously in force).

Del Vecchio does not distinguish between a juridical system and a system of equity. He does not consider the references made in the codes to equity or to the nature of things to be expressions of values different and alternative with respect to juridical references. For him, rights and equity are two reciprocally integrated sources; equity constitutes 'a perennial source of renewal and re-integration for the whole juridical organism'.

There are, however, norms that reproduce principles; norms that reproduce them only in part, and gaps that may be filled with the help of principles. The problem of the will of the judge does not escape Del Vecchio nor does he confuse the *jus conditum* with the *jus condendum*. Where there are norms, these must be applied even though they do not respond to criteria of rationality and equity. In other words, principles, 'having a character of vitality and of absoluteness' cannot have the value of special norms that constitute the system, but can be used as a frame of values in order to clarify and complete the rules of positive law'. In the application of norms, principles make explicit the *ratio legis*. In the case of gaps, they regulate the material. Del Vecchio assigns to principles, according to natural law, an interpretive and a 'corrective' function.

1.1.11. The general principle of the legal system of the State

The outcome of the second phase sees the approval of the formula established by Article 3 of the prelaws or general provisions (1939) which in the 1942 version becomes Article 12. One refers to this article for controversies in which a decision is impossible to formulate by way of a precise disposition. Only subsequently, when doubts still exist, is the judge directed to general principles 'of the legal system of the State'. The most reductive intepretation this formula would seem to consent only to an interpretive and integrative use; and one attends not to all the principles of law, but only to those so general as to be part of the legal system 'of the State'. One could not have invented a formula more rigid or positivist, and it was the fruit of a casual choice that other, more bland formulas were rejected [see para 1.1.6].

The formula was more extended in the first version proposed by the commission where the limitation of 'general principles of law'—'general principles of the law in action' was foreseen. This was to exclude the risk of an actively legislating judge (that is revived in Article 1, paragraph 2 of the Swiss Code) as well as to satisfy 'the reasonable needs of the legal culture and to serve judicial practice'. The formula was maintained in the Report of the Minister of Justice presenting the new text of the Code to the King of Italy. With reference to law in force, one could prohibit the interpreter from bringing back into the sphere of the legislative system those norms to which the system itself is connected in its origins and historical development.

Any tendency 'to excessive generalizations and abstractions, referring to foreign laws and thus altering the peculiar lines of our national legislation' would thereby be impeded. But the text pleased no one.

In the Report of the Minister of Justice, the reasons for the final choice of words are stated thus:

> The specification introduced in the definitive project with respect to the general principles of law, in the sense that such principles must be sought within the sphere of the legal system in force, has encountered the full favor of the Parliamentary Commission. Nevertheless, I believed it opportune to introduce in the text of Article 3 a modification, not merely of a formal nature, to express more clearly and more completely this concept. In place of the formula 'general principles of law in force', that might have appeared to limit the work of the interpreter, I held 'general principles of the legal system of the State', to be preferable.

Here the term 'system' is comprehensive in its meaning, beyond the norms and institutions, and even the political-legislative orientation and the national scientific tradition (Roman law, common law, etc) with which it is in harmony. Such a system, adopted or sanctioned by the State, that constitutes our positivist system, whether public or private, will give the interpreter all the necessary elements in the search of the regulative norm.

As we see, the call to the national scientific tradition, that today is considered a mere ornament, was the mode of tying the values suffused in the system and in place at its base to the law in force. Some had made clear its role under the denomination of the dogma of private law.

That the interpreter must extract the principles from the legal rules in force and be bound by them, is another subject. However, the interpretation of rules passes beyond the literal confines of the rules themselves.

1.1.12. The legal-realist thesis

We have reached the present debate, having warned several times about the tension between formal interpretation and conceptual interpretation, as well as the unconscious use of formulas. Of the valuable contributions that doctrine has gradually elaborated, we take into account, above all, the voices of the writers of encyclopaedie or commentators of the Civil Code. In this context the position of Giovanni Tarello stands out, demonstrated within a research dedicated to the interpretation of the law (1970).

The legal-realist position of Tarello begins with the presupposition, shared by among others, Betti, but also by the formalist culture, that rights do not spring only from statutes ('not all of the discipline of society can be found in the totality of the statutes'). That is because the interpreter already makes additions in the moment that he effects merely literal interpretation of a statutory provision (unless the statute contains all the definitions of all the terms used, which rarely happens). The law cannot foresee all the specific concrete instances that are possible in reality. The search for the norm to complete the system begins here. Tarello explains that this procedure is assisted by the ideology of completeness of the system. Article 12 of the General Provisions or (prel) to the Civil Code begins with this premise because it adopts analogy and general principles to complete the system; it is therefore a norm of closure. The judge must give content to the analogical interpretation as well as, and above all, the general principles. Still, completeness is belied by the existence of norms which are conflicting, such that, if all statutes were the reflection only of the law, we would find ourselves confronted by a contradictory system. The question is resolved with recourse to three criteria: the criterion of hierarchy (Article 1 prel), the criterion of posteriority (Article 15, prel), and the criterion of speciality. But these three criteria require the intervention of the interpreter just as the application of the laws requires systematic interpretation.

In this context general principles are one of the diverse techniques utilized by judges in the interpretation of laws. Tarello warns that principles mask the *analogia juris*; they mask a favour towards some interest (eg the conversion of the contract, the protection of a debtor's interest, the interest of the employee, etc). Moreover, they mask the ideology of the interpreter, especially when he reproduces the values of the ruling regime (as happened for the principles codified in the Labour 'Charter' during Fascism). The argument beginning from general principles is a blank scheme that from time to time serves to cover disparate operations.

But principles can be understood in a different way, that is, as values underlying the system, utilized by the judge almost as if they were fundamental sources. This is the thesis of Ronald Dworkin. In his critique of positivism, Dworkin distinguishes between rules and principles. Rights are not a system of rules, but of rules and standards, that is of principles, of politics and of retro-standards. A principle is a standard that must be observed not so much as it provokes or maintains a situation (economic, political or social), but inasmuch as it expresses an exigency of justice, of correctness, or of any other moral dimension. For example, the standard that no one must draw profit from his illicit act, is a principle. According to Dworkin, principles are therefore different from rules, but are a part of the law. Their difference is above all logical. The enunciated norm is expressed in a precise way, while the principles do not determine the exposition of conditions that render their application necessary. Another difference consists in the fact that principles have a dimension that rules do not have; this dimension is given by the weight or importance. Principles serve to give content to general clauses inserted in the rules. What is more, only rules impose results, while principles do not. In reality, principles can be recognized *ex post*, that is, after their application on the part of the judge.

The fact that in common law the weight of precedent is much more relevant than in continental rights, weighs heavily on Dworkin's thesis. Moreover, it is the fact that beyond the influence of Roman law on common law, there has never been in that culture a dominant position of brocards, traditional principles, or additional techniques, as has developed in the continental countries and in Italy in particular.

In any case, it is not possible to stop at the positivist conception. What one can do is take into account the positivist exigency concerning the control of judicial discretion, the consistency and logic of motivation, and above all, the awareness of the use of the expression 'principle'. This along with the technique of employing the principle that is singled out either for historic recognition or out of spontaneous, natural expression, or as an *ad hoc* creation to resolve a controversial question.

Along this line, which demystifies principles considering their historical function and content, we place François Ewald, a student of Michel Foucault. Ewald advanced his thesis from the presupposition that laws are the fruit of a system of the allocation of power, and that therefore systems of the law in action that exist concretely from one historical phase to another express the values of the society that creates them. He then elaborated that general principles (here understood in the acceptance as the foundation of a system) and unwritten rules latent in the juridical tradition of the civil nations, are norms that the jurist follows. These comprise a kind of 'natural empirical law' that, as distant from the classic natural law as from dogmatic positivism, consents to value the legitimacy of normative provisions and to enrich positivist data. Thus, general principles are retraceable in the history of laws and are the expression of the memory of our juridical tradition.

This position, certainly acceptable, although partial in the definition of the role of principles as well as in their historicity, can nonetheless be placed within the range of positivist criticism. But it has provoked the criticism of those who hold that the natural law model is vital in the history of rights and that principles must be situated in a more circumscribed dimension.

1.1.13. The composite function of principles

We can present the results of research obtained up to this point in a brief summary. It deals with assertions that find their foundation in what is espoused in the preceding paragraphs.

1. The individuation of functions which general principles fulfil is vague and arbitrary as is the categorization of principles, their creation or their identification in the law in force.
2. This vagueness and arbitrariness, however, should not be surprising as it is typical of all interpretive activity. What is important is that the interpretive activity responds to the canons of logic, to common sense, and to practical utility.

   A fundamental function fulfilled by principles is thus the role that they play in legal reasoning. As Struck has clearly brought to light, principles, and therefore the juridical topos, serve the application of norms from the moment that no juridical rule or value is absolute. There is always the case in which, depending on the circumstances, the rule must be limited and the value must yield to considerations that are superior.
3. In the general opinion and in general practice, principles thus fulfil a function much broader than the one entrusted to them in Article 12 of the prelaws or General Provisions of the Civil Code. On these hinges the system of private law, consisting of positivist sources and all that can be derived from its interpretation, its manipulation, and its construction in the system. Principles thus play the role of 'foundation' of the system. In the non-codified sectors, administrative law and international law, principles fulfil a still more relevant function, that of a normative frame of reference.
4. In case law principles obviously play the role recognized for them by Article 12 of the General Provisions placed before the Civil Code, that is as a rule applicable to concrete instances when the text has gaps, is imprecise, or is lacking in some way.
5. In the case law, principles are often invoked for the purpose of mere embellishment in that they corroborate the application of a positivist rule. Thus, they serve to reinforce the settlement of the decision and assign the greatest possible internal consistency to the reasoning.

6. Where they are created *ex novo* by the judge, they serve to legitimize rights created by case law. To mask they arbitrariness of the decision, the judge will provide for the introduction of a legitimizing shield which are the principles invoked.
7. Principles constitute the modern *koiné* of jurists belonging to different systems. This is for reasons deriving from existing data as well as for the formation of a uniform juridical culture derived from the circulation of juridical models or for the formation of a uniform commercial practice of arbitration.

   International positivist sources of law tend to fuse the normatives of the Member States (from time to time, by way of institutions of parallel systems, as happens for the EC system, or by way of conventions, as happens for the Council of Europe, or through treaties).

   The circulation of juridical models occurs either as an effect of the uniformity of the positivist data or sources of law (as happens for the reception in the internal systems of models from EC law acquired from other internal systems and imposed on all Member States); or as the effect of cultural exchanges and comparisons.

   Commercial practice tends to be inspired by uniform principles; in the same way, international arbitration tends to follow principles gathered from civil societies.

   Today, principles fulfil the function that at one time was fulfilled by Roman law: they tend towards the fusion of systems diverse in tradition and internal history.
8. Principles fulfil the function of 'policy': they express the policies of the aims of the legislator and, in general, of the interpreter which in a more or less conscious way operates according to a table of values. This policy, understood to make expression and application of principles, can either be express or implied.
9. The 'implied' principles serve to elaborate decisions formally presented as consistent with clear or express principles, but substantially inherent to the policy of the interpreter's rights.
10. Principles expressed in a dialectical way with their reciprocal (or opposite), fulfil the function of creating a balancing process that will be mitigating the interests in play, orientating the social engineering, and facilitating the mediating function of the judge.

Principles fulfil many other functions, as we have sought to demonstrate so far in this work and as has been brought to light by many authors who in different epochs have assumed them as the object of their reflection. As it is not possible to identify at any one time and forever all principles, and as it is not possible to catalogue at one time and forever all principles, so, in the same way, it is not possible to list all the functions which principles fulfil; or that such functions are fulfilled contemporaneously.

In any case, principles appear as a factor that cannot be eliminated in the art and in the process of creating norms and of interpreting them; or, what amounts to the same thing, they are indispensable instruments in the development of law.

1.2. 'UNJUST' DAMAGE AND THE ROLE OF NEGLIGENCE: HISTORICAL PROFILE

1.2.1. Introduction

In scholarly doctrinal works, there is usually little occasion for a historical treatment of civil code provisions. There is a tendency among scholars to focus narrowly and ignore the history of their speciality. Historians, on the other hand, may tend to theorize too broadly for these purposes. Bearing this in mind, we see that in Article 2043[1] regarding fault liability, the Italian Civil Code reflects almost word for word the norms and the contents of its predecessors. The terms of the provision refer back to 'principles', adages, and Roman notions. The various arguments about the subsection on negligence have referred constantly to the importance of legal tradition; in fact, this tradition is so valued that it has at times overruled the letter of the law. With the support of historical studies, this tradition reached the 1960s almost unchanged. Civil lawyers then found it necessary to take on tasks that were traditionally reserved for historians.[2] Thus, we have shown an awareness of the importance of tradition.

But how solid is this tradition? Were the historical sources really intended to convey the meanings that some modern scholars would have us believe? When reference is made to the past, what exactly are the source's historical roots: French, Pandectist or authentically Roman?

Finally, how was the notion of 'unfair' damage introduced into the Italian Civil Code? And what is the relationship between that code and the German Civil Code (BGB), which has, delictually speaking, features similar to common-law tort systems? Is the BGB an alternative model to the French codification or just a kind of limitation upon it? To these initial questions that any code interpreter must address, we can give a clear answer.

It is not necessary to trace the internal history of the '*Lex Aquilia*'. This ground was covered excellently by G Rotondi, as well as by various Roman historians. Further, we have no need to search for ancient sources, as was recently undertaken by Jolowicz and Markesinis, who made a schematic

[1] Art 2043 provides: 'Any fraudulent, malicious, or negligent act that causes an unjustified injury to another obliges the person who has committed the act to pay damages.' Mario Beltramo et al *The Italian Civil Code and Complementary Legislation* 209 (trans, Book 4, 1991).

[2] On this subject there is an excellent work by Gianfranco Massetto, a renowned historian, on the topic of 'extra-contractual liability' which was published in the *Enciclopedia del Diritto* (39th edn 1988) 1099.

comparison between various tort systems–Code Napoleon, BGB, and other modern systems, which were preceded by the *Lex Aquilia,* as if this Roman legislation were a unifying model for all the modern systems of liability.[3] It may now be common knowledge, but only recently were the above systems considered to be similar. Then it became clear that tort and crime are but two aspects of the same matter. It also became accepted that the notion of 'tort' originates in Roman '*culpa*', and that the Roman sources, being rich in nuance and detail, offer a wealth of insightful literature.

The interpretive study proposed here is quite different. Its purpose is to try to understand, by examining the sources that may have influenced the outlook and culture of the 1942 legislators who authored the Italian Civil Code, how the actual system of fault liability was conceived, with no pretension, however, of being a complete and definitive treatment of the subject.

New questions that need to be answered are then raised. We will consider how the Roman sources were adapted in the fault liability field by the jurists of the 1600s and 1700s to conform to their own outlook, heritage, and philosophy. Also to be addressed is the different relationship existing between civil liability sanctions and criminal punishment for fraudulent and negligent acts. We need also to understand where human behaviour ends (and with it the principle of civil liability) and where casualty begins. We must also consider situations where an unintentional human act coincides with an unavoidable act of nature. These are problems and questions that have yet to be answered. Regarding sources, we will investigate the impact of the Jesuit and Jansenist '*querelles*'. These quarrels concern man's free will (*arbitrium*), his control over his daily life, and doubts concerning the relationship between God and man. All of these have influenced ethical concepts and therefore the relationship between negligence and sanctions in civil law. In fact, the initial findings of the ancient authors indicate a close connection between ethical principles and liability within a legal system. It goes without saying that ethical principles of recent centuries, even if permeated with Christian values, are more closely related to our system than to the ethical values in Roman times.

A brief analysis of some of the most popular and well-known sources will support this argument. It will also prompt questions and help us to understand the novelty contained in the deceptively simple construction of Civil Code Article 2043.

[3] FH Lawson and BS Markesinis, *Tortious Liability for Unintentional Harm in the Common Law and the Civil Law* (1982).

1.2.2. Historical antecedents

In the fourth book of Mario Viviani's work,[4] which is dedicated to liability arising from criminal offences, he cites those usages or practices (*praxis*) that, in reference to free will (*arbitrium*), connect human actions and their consequences to the will. 'It is said that what we want to do or not to do depends on our choice, and its opposite is due to our choice.'[5] Viviani quotes extensively from St Thomas Aquinas, St Augustine, and Plato's *Gorgia*. The author examines several types of torts. Theft, robbery, and finally damage are regulated by the *Lex Aquilia* and are distinguished. The question of sanctions for damage arising from self-defence is analysed here, taking into account the Bible.

In the analysis of obligations arising from 'quasi-crime' Viviani offers some examples (hotel-keeper, carriers, etc), which highlight the subjective fault basis of the action ('the wrong of one person cannot be attributed to *another*'—'*delicutum unius non debet alteri imputari*'). The justification for third-party liability due to negligence in the selection of people who proved to be unreliable or untrustworthy is then given. In a concise sentence, the problem of reconciling the subjective basis of the responsibility for damages with 'third-party liability' is again called to mind.

The writings of Johann Gottlieb Heinecke (Heineccius, 1681–1741) are also important and well known in Italy. His treatise on torts demonstrates his knowledge of tradition, his convictions about fault liability, the unquestioned role of negligence, and the secondary significance of exceptions related to liability arising from personal conduct.[6]

Heineccius's description of the tort categories is systematic. He specifies the characteristics of crime and quasi-crime separately, thus avoiding the creation of a universal tort system as well as the general clauses so characteristic of the French system.[7] Heineccius introduces the obligations arising from crime in Book IV of his *Recitazione*. The act originating the obligation can be either lawful or unlawful. A lawful act arises from the will of the parties and is called 'convention'; an unlawful act is called a crime or misdeed. According to the author, Justinian's treatment of crime in the *Institutes* deals almost exclusively with the crime of theft, and Heineccius feels a need to include in his treatise other types of tort, as well as a general preface.

[4] M Viviani, *Rationale Instrfutionum Juris Civilis* 303 (Rome, 1623).

[5] Ibid (*'[I]d dicitum positum in nostra facultate quod et agere et non agere valemus, et cuius opposifum in nostra facultate est positum'*).

[6] See Johann Gotrlieb *Heinecke, Elementa Juris Civilis Secondum Ordinem Institutionum* 349, §1112 (Neapolitan edn 1778); Johann Gottlieb Heinecke, 4 Recitazioni di Diritto Civile Secondo L'Ordine delle Isttuzioni di giustiniano 163 (AL Naplas trans, 1830).

[7] Art 1382 of the French Civil Code provides: 'Any act whatever of man which causes damage to another obliges him by whose fault it occurred to make reparation.' C Civ Art 1382 (Crabb trans, 1977).

His general preface refers to both crimes and quasi-crimes. It differentiates real crimes (fraud), quasi-crimes (negligent acts), public crimes (threats to state security), and private crimes which encompass harm to 'citizens' rights and property.' According to the Italian translator of this work, 'crimes' include only those acts classified as offences.

His general definition of 'crime'[8] separates 'act' from 'thought.' An act is something apparent and expressed. It is a thought which has materialized into an action. An 'unlawful' act indicates a violation of a 'civil or natural law' (we recognize here the similarity to the notion of 'unfair damage', which means damage caused *contra jus*). Further, this act has to be 'spontaneous', that is it cannot be coerced. The obligation to make the victim whole applies only when possible (for example, if the victim dies there can be no reparation).

In treating the crimes of theft[9] and robbery,[10] Heineccius addresses the *Lex Aquilia* and the subject of injuries.

The author defines *damnum injuria datum* as 'any harm to personal property or rights caused by a person with no legal justification'. Here again we note the similarity to the second part of the modern definition of 'unfair damage', that is, damage caused *non jure*. Harm to a person's property and rights can also occur as a consequence of a crime, for example the killing of a person. The author clarifies that in this case several legal actions will co-exist. The main interest protected is personal property; the damage caused must be unjustifiable, which means that it must not arise from the exercise of a legal right (*non jure factum*).

Whether the damage arises from a fraudulent or negligent act or a failure to exercise due care is irrelevant: Under the *Lex Aquilia* slight fault is actionable ('*in lege Aquilia et levissima culpa venit*'). Depending upon the degree of negligence, the case will be classified as a crime or quasi-crime. In the description of tort, the author continues with examples and arguments taken from Roman sources: damage caused by servants or animals and damage to trees and objects. Finally, the subject of injury to persons is introduced. The injurer is obligated to pay for the medical expenses of the injured; he is responsible for '*lucrum cessans*' and '*damnum emergens*'.

A superficial reader reviewing these sources could argue at this stage that in Heineccius's time it was only necessary to update the interpretation of Roman sources in order to discover the enforceable legal rules. However, here Heineccius abruptly changes the scenario; he questions whether the *Lex Aquilia* still has currency, and he highlights all of the arguments against it. Today, he says, there is no distinction between servants, or different types

[8] Ibid ('[A] crime is an unlawful and spontaneous act, by which a party is obligated to suffer a punishment, and to repair the damage if possible').

[9] Ibid § 1039–70.

[10] Ibid § 1071–9.

of animals, or among the different means of causation. The damage, whether '*corpore*' or not, is not doubled because the party denies it, and so on. Thus Heineccius, rather than preserving and updating the portion of the sources which remain valid, adopts a drastically simplified solution. He derives the modern concept of damage from the natural law and *patrii statuti* instead of the *Lex Aquilia*. A quotation of Tomasius follows.

There follows a dissertation on injuries, libel, damage to reputation, and so on.[11] We finally arrive at an explanation of obligations arising from quasi-crime.[12]

Heineccius opens up a polemic on the work of Struvio regarding the definition of 'quasi-crime'. Feeling strongly about his own theory on the subjective basis of tort, he cannot accept the concept of third-party liability when no negligence has occurred (which in his opinion is Struvio's theory). He insists on the definition of quasi-crime as 'a tort committed with negligence but without fraud'. Hence a lessee is liable for his servant's tort because 'he has failed to admit in his house a more diligent subject'—not because of third-party liability.

At this stage his thesis becomes clear. He provides a description of six types of quasi-crime: (1) an unfaithful judge; (2) scattered and thrown objects (*de effusis et dejectis*); (3) suspended and hanging objects on passageways; (4) damage to clients' chattels caused by sailors, hotelkeepers, and grooms; (5) aiding and abetting; and (6) 'dissimulation' (giving consent to the commission of a crime).

The Neapolitan editor's footnote is also quite interesting. He recalls, without noting any contrasts and almost as a natural sequence, the liability rules of the two Sicily Kingdoms which derive from the Napoleonic Code.

Let us return to Heineccius's dialogue with his interlocutors. Among them we have Struvio (Giorgia Adamo Struvio, 1619–92) whose *Jurisprudentia Romano Germanica Forensis* is well known in Italy.[13] In reference to crimes, Struvio uses the Roman divisions of the subject.[14] As a general definition of crime, he insists on an act in itself illicit (*factum in se illicitum*) committed spontaneously and in violation of the law. The obligation to pay damages and to submit to sanctions arises from such actions. After treating *furtum* (theft) and *iniuria* (libel), the author deals with *damnum iniuria datum*, which is the damage caused to a person or his chattels due to fraud or negligence, no matter how slight. He highlights the point that in crimes, damages consist of a sum of money and in cases of physical iniury (reference is made to the *Lex Aquilia*) this will include medical expenses and worker's compensation (*operae, quibus quis caruit*

11 Ibid § 1096–111.
12 Ibid § 1112–25.
13 Giorgia Adamo Struvio, *Jurisprudentia Romano Germanica Forensis* (16th edn 1739).
14 2 ibid tit. XXIII at 436.

aut cariturus est ob vulnus), and, if requested by the victim, an amount for pain, grief, scars, and deformity. Further on, Struvio discusses quasi-crime,[15] citing the same examples as Heineccius. The crux of his theory lies in the recognition of third-party liability—liability based on something other than personal conduct. Struvio's modernity lies in not insisting upon proof of the subjective negligence of the tortfeasor.

Grotius also differentiates between *casus* and *culpa,* that is, between accident and fault. *Culpa* (negligence) implies conscience and action, despite the lack of any desire to cause the damage. As stated in the Aristotelian ethic, fault is similar to the principle of responding for one's behaviour.[16] In dealing with damage per *injuriam,* Grotius states that once it has been perpetrated, the obligation to make good on the damage arises naturaliter.[17]

The writings of Vinnius (1588–1657) are also relevant to this discussion. According to Orestano,[18] the works of Vinnius were well known and widely used by Italian scholars teaching civil law up until the first half of the 1800s. Vinnius's most used works are the four books concerning *Institutuinum Imperialium Commentatius Academicus et* Forensis,[19] with footnotes from Heineccius, and the four books concerning *Partitionum Juris* Civilis.[20]

In reference to third-party liability, Vinnius mentions damage caused by objects and animals. He does not, in any event, mention 'negligence' as a premise for damage liability.

Voet (1647–1714) does not present any particular surprises on the subject. His *Commentarius ad Pandectas*[21] defines 'crime' as a verbal offence or action based on fraud or negligence and *contra jus* (against the law). Such description refers mainly to crimes against a person's rights and property.

1.2.3. The modern evolution

The problem of personal negligence for third-party liability remained unresolved until the 1865 codification, in Italy, which, as we know, creates a synthesis (*crasi*) of the two opposite theories. In fact, even though it supports (at least literally) the non-liability thesis, the Code still recognizes

[15] 3 ibid tit. XXVI at 442.

[16] 'Culpa affinis est qui in se habet agendi principium', Grotius, *De Jure Belli Ac Pacis* 514 (Amsterdam 1646).

[17] Ibid at 289.

[18] Riccardo Orestano, *Introduzione allo studio del diritto romano* (1987) 81 .

[19] Vinnius, *Institutionum Imparíclium Commentarius Academicus at Forensis* (Naples 1771) 770.

[20] Vinnius, *Partitionum Juris Civilis* (Venice, 1793) 185.

[21] Voet, *Commentarius ad Pandectas* (XLVII edn, Colonia 1778) tit. 1, 802.

that a person is liable for damages caused by his own actions or by persons for whom he is responsible or by objects in his custody.

Indeed, the textbooks used by practitioners (*pratici*) and by civil law students in that period summarize and reproduce the rules of Roman law. The work of Carlo Redi is an exemplary model.[22] His definition of *delictum* is every illicit wrong done willingly against the law.[23] He then describes the different types of crime (theft, robbery), damages *ex Lege Aquilia*, injuries (insult, offence) and finally quasi-crimes (with no mention of the law applied at that time). The usual examples (a judge's bad decision '*effusiones et deiectiones*'; *posita et suspensa*; hotel-keeper and carrier liability) are found here as well.

We can now see how the Roman sources can be read, interpreted and manipulated to support both the principle of 'no liability without fault' and the opposite principle of objective liability that recognizes third-party liability (for objects or animals in custody or for employees) with no need to prove personal negligence.

The Roman sources being predominantly a system of typical paradigms is constructed by using case methodology to identify the different types of tort.

How does the transition occur from a system based upon typical cases to a system founded upon abstract principle?

We see the change occurring in Domat and Pothier. The former describes in minute detail the different types of tort, but prefaces the description by giving a general concept of tort. The latter simplifies the matter and draws some general guidelines for the Code's norms on crime and quasi-crime, insisting mainly on imputability.

Domat, unlike the authors studied so far, starts from a wide and unitary concept of torts. He takes into consideration not only all the facts expressly forbidden by the law, but also those in conflict with equity, honesty and society's morals, 'even if the same are not provided for by written law'.[24] Thus, we begin our outline of the concept of 'unlawfulness' (*illiceita*), which will be discussed later. This leaves out reference to tight guidelines regarding specific rules, and strives to evaluate general behaviour. In other words, we are approaching the creation of a 'general cause'. Domat explains: 'Anything against equity, honesty and society's morals is against the principles of the Laws and God's Law.'[25]

Further on, Domat provides an explanation for such rules: men are united in a society by a certain order which obligates them to refrain from damaging the rights and property of others and also obligates each member

[22] See Carlo Redi, *Institutiones Juris Civilis* (Florence 1841) 225.
[23] Ibid ('omne factum illicitum sponte contra jus admissum').
[24] Domat, *Lois civiles, in* 1 *Œuvres Complètes* (J Remy ed, Paris 1835) 467.
[25] Ibid.

to maintain his possessions in such a way so as to not damage another's.[26] In Domat's words, an orderly, civil life requires sanctions against damages which are caused by personal conduct of employees, by objects owned or by animals used.

The norms of the code civil are born in this microcosm: each member of society (citizen) deserves a peaceful life, and this can be achieved if each member has control over certain things which are controllable, such as personal behaviour, possessions, employees, and the use of animals. These are the reasons for this legal regulation.

In his description of torts, Domat does not at first refer to damage. It is mentioned in the context of commitments created without a previous contractual obligation ('extra-contractual', as we would say). He then deals with the giving (*datio*) of things, that is the giving or receiving of a sum of money not due, for unlawful reasons.

In Domat's classification of negligent damage, he distinguishes negligence which causes a crime or tort from that which produces breach of contract. For example: the failure to consign an object that has been sold or the failure to make repairs to a rented house. He also contrasts these from negligence, which is not connected with a crime or tort or agreement but is simply due to imprudent behaviour or the custody of an animal or object.

Domat is therefore the first one clearly to differentiate those matters unified by the common denominator of fault, and to distinguish between torts and crimes since the latter belongs, in his view, to a field of the law which should not be mixed with civil matters.[27]

It should be noted how Roman sources are also taken into consideration by Domat, especially in citations to the Digest. These receive an interpretation quite different from that given by the historians and jurists of Domat's day. Domat does not follow the typical Roman arrangement, nor does he mix together crimes and torts. After enunciating the definition of tort, which he insists has to be anchored in negligence, he gives some examples. These examples are of course taken from the Digest, as well as from daily life.

Remy, who is the editor of the authoritative 19th century edition of Domat's work, presents some references to the 'code civil' and also includes in a footnote the French Court's first decisions (*arrêts*). One of these decisions concerns the liability of a building owner for damage to a third party arising out of the use of the owner's property and his servants' negligence. The owner is responsible even if such damage occurred in his absence or without his knowledge. In the case of undivided ownership, all owners are jointly liable unless the property is divided. Teachers, craftsmen and anybody who boards pupils, apprentices, or others for reasons of commerce

[26] Ibid At 473. [27] Ibid at 470.

or industry are liable for their actions.[28] The same applies for objects suspended or thrown from a building.

Domat tries to adapt the Roman rules to the contents of the French customs (*coutumes*). Regarding damages caused by animals, Domat examines several cases and cites a general rule: if the owner or custodian of the animal was in a position to avert the damage, he is responsible because he stands to benefit from the animal's use.[29] In reference to damage caused by buildings, the owner is always liable except for fortuitous cases or if he proves to have exercised his own right.[30]

We may ask, why does Domat focus on damage caused by objects, people, and animals? These examples can be easily linked to their Roman sources and to the frequency with which damage of this kind occurred at Domat's time in the agricultural world. Unlike scholars in the Roman–German tradition, Domat is not satisfied with a simple list of cases. He elaborates general rules for human society. That is, all cases are governed by general rules which should correspond, in a descriptive order (the order of civil society) to the definition of tort found in the opening of his treatise. The 'grand' author enunciates here his general rule, with notes referring to other types of damage caused by negligence, excluding offences (*reati*) and crimes:

> All losses and damages which may occur through the act of a person, whether due to imprudence, rashness, ignorance of what one ought to know, or other similar faults, however slight they may be, must be repaired by him whose imprudence or other fault brought it about.[31]

The above general enunciation and the text of the Code Napoleon Article 1382 correspond exactly. In fact, the latter states: 'Every act of man which causes damage to another obliges him by whose fault it occurred to repair it.'[32]

Pothier (1699–1772) restates the position that crime and quasi-crime are a third and fourth source of obligation: a crime is an act by which a person, with fraud or malice, causes damage or tort to another; a quasi-crime is an act by which a person, without malice but with unjustified negligence, causes harm to another.

Pothier, in his concise and clear style, derives implicitly from the above definition the essential elements of tort: the subjective element (fraud or negligence); the objective element (damage); the knowledge, which implies

28 Ibid at 472. 29 Ibid at 474–5. 30 Ibid at 478–9.

31 'Toutes les pertes et tous les dommages qui peuvent arrivé par le fait de quelque personne, soit imprudence, légèreté, ignorance de ce qu'on doit savoir, ou autres fautes sembiables, si légères qu'elles puissent étre, doivent étre réparées par celui dont l'imprudence ou autre faute y a donné lieu.'

32 'Tout fait quelconque de l'homme, qui cause à autrui un dommage, oblige celui par la faute duquel il est arrivé à le reparer.'

imputability (much consideration is given to cases of damage caused by minors, incapables, and the mentally insane); and the chain of causation.

In reference to quasi-crime, which as defined by Struvio involved, 'acts for which we are liable even if caused by others,' Pothier does not insist on the necessity of negligence when referring to custodians, masters, and parents. Nonetheless, he relieves parents of all responsibility if they can prove that they could not have prevented the child's act. This exemption, however, does not apply to owners and employers, for reasons of social policy and 'deterrence': 'This liability has been established in order to make masters careful to use only good servants.'[33] Obviously, however, masters and employers are not liable for torts caused by servants and salesmen acting outside of their employment.[34]

Pothier's dissertation on torts ends here. The codifiers had only to produce a synthesis (*crasi*) between Domat's and Pothier's writings. As can be seen in Fenet's documents, this is what occurred.

The concise norms of the Code Civil soon became a source of analysis for the doctrine and the jurisprudence. Among the commentators we cite two examples, one belonging to the systematic model, the other to the exegetic one. The transformation that occurred, whether expansive or restrictive, over almost two centuries of application, will be discussed later.

KS Zachariae's version defines 'crime' as 'any unlawful act by which a person offends against, purposely and with malice, somebody else's rights'.[35]

The definitions of 'crime' and 'offence' are followed by a discussion of the distinction between the two terms, which are considered parallel but not synonymous. A crime is a harmful, damaging act which has the following elements: (a) illicitness, that is, a prejudice to somebody's rights, which derives either from an action or an omission; (b) absence of justification for such action; (c) imputability; and (d) a subjective element: fraud for crime and negligence for quasi-crime. As we can see, the core of the entire theory of torts lies in this concise and clear analysis. It is still today endorsed by jurists, with the exception, of course, of the definitions of crime and quasi-crime. All of the characteristics indicated above for crimes are repeated for quasi-crimes,[36] which he believes are based on negligence.

Without negligence, an act cannot be considered a quasi-crime; the existence of negligence must be proved by the injured party.[37] Third-party

[33] 'Ce qui a été établi pour rendre les maitres attentif à ne se servir que de bons domestiques'.

[34] *Pothier, Œuvres de Pothier* (Dupin ed, 1835) 64, 141.

[35] KS Zachariae, *Corso di Diritto Civile Francese* (Aubry and Rau trans, 5th edn 1868); 2 KS Zachariae, *Corso di Diritto Civile Francese* (Attanasio and Del Core trans, Naples 1847) 110 [hereinafter Zachariae].

[36] Zachariae, *supra* n 35, at 113.

[37] Ibid at 113.

liability, for which the law attaches legal responsibility, is treated like quasi-crime whenever the tortfeasor is negligent.

The superb treatise of Toullier[38] may be considered next. He starts from the terms of Code Article 1382 in order to clarify that the expression '*fait*' is intended in its broader meaning, including mistakes and omissions. The expression '*faute*' refers to the objective illicit act (*quod non jure fit*), not to the subjective feeling.

He concludes that it is forbidden to prejudice someone else's rights[39]—namely individual rights, personal rights, ownership, and other real property rights. Toullier includes possession, among other real rights, provided it has lasted for over a year. A very detailed case study of jurisprudence and legislation follows, concerning mainly arson, real property, leasing, etc. There is also a specific discussion on norms concerning third-party liability for persons or objects in custody.

Toullier is very sceptical regarding the link between negligence and liability. How can third-party liability be justified when reason and moral principles indicate that civilized people should be measured by the subjective standard of negligence? Toullier analyses the Roman sources and determines that the Romans also based third-party liability on negligence.[40]

Toullier then believes that the Code considers third-party liability to be based upon exceptional cases imposed by the law or by an expressed or implied agreement, for example, hotel-keeper or carriers' liability. These norms, though severe, are considered necessary for safety reasons.[41] He also proposes a restrictive interpretation in reference to parents' responsibility. For masters and employers, he does not recognize that this is a type of third-party liability. They are responsible for damage because they ordered somebody to do something on their behalf.[42] The same concept applies to a servant's fraudulent acts, such as stealing from a neighbour's crop, provided the servant is not a criminal.[43] Toullier justifies the liability as follows: masters and employers use servants and salesmen to operate on their behalf; therefore, any damage occurring as a result of the actions of the latter must be considered as if caused by the masters and employers *directly*.

Toullier notes that the Code excuses the liability of parents and teachers who can prove that they could not have prevented the damage. He explains why it does not do the same for masters and employers. The author recalls the argument, which occurred during the Code's compilation, between Tarrible who was in favour of the exemption and Bertrad de la Greuille who was against it. To resolve this issue, Toullier cites Pothier, who denies

[38] Toullier, *Le Droit Civil Français Suivant L'ordre de Code* (New Belgian edn, Bruxelles 1838) 48.
[39] Ibid at 50.
[40] Ibid at 101.
[41] Ibid at 109.
[42] Ibid at 117.
[43] Ibid at 117 n 4.

the exemption with respect to acts by servants and employees within the scope of their employment.

In other words, the subjective character of an act—and therefore the liability for it—is maintained by treating the act of the servant or employee as an intermediary link to the employer.

If damages are caused by objects, they, too, are rationalized in terms of negligence. Thus, 'if a building collapses the owner is responsible because it was his duty to maintain it in good order'.[44]

When the draft of the Civil Code norms was written, the question of liability for negligence and the exceptions thereto were not straightforward and clear. To better understand the different approaches to the regime of liability, we should now have a look at the other legal systems which were in force in Europe at that time.

The Austrian Civil Code came into force on 1 January 1812, under Francis I. It was extended to the state of Milan on 1 January 1816, with the understanding that the Italian translation of the Code would prevail over the Austrian text. The Code follows Gaius's arrangement of the civil law by subdividing legal topics into subjects (persons, property and possessory rights, and norms common to both). The resulting picture, however, is more complex than the linear and simplified Code Napoleon. In fact, when the stratified layers of rhetoric are removed, the Austrian Civil Code appears surprisingly modern. The general rules regarding contracts are placed in the Code's Second Part, which concerns personal and real property rights. The opening article states: 'Personal rights in property, under which one person is obliged to some extent to accomplish something for another, are based either directly on a law, on a legal transaction, or on damage suffered.'[45] We can instantly see here the tripartite sources of the field of obligations (*ex lege, ex contractu, ex delictu*).

Yet in the succeeding chapters where general and particular contracts are dealt with, obligations arising from the law are not included, and the principles related to tort are placed at the end of Part Two under the heading: 'Right to Damage and Satisfaction.'

The Austrian legislator's main concern is to categorize different types of damage, whether contractual or extra-contractual, by the use of similar norms. This classification should take into consideration the damage's cause, namely a breach of contract or a tort. Paragraph 1295(1), using a formula similar to Napoleon Code Article 1382, reads: 'A person is entitled to demand indemnification for the damage from a person causing an injury

[44] Ibid at 131.

[45] *Allgemeines Bürgerliches Gesetzbuch* (ABGB) § 859 (Austria). The English translation appearing in the above text and in subsequent text is taken from Baeck's edition of *The General Civil Code of Austria* (Oceana 1972).

by his fault; the damage may have been caused either by the violation of a contractual duty or without regard to a contract.'[46]

In this highly descriptive Code, damage is defined as 'every detriment which has been caused to any person in regard to his property, his rights or his person'. Such damage refers to the direct loss (*damnum emergens*), which, the Code states, must be distinguished from the *lucrum cessans*—namely 'the loss of profits which a person expects according to the usual course of his affairs.[47]

What is the cause of the damage? Paragraph 1294 answers: 'Damage arises either from an illegal act or an illegal omission of another, or from an accident.' It is further specified in paragraph 1306: 'A person is generally not responsible for damages he has caused without fault or by an involuntary act.'

Paragraph 1311 then says: 'Mere accidents affect only the person to whose property or person they occur.' Negligence is the crux of the system. There is to be no liability without fault, and when in doubt, '[t]he presumption prevails that damage has arisen without any fault on the part of another'.[48] The burden of proof is on the injured party.[49]

Damage, by definition, must be faulty and 'illegal'. Illegal damage is caused 'either wilfully or not wilfully'.[50] Wilful damage is based either on a wrongful intention, when caused with knowledge and willingness or on an omission, when caused by ignorance or lack of care of duty. Fault (*Verschulden*) includes, in this text, both act and omission if there was a duty of care.[51] According to Basevi[52] wilful damage would best be translated as '*danneggiamento*', corresponding to the original 'Beschädigung'; Ellinger also agrees with such a definition.[53]

The above system, though obviously redundant, clearly states that a tort must be connected through a chain of causation to fraudulent or negligent behaviour on the part of the responsible party;[54] furthermore, damage must qualify as 'illegal'. The indiscriminate use of 'act' and illegal 'damage' derives from the norms which at times sanction the behaviour and at other times the effects of that behaviour.

There is no third-party liability then, except for some specific circumstances which correspond to those in the Code Napoleon, namely: (a) custodians of the insane and underaged are responsible for damages caused

[46] Ibid § 1295(1).
[47] Ibid § 1293.
[48] Ibid § 1296.
[49] Ibid § 1298.
[50] Ibid § 1294.
[51] Ibid.
[52] Basevi, *Annotazioni pratice di diritto civile austrico* (VI edn, Milano, 1855) 578.
[53] Ellinger, *Manuale di diritto civile austriaco* 289–90 § 1294 (G Rotondi trans, Milano, 1853).
[54] Ibid § 1313 ('A person is not generally liable for the illegal acts of another in which he has not participated.').

by their *protégés* when the former have neglected their duties;[55] (b) employers are responsible for damage caused by employees only if they have been illegally hired or if they are, by reason of their nature, dangerous individuals;[56] (c) employers of incompetent or unfit employees are responsible for them;[57] (d) hotel-keepers and carriers are responsible for their employees' damage;[58] (e) the owner of a building from which an object falls is liable for damage caused;[59] and (f) whoever incites or irritates an animal or provides improper custody for it is liable for any damage it may cause.[60] But since an animal, unlike an object, is mobile, chances are that its custodian's contribution to the accident in terms of actual causation is marginal. The paragraph adds: 'if no one is convinced of negligence, the damage which occurred should be considered as a fortuitous case.'

As far as protected interests are concerned, it can be seen that the Code creates a general scheme of typical and atypical cases. In fact the definition of damage makes reference to harm caused to property,' to 'rights' and to 'persons'. This categorization is tempered both by the adjective 'any' harm, and by use of the expression 'rights'. Ellinger stresses that this term refers to 'civil and political rights to which any citizen is entitled, and not to legal action for contractual obligations'.

Looking through the subsequent articles, we note that the type of damage taken into consideration is mainly that related to property and possessions. Nonetheless, the level of precision relating to the regulation of physical and moral damage[61]—so lacking in the Italian legal system—is surprisingly high. The Code deals with 'permanent injuries, injury to a female who cannot, because of her gender, improve her standard of living with her own means',[62] recognition of the right of parents to receive compensation for the loss of a child,[63] and finally with female seduction,[64] loss of freedom[65] and damage to one's honour which causes pecuniary loss.[66]

Damages relating to physical injury include compensation for lost gains (*lucrum cessans*) and possibly for future damage stemming from permanent injuries caused by the accident, as well as expenses for medical care and suffering. In cases of negligent or fraudulent damage to property or possessions, thorough compensation or indemnity can be obtained.

According to paragraph 1323, there are no *lucrum cessans* damages recoverable in the case of injury to property.

If the action causing the damage was forbidden by the criminal law, or there was malice and impertinence, 'sentimental value' may be demanded instead of the usual 'estimated market value'.

[55] Ibid § 1308–9.
[56] Ibid § 1314.
[57] Ibid § 1315.
[58] Ibid § 1316.
[59] Ibid § 1318.
[60] Ibid § 1320.
[61] Ibid § 1325.
[62] Ibid § 1326.
[63] Ibid § 1327.
[64] Ibid § 1328.
[65] Ibid § 1329.
[66] Ibid § 1330.

We come now to the period of the Unified Code (1865) in Italy, which is the best-known and most compelling period in history for civil law scholars specializing in this subject. The Italian Unified Code reproduces, almost completely, the text of the Napoleon Code, with parallels corresponding to the previous codes. It establishes six liability norms, including a general principle of responsibility based on negligence;[67] rules recognizing third-party liability with the exception[68] of parents, teachers, tutors and craftsmen; and rules of liability for damage caused by animals[69] and objects.[70] In a work by G Foschini[71] treating the Civil Code of the Kingdom of Italy, the new norms are compared with the previous ones, but without comment, the new norms being apparently 'self-explanatory'.[72]

Problems arising from the application of the Unified Code are extensively dealt with in the jurisprudence of this period. It is further settled that 'act' includes omission (or negative action) as indicated in the Code's general principles. Thus, reticence, meaning omission and concealment of the truth, obligates one to make good any damages.[73]

The extensive coverage of the Code's general liability clause is highlighted. In fact, the phrases used in this norm are so 'absolute' and 'general' that there are no conceivable limits. 'The law (it is stated) does not mention the injured party; the only concern is the damage which, by virtue of its occurrence, obligates one to repair. Hence, in case of homicide, anyone who claims lo be damaged by the crime is entitled to recover his loss *jure proprio* (in his own right), and not simply as an heir of the injured party.'[74] The principle stating that 'everybody is liable for his own fault' is further reiterated.[75]

When describing the conditions under which an injurious act becomes a civil tort, the Italian decisions take into account the theories of Domat, Pothier, and Zacharie concerning whether: (a) the act is against the law; (b) the act is imputable to the acting subject; or (c) the subject acted with the knowledge and the intention to cause such damage.[76]

[67] Unified Civil Code Arts 1151, 1152 (1865).

[68] Ibid Art 1153.

[69] Ibid Art 1154.

[70] Ibid Art 1155.

[71] G Foschini 430–31 (Chieti 1867).

[72] Forschini's tables are as follows: 1151 = Frane 1382; Rep 1336; Parm 2085; Alb 1500; Est 1393; 1152 Franc 1383; Aust 1294, 1295 e 1296; Nap 1337; Parm 2086; Alb 1501; Est 1394; 1153 Franc 1384; Austr 1313; Nap 1338; Parm 2087; Alb 1502; Est 1395; 1154 = Franc 1385; Austr 1320; Nap 1339; Parm 2088; Alb 1503; Est 1396; 1155 = Franc 1386; Na 1340; Parm 2089; Alb 1504; Est 1397.

[73] C Palermo, 10 Apr 1894, Crisafulli c Genio Militare-C.G. di Pal, 1894, 234; C Roma, 11 Dec 1893, Com di Cagliari c. Zappati CSR, 1893, ii, 359.

[74] C Torino, 30 Apr 1883, Lanza c. Ferrovie AL-L, 1888, II, 524; C Roma 20 May 1889, ric Mamazza L. 1889, I.

[75] Cass Florence, 16 May 1889, L. 1887, II, 295.

[76] C Roma, 28 May 1888, Rosini c Anelli, L, 1889, 1,548.

Negligence, it is stated, is either contractual (Article 1224) or extra-contractual (quasi-crime). While the same legal concept applies in both cases, the 'cause' and the degree of negligence differ. In fact contractual negligence originates from a contract, whereas extra-contractual negligence arises simply from human behaviour. Contractual negligence has several degrees: slight negligence (or failure to use great care), ordinary negligence (failure to use ordinary care), and gross negligence (failure to use even slight care). Extra-contractual negligence does not have internal gradations. Tort liability arises even for slight negligence: '*in lege Aquilia et levissima culpa venit*'.[77] Furthermore, contractual negligence generates, in any case, liability to make good the loss, while tort negligence creates liability only when there is a violation of a legal duty, which exists by virtue of society's expectations regarding interpersonal conduct.[78]

Roman sources are often mentioned, though they are modified in the process. For example, the *actio institoria*[79] is cited to justify third-party liability of masters and employers based on the assumption that an employee looks after his employer's interests.[80] The *actio de pauperie*[81] is quoted to justify master and custodial liability. Several arguments have been raised by jurists as to whether to recognize proof which would release the master or custodian. According to the Supreme Court of Turin,[82] such liability occurs regardless of negligence. The Supreme Courts of Rome[83] and Florence,[84] however, take the opposite view on the basis that the Code provision introduces a presumption of fault *juris tantum*, which can be overcome by proving the contrary. Jurisprudence, then, reflects the arguments and doubts embedded in the doctrine.

The important debate which took place at the end of the century (as already mentioned in another part of this work) originates right here, the main points of contention being the principle of negligence versus theories of strict liability (no-fault liability). The great jurists of that epoch favoured a dyarchy: the principle of no-fault liability was justified by the needs of social order. Today we would call it social solidarity. With the beginning of the industrial era, the principal arguments sustaining no-fault liability became the proliferation of 'anonymous' forms of damage, the need to offer

[77] C Roma, 8 June 186, X c Gualandi and others, L, 1886, 11, 253; F, 1886 1, 714; AGI, 1886,1, 264, e GI, 1886, I, 1, 479.

[78] A Venezia, 18 May 1888, De Boni c Antonini, L, 1888, II, 339

[79] *The Institoria actio* was an action in which an actor has contracted with an institor to instigate another's performance.

[80] Cass Florence, 14 May 1883, L 83, II, 44

[81] The *Actio de pauperie* was an action brought for damage done by an animal without fault of the owner, but for which the owner is still liable.

[82] 3 Mar 1882—G.I. 1982, I, 1, 425

[83] 16 Aug 1894; L. 1994, II, 487.

[84] 30 Dec 1989—L. 1990, 299.

damages to the victims who could not prove fault, and the need to introduce some form of welfare in the working-class world. This thesis was supported also by scholars such as Barassi, Cogliolo, Coviello, Gabba, Chironi, and Venezian.

We are now approaching the eve of the modern codification. Toward the end of the 20th century and the beginning of the 21st, another factor arose which was eminently doctrinal and academic: the successful dissemination of German Doctrine.

As we know, the exegetic phase of the Italian Civil Code was followed by a phase of high esteem for the Pandectist theories and their systematic approach. Questions were raised as to whether there was an actual revival of Roman law, or whether its influence was only conceptual and indeed whether such influence was actually felt in civil tort liability.

Answering the above questions is not easy. Some attempt can be made, however, by comparing the Italian translation of the Pandectist manuals that were used by Italian jurists, with the contemporaneous Italian manuals then in use. We will take into consideration some of the Pandectist authors such as Savigny (1779–1861), Puchta (1798–1846), Arndt (1803–61), and Windscheid (1817–92), all of whom have different cultural and ideological backgrounds.

Savigny's *Treatise on Obligations*[85] states precisely that a tort is the violation of a right, a 'dominion' exercised by a person who is not entitled to exercise it. This dominion is defined as 'an illegal and unfair taking.' The author takes us to an abstract and conceptual field where will and power prevail. In the criminal area, the author implies the requirement of an intention to violate a right (fraud–malice), or the violation of a legal duty of care (negligence–fault). The treatise continues with trial proceedings (*actiones*), an analysis of sources and a discourse on private sanctions. Lastly, Savigny remarks that '*iniuria*' is an expression that should apply only to libel (a prejudice to someone's honour).

Savigny's followers are considered to be more conventional than he was. They take some of the Maestro's theories and erect an abstract system of torts. They also suggest an examination of tort sources, yet their treatment of the subject is quite modern. In fact their works contain the two main elements which later influenced the BGB code and the modern juridical thought: negligence as the basis of torts and violation of subjective rights as the criteria for damages.

Puchta quotes, by way of footnote, the Roman sources[86] and outlines a definition of tort that was endorsed by Italian doctrine up to some decades

[85] Savigny, *Trattato sulle obbligazioni* (G Pacchioni trans, 1915).
[86] Puchta, *Cors di Istituzioni* (A Turchiarulo trans, 1 st edn, Naples 1854).

ago. Two conditions, he says,[87] must coincide in order to have a tort: (a) an objective condition, which is the violation of someone's 'right', and (b) a subjective condition, which is the tortfeasor's negligence understood in its wider sense.

With reference to the consequences of torts, damages and sanctions are mentioned. The author follows the Roman tradition. There are no variances concerning the different types of tort.

An important innovation, however, is that a tort must be perpetrated intentionally—with fraud, malice or negligence, and *non* jure—meaning that the tortfeasor was not pursuing a legal right.

This was the basis of the modern definition of tort, and it was adopted by the BGB.

Arndt further clarifies the relation between tort, will, and negligence.[88] He emphasizes that 'every tort implies an objective element, the offence, and a subjective element, the connection between the offence and a person's will, which makes such person responsible and liable. This second aspect is designated by the word "negligence" ', meaning *culpa* in a general sense. There is a further passage: negligence makes the tortfeasor appear as 'the author of a legal violation, one who commits an *injuria* (harm, offence)'. The connection between will–negligence–tort and also between negligent violation of a right–tort is thus established. The *Lex Aquilia* is the parameter used 'to fix the limits within which actions are contrary to the law; any action exceeding such limit is therefore by definition a fortuitous case'.

Crime is also treated in the section describing the sources of obligations. The subject of damages and alternative sanctions is discussed early on (sanctions are considered obsolete), while theft and damage are covered in the final pages, on the basis of *Aquilian* principles. We may be surprised to find Arndt's paragraph 324, concerning damage, became the exact basis of BGB paragraph 823: 'anyone acting with negligence, and therefore in a tortious manner, who damages, destroys, or diminishes something (property or possessions), and anyone who, with malice or negligence, physically injures a free person, is always liable toward the injured party, to make good damages for the harm caused, *damnum injuria datum*'. Arndt considers the *Lex Aquilia* to be the general legal action for damage,[89] and its general principles are relied upon when describing specific cases such as fire, tree-cutting, etc. Further on, Arndt considers damage caused by third parties, animals, and objects. In paragraphs 831, 833 and 836 of the BGB, we find the same subjects covered in detail.

[87] Ibid at 241.
[88] Arndt, *Trattato delle Pandette* 161 (F Serafini trans, 3rd edn, Bologna 1877).
[89] Ibid at 279.

As we analyse the above writings, the conflicting views about negligence become immediately evident. To some authors, negligence is a criterion by which to evaluate human behaviour and negligence should be considered as violation of a duty of care. For others, it is synonymous with the violation of legal rights, and, as such, it focuses on the effects of behaviour rather than on (its mode) its interior basis.

Windscheid's dissertation is considerably different. It is extremely comprehensive and accurate in analysing the Roman sources.[90] Windscheid deals with tort in two stages: first, in reference to legal acts and legal relations; second, in regard to *choses in action*.

In reference to tortious behaviour the author distinguishes two types: the violation of an individual's subjective right and the violation of a specific prohibitory law. An action is tortious either because of its effects (for example the stealing of someone else's possessions) or because 'the author is blameworthy' for such conduct and negligence is implied. Negligence (*culpa*) is a unified concept, 'whether it applies to the protection of property or obligations', to contractual or extra-contractual matters. It always refers to a reasonable man's behaviour. Negligence entails imputability, meaning 'the psychological status of the subject allowing his/her to be responsible for the consequences of his/her will, action or omission'.[91]

In relation to the second stage, the writer deals with damage caused by fraudulent actions (defining these cases as 'credits arising from crimes and similar matters').

Even though he fails to formulate a general rule, Windscheid does examine the Roman sources in order to ascertain which sources remain valid and why. Also, he places in relief the integrating theory of German law. Several cases are analysed: theft, robbery, damage, damage caused by animals or objects, fraud, harm to creditors, disturbance of one's possession of things (*beni mobili*), actions against someone's will, actions against someone's protests interference with the right of burial, violation of duty, and unfair litigation.

When speaking of a 'damaging' action, the author cites negligence. In an action for negligence, he says, damages are due only if the harm or injury qualifies as unfair.[92] Unfairness occurs when the tortfeasor is negligent and has no legal right to cause the damage. Damages can be claimed either by the owner or the possessor of the damaged property (even if, in the possessor's case, they must be claimed against the owner).

Windscheid does not give a satisfactory and complete answer to the dogmatic problems mentioned above, even we can see that his analysis is

[90] Windscheid, *Diritto delle Pandette* (Fadda and Bensa trans, 1904) 342.
[91] Ibid at 406.
[92] Ibid at 357.

constructed upon a solid basis. In reality, if we compare his analysis with that of Domat or the French exegetical authors, we can see how limited the Pandectist influence was on interpretation of the French Code. In the drafting of the BGB, such influence was heavily felt (Windscheid actually exercised a personal influence), but in the Italian doctrine, the Pandectist influence was irrelevant, both at the end of the last century and at the beginning of our own. The Unified Code's provision on civil liability, unlike the fields of contract and legal relation, is not indebted to the Pandectist school. The clear norms of the Code Napoleon are poured into the Unified Code, and appear more suitable than the principles derived from Roman sources, or from the schematic BGB. Actually, the choice of civil liability principles gives the impression of a continuous alternation between courses and counter-courses. Roman sources may be kept in the background but they may emerge when needed to support and strengthen a principle or an interpretation by certain supporters. Domat's and Pothier's views are sometimes reconsidered critically, at other times ignored. Other serious conceptual or lexical questions may also be ignored in the interest of simplification or simply due to indifference.

Since our main concern is to search for the roots of the present liability in Italy, we will examine, without pretence of completeness, the analyses found in two manuals and one systematic treatise.

Biagio Brugi's manual, first published in 1904,[93] considers crime and quasi-crime as sources of obligation. The author draws a distinction between the 'Roman doctrine of obligations *ex delicto*' and the liability laws currently in force. Furthermore, he differentiates the typical system of criminal law from the atypical civil tort law. Also, imitating the German Civil Code, he tries to substitute the double notion of crime–quasi-crime in place of tort.[94] Displaying a modern way of thinking, Brugi speaks of liability for parents, tutors, etc, in terms of implied fault. He discusses consequential obligations related to ownership, such as owning a building, or having animals in one's custody. The author regrets that the Code does not lay out the precise limits of the word 'damage' nor provide a method of calculating it.[95] The measure of damages is simply a question of fact left to the judge's discretion. We must recognize then that Brugi is a Romanist who pays attention to the Pandectist scholars and to the BGB, which at the time of the author's writings, had been in force for only a few years.

Emanuele Gianturco's treatment is more lapidary. He is not inclined to

[93] His citations are taken from his work *Istituzioni di diritto civile italiano* Biagio Brugi, (1923) 562.

[94] Ibid at 564.

[95] Ibid at 569–70. He defines 'damage' as 'any injury suffered, which should not be suffered, in property, health, honor'.

discuss the basis for the liability system.[96] His exposition indicates the elements of tort (imputability, moral and material damage, man's fault with the exception of fortuitous cases). Social laws regarding labour relations are noted in reference to quasi-crime. It is further specified that employers' and masters' liability is applicable because of the *mala electio est in culpa*. The Roman '*actio de effusis et deiectis or noxae deditio*' should no longer apply. Here the discussion ends.

We have finally arrived at the threshold of the new codification.

Giovanni Pacchioni is extremely precise and complete in his treatment of the subject. One full book of his treatise 'Italian Civil Law' is dedicated to tort liability, and he still uses the old nomenclature 'crimes and quasi-crimes'.[97] Still Pacchioni's approach is absolutely modern. His historical introduction shows the obsolete areas in the *Lex Aquilia*. It also shows what traditional principles are worth keeping. He specifies, above all, that the requirement of injury (*damnum iniuria datum*) did not have a connection with fault but was simply indicating that the damage was '*non jure*'. In other words, he rejects the interpretation which connects damage to the question of imputability, even though that theory was supported by many scholars. For Pacchioni, the *Lex Aquilia* was originally based on the 'chain-of-causation' principle, and the concept of negligence was introduced at a later time.

Pacchioni then draws parallels between the theory and design of general contract and the theory and design of general tort, and he abandons the bipartite classification.

Any tort produces the same effects, whether based on fraud, fault or no fault.[98] Thus, doctrine, as we can see, reached an important conclusion even before the new codification took place, namely the consideration of liability without fault as a possible (and not merely exceptional) criterion of imputability. This view was reached with some difficulty once again in the 1960s, by the further elaboration of doctrine, though sometimes jurists still ignore it.

Pacchioni also opens up another facet of the question that we have only briefly mentioned in this historical account. This is the issue of 'illicitness'. What is the meaning of 'tort?' Pacchioni's suggestion is to invert the prior thinking by considering a tort to be the violation of a 'social duty of care', instead of the violation of a personal right.

On the controversy between fault and no-fault supporters, Pacchioni takes an intermediate position. He criticizes those who want to extend fault even to cases where fault 'shines only because of its absence'.[99] But he also

[96] E Gianturco, *Istituzioni di diritto civile italiano* (Lessona ed, 1 st edn, 1929) 150.

[97] G Pacchioni, *Diritto civile italiano* (1940) vol IV–F, pt I1.

[98] Ibid at 48.

[99] Ibid at 207.

criticizes the doctrine of 'pure causation,' which he considers of German lineage (it was supported by Gierke against Windscheid, but did not penetrate the BGB). The principle, *ubi commoda,* which justifies no-fault liability in terms of risk, is to be considered 'a general principle of law'.[100] Yet this principle should not be considered as a unifying element for all the cases of no-fault liability. Indeed, each situation has its own justification. Here we come to the crux of the argument which divided the doctrine, at the beginning of the sixties.[101]

Thus, in Pacchioni's view, we have no-fault liability only: (a) when carrying on activities dangerous to society; (b) when carrying on personal activities (called by the author biological) by using dangerous means; or (c) when the activity is carried on by an insane person.

Pacchioni's ideas are inscribed in the codification. Yet, whether because of the ambiguous phrases used in the Report of the drafters, or because of the normative text which does not state explicitly the choices made, the old arguments are not put to rest. In other words, it seems that the codification does not solve the issue of a bipolar criterion concerning imputability, nor does the code resolve the question of the criteria to be used to individualize the rights deserving legal protection.

We noted earlier the weak influence that German theories had on civil liability, and this observation is confirmed when the new tort regime is codified.

Here, more or less consciously, the concepts and choices are exposed, but only to be criticized or rejected, in most cases. This is particularly apparent in several sections of the preliminary draft.

First, it is stated that the phrase 'illicit facts' seems more appropriate than 'illicit acts' since in other parts of the same book,[102] the word 'acts' has referred to 'legal relations' (agreements).[103]

Secondly, it is clarified, in reference to the meaning of the general clause, that:

> the basis of liability, in this general clause, remains negligence. The German code does not contain a general disposition of this kind. Instead, it has a series of specific dispositions from which interpreters can derive a general theory. Even in such a code, however, the most important cases are related to liability for intentional injuries or negligent injury to the right to life, personal integrity, freedom or any other human right, or for breach of a law protecting a person.[104]

The analytical spirit of the BGB norms, summarized above, creates a

[100] Ibid at 222.

[101] Pietro Trimarchi and Marco Comporti (who altered the unifying criterion by basing it on risk) should be put on one side, and Stefano Rodotà on the other.

[102] CC Arts 154, 164 and Arts 1324, 1334 (Italy).

[103] RR, n 263.

[104] RCR, 24.

laborious and unclear system which is discarded by the Italian drafters. They feel that they should not 'get lost in a meticulous case load'. They prefer to follow the Swiss[105] and Austrian Codes.[106] Some accommodations have been incorporated into the negligence principle, which after all already cohabited with negligence in the main base of the tradition.

Thirdly, in the remarks of the Guardasigilli (Garde des Sceaux), we find practical doubts being expressed as to the appropriateness of this principle under contemporary social conditions:

Generally we have maintained the principle that the author's liability of a damaging fact must be based on his/her fault/negligence. A doubt has arisen concerning the necessity to change, for practical reasons, the burden of proof, meaning to require the author responsible to prove his lack of negligence, while still keeping in mind the rule of no liability without fault. I said for practical reasons because probably it would be easier [for the author] to collect proof which ascertains or excludes, the requisite negligence. Reserving the right to meditate further on this problem. I have in the meantime elaborated Article 764 in the traditional way; namely the injured party has to prove the negligence of the injurer.[107]

It is evident from the King's Report that we prefer to remain anchored to tradition, even though we may want the judge to create simple presumptions that facilitate the burden of proof for the injured party:

[I]n case of fault liability, the traditional principle, by which the burden of proof is on the injured party, applies (Article 882). In some special cases, such principle presents difficulties to the injured party. Then the judge can obviate these obstacles by utilizing to the maximum extent simple presumptions and common sense rules. Therefore the innovating tort theory which was based on shifting the burden of proof from the injured party, who affirms negligence, to the injurer who denies it, seemed unnecessary.[108]

As it is known, the unfairness of damage is mentioned in the general clause with the following justification:

To clarify Article 1151 of the 1865 civil code, it is therefore specified that negligence and (injury) *injuria* are two different concepts; as such an action or an omission is a source of liability, therefore imputable, when committed with fraud and negligence and to harm one's legal sphere of rights. Therefore there will not be liability (when a damage is caused) in case of legitimate defence, in fact one has the right to defend himself even if causing damage to his/her aggressor (assailant); damage caused under such circumstances cannot be qualified as unfair. In other words, we have injuria only when one's sphere of legal rights is infringed (violated) without justification.[109]

[105] Code Civil Suisse [Cc] Art 41 (Switzerland).
[106] ABGB § 1295.
[107] RG, 651.
[108] RR, n 264.
[109] RG, n 267

Such words, even if they may appear insignificant today, are rich in history and experience.

The subject of employer liability raised another revealing question. Basing liability for employers upon fault in the surveillance or selection of employees (*culpa in vigilando and in eligendo*) raises doubts because there is the need to exclude fault liability when compulsory employment laws apply.[110] To recognize that fault could not operate in cases of compulsory employment. Was that a verbal manifestation of solidarity towards the category of 'Employer?' Here we find the origin of need to use a double fiction, or even manipulation, which seeks to justify liability on the basis of fault, though it conflicts with the literal interpretation of the text as well as with the uniform orientation of the doctrine of that time.

The one truly innovative feature concerns liability for dangerous activities. Here the code authors prescribe an intermediate regime of fault and no-fault liability.[111]

Another innovation has much less value. This transfers the liability for vehicular accidents from the Traffic Code to the Civil Code.[112]

Finally, moral damages are recognized, closing an old and persistent controversy.[113] Moral damages will be awarded only in the cases contemplated by the law, since social views are subject to change.[114]

Thus ends our historical profile of the Italian Civil Code's liability articles. The Civil Code was unable to overcome the impasse on negligence, and could not establish the connection between *culpa* and *iniuria,* which one had managed previously in the pre-revolutionary period.

1.3. THE ITALIAN WAY TO *DRITTWIRKUNG*. CONSTITUTION AND THE CONTRACTUAL RELATIONSHIPS BETWEEN PRIVATE PARTIES

1.3.1. Preliminary remarks

Before dealing with certain aspects of the constitutionalization of private law, a few preliminary remarks are in order, for the benefit of those who are not familiar with the Italian legal system. The Italian system is based on a written Constitution (1948), on ordinary laws (including the Codes and especially the Civil Code of 1942) and on special laws. Case law has for only a few years been regarded as a source of law, secondary to actual legislation. The Constitution (1947–8) consists of a bill of rights and legal rules on the organization of the State and the constitutional authorities, one of which is the Constitutional Court. Private law, in the strict sense, is the law governing relationships between private persons, and in the wider sense, the

110 RR, n 656.
111 RR, n 265.
112 Art 2054.
113 Art 2059.
114 RR, n 273.

law governing private persons in civil and commercial contexts and in their relationships with public bodies.

The bill of rights deals with the fundamental rights, or liberties.

The Constitutional Court (pursuant to Articles 134–7 of the Constitution) determines, *inter alia*, disputes relating to the constitutional legitimacy of laws and other enactments having the force of law, made by the State or by the Regions.

Application to the Court can only be made by an ordinary or administrative judge, who refers to it a matter which he has been asked to decide on its merits or as to its constitutional lawfulness. There is no provision for private persons to apply to the Court directly. This means that the Court does not revise the judgments of other courts, but makes a pronouncement as to the constitutionality of a legal provision (eg article of a Law) which the referring judge is considering applying to the facts before him, but as to which he has expressed reasonable doubts as to its constitutionality (ie compliance with the Constitution).

For a long time it was argued that the provisions of the Constitution were directed *only* to the legislator; but for several decades now, it has been generally agreed, partly as a result of the evolution of the case law of the Constitutional Court, that the provisions are aimed at *everyone*. Thus, at least in part, wherever possible, they also apply to legal relations between private persons.

Generally, when one talks about the provisions of the Constitution applying to legal relations between private persons, one is making several assumptions:

(a) that the legislator, when attempting to regulate matters of private law, has complied with the Constitution;
(b) that those provisions of the Constitution that relate to matters of private law apply to legal relations between private persons;
(c) that interpretation must be in accordance with the Constitution; that is, that legislation on private law is to be interpreted in the light of the rules of the Constitution; this is done on general principles such as the general terms 'public order', 'good practice', 'honesty and good faith', 'fairness', 'unjust wrong', etc.; and by the use of general formulae, such as 'the nature of things', 'actual circumstances', and of standards of evaluation such as diligence, honesty, etc;
(d) that private persons spontaneously comply with the rules of the Constitution in their dealings.

It is in these various meanings that we speak, in Italy, of the Constitution *directly* applying; or applying *indirectly*; or by mediation; or of its *effects upon third parties*; or of its applying *vertically* or *horizontally*.

These are particularly besetting questions for the fundamental rights.

Many of the fundamental rights relate to the legal relationships dealt with by private law. The Constitution elevates to the level of fundamental rights of persons, whether natural or legal, (*diritti soggettivi*), some of the interests (or values) relating to persons, such as equality, dignity, solidarity, health, and work. It codifies some of the fundamental liberties, such as personal liberty, freedom of association, religious freedom, and so on. All of these are matters proper to private law in the wider meaning stated above. A further distinction is made, between those provisions of the Constitution that confer importance upon fundamental rights (as recognized and protected by the Constitution and in other binding legislation such as the EC Treaties or the international Declarations or Conventions on the so-called rights of man or human rights) and those provisions of the Constitution that do not relate to such rights. In the Italian legal system, the so-called economic rights, such as the right of ownership, the right of the individual to carry on business, freedom of contract, the right to leave one's assets by will, etc are not treated by the Constitution as fundamental rights but as limited by considerations of public policy.

On the basis of the above summary:

1 Any provision of legislation that conflicts with these values (or principles) can be declared to be unconstitutional. This means that the values (or principles) act as *prohibitions*, which the legislator must observe, and as *boundaries* within which the power to legislate must be exercised;
2 The judge, who is subject (only) to the law, must apply the rules of the Constitution, as it is the basis of the entire legal system. Thus he is not at liberty to discriminate between public and private legal relationships when deciding whether to allow or exclude the application of the rules of the Constitution to them; and
3 The question of compliance by private persons with the values (or principles) of the Constitution as expressed in its various provisions, in the regulation of the legal relations between them, is more complex and problematical.

One fundamental question is whether freedom of contract can be exercised in a way that ignores the Constitution or is actually in conflict with it. Since private persons must comply with the law, and therefore also with the Constitution, when regulating the legal relations between them, and since restrictions upon private persons are of legal importance and have effect only to the extent that they are lawful: in the event of non-compliance with the rules of the Constitution by private persons, it will be necessary to establish whether the non-compliance affects the validity of their legal relationship and whether the rules of the Constitution can supplement those purporting to govern their relationship. If a law that has permeated their legal relationship is held to be unconstitutional, the question is, whether it can be judged to be so by the ordinary judge, or whether it is only the Constitutional Court, on the basis of the opinion of the competent ordinary judge in his referral to it, and on the basis of its own opinion, that can establish the unconstitutionality of the law and thus the application of the principle expressed in its judgment to the legal relationship between private persons, through the medium of the competent, ordinary judge.

One must also bear in mind that the expressions 'directly apply' and 'indirectly apply' are still clouded by ambiguity. The facts of many cases are classified either in the first or in the second category; and in the various legal systems, the nomenclature, the analysis of the system and the evaluation of the effects of interpretation (or application) of the Constitution are not uniform but very diverse.

There are differences, in the various legal systems, between the concepts of direct application as dealt with in doctrinal writings and decided cases; and each legal system must be considered separately, because a particular model is never merely transplanted from one system to another by simple mechanical observation: it will give rise to attitudes of rejection, or to a marginal and problematical acceptance, or substantial adaptations. Bearing this in mind, there are at least three different models with which the Italian model can be compared: the German model, and based upon it, the English,[115] and the French.

The Italian model is close, but not identical, to the German model. Although the two models have aspects in common, such as the structure of the system, the written nature of the Constitution (long and rigid), and a Constitutional Court, in the German model the private individual has direct access to the Court and the Court has powers to overturn the decisions of ordinary judges. These are features which the Italian model, as already stated, does not share. The French model is still under construction. The English, in view of the non-existence (so far) of a written Constitution, has fallen back on the fundamental rights recognized and protected by the European Convention on Human Rights and on the Human Rights Act of 1998.

1.3.2. The Italian model of Drittwirkung

The case law produced by the Italian Constitutional Court is vast, dating as it does from 1956, the year the Court was set up. It is not possible within

[115] See the introductory essays in Markesinis's collection *The Impact of the Human Rights Bill on English Law* (Oxford, 1998). On the bearing of the Constitution upon relationships between private persons see Markesinis, 'Comparative Law—A Subject in Search of an Audience', in *Modern Law Review* (1990) 10 ff.

these pages to run through the entire output of its decisions on matters relating to private law.[116] It is appropriate therefore to exclude from our consideration the Court's interventions in the wide areas of family, inheritance and property law, and to devote some time instead to some aspects of the Italian style of *Drittwirkung* in the matters of the rights of the person and legal relationships of obligation.

It is also appropriate to point out that at least since the 1960s and particularly since the 1970s even ordinary judges, whether deciding as to facts or as to lawfulness, have started to apply the provisions of the Constitution. This technique of interpretation is easily apparent in the computer databases of court judgments.

(i) Status and the principle of equality

A fundamental principle of the Italian Constitution is the principle of equality (Article 3).[117] This principle has become established as a protected situation relating to the legal or natural person and it is possible to trace various acceptations of it in the case law relating to the Constitution. One of these specifically relates to the prohibition against discrimination and the concomitant right of the legal or natural person, to equal treatment in the like circumstances. When comparing circumstances, none of those qualities or distinguishing characteristics indicated, for the purpose of protecting the individual, in Article 3, clause 1 of the Constitution for the purpose of protecting individuals (sex, race, language, religion, political opinions, or personal and social circumstances) may be used as a means of discrimination. Another acceptation consists in perceiving equality as a limitation upon every aspect of the power to legislate: the power must be exercised according to the standards of what is coherent and what is reasonable.[118] In the Italian legal system, as we shall show below, the principle of equality is held not to affect freedom of contract to the extent of making it legitimate directly to apply Article 3 of the

[116] Recognition effected egregiously by Cerri in '*La Costituzione e il diritto privato*' in *Trattato di diritto privato* P Rescigno (Turin 1987) [Vol] I 47 ff; and (1991) [Vol] XXI, 697 ff.

[117] 'All citizens have equal social dignity and are equal before the law, without distinction of sex, race, language, religion, political opinions, personal, and social conditions.

It is the duty of the Republic to remove those obstacles of an economic and social nature which, really limiting the freedom and equality of citizens, impede the full development of the human person and the effective participation of all workers in the political, economic and social organisation of the country'.

[118] In the judicial culture of private law the pages dedicated by Pietro Rescigno to this problem are still unparallelled. Among the vast learned output of this master, one may be permitted to refer to Chapter II of the volume I of the *Trattato di diritto privato* edited by him (Turin 1982).

Constitution to re-balance the relationship between the performances of mutual obligations in a contract.[119]

But this assumption is not universally valid. The statutes by which people inaugurate societies (or clubs) are also described as contracts. They are contracts of association; and even the rules or statutes by which the internal life of a society is regulated (its rules of membership) or by which individuals join it, are negotiated legal documents. Can these manifestations of private autonomy be affected, if they are in conflict with the provisions of the written Constitution?

The problem has not been resolved directly, but it has been touched upon in a judgment of the Constitutional Court relating to the power given to the Jewish Communities to tax all their respective members, by the Royal Decree of 30 October 1930, no 1731 (now amended by the Agreement between the Jewish Communities and the Italian State of 27 February 1987). Membership of the Communities was, according to the then legislation, now repealed, obligatory. The Communities were entitled to levy tax from any ethnically Jewish individual, even if he did not practise the Jewish religion or follow its precepts. The legislation was not discriminatory at the time it was introduced; on the contrary, it was the Communities themselves who requested it from the Italian State, so that they could have greater power to claim payment of taxes from their registered members. The Constitutional Court, in its judgment of 30 July 1984, no 239[120] found, however, that the legislation was in conflict with Article 3 of the Constitution. This was because the obligation to pay the contribution depended on the fact of being Jewish and resident in the relevant territory. Thus it constituted discrimination on the basis of race and religion. But the legislation was also lambasted because it was contrary to the principle of freedom to form or join associations under Article 18 of the Constitution inasmuch as that principle also implies the freedom not to join or belong to associations. To state this in the words of the Court:

> to oblige a person to belong to a Community merely because he is Jewish and resides in the territory pertaining to that Community, when his membership is not accompanied by any manifestation of a wish to belong, is in breach of the freedom of association that is protected by Articles 2 and 18 of the Constitution.

[119] The declaration of nullity of terms imposed by the stronger party to the contract on the weaker party is dealt with in ordinary law. In the [context of the] rules of the Civil Code the individual—exceptional—circumstances are defined in which at the behest of one of the parties it is possible either to reduce the performances required by the contract to parity [equity] or to order rescission or termination [of the contract] on the grounds that it is excessively onerous. It is only since EC Directive no 13 of 1993 was brought into force in Italy that articles 1469 ff of the Civil Code also enable the judge to verify whether there is a significant imbalance between the [required] performances, not so much from an economic as from a legal point of view.

[120] In *Foro italiano* (1984) I, 2397, with a note by N Colajanni.

The most frequent interventions of the Constitutional Court concern the application of the principle of equality at work, with particular regard to parity between the sexes and the protection of the working woman.

On the question of economic or business activity carried on by private persons and its relationship with their status and citizenship, it is worth noting the judgment of 30 December 1997, no 443.[121] It declared that the legislation preventing businesses with an establishment in Italy from using, in the manufacture and marketing of their products, ingredients that were permitted by EC law to businesses having establishments in other Member States of the EC, was contrary to the Constitution.

The foregoing examples are illustrations of *indirect* applicability: they indicate acceptance that the question of constitutionality can have a bearing on a legal relationship that is normally governed by private law.

There has as yet been no instance of *direct* application. A hypothetical example of this could be the question whether rules of membership could validly exclude a member of a society, on the basis of one of the criteria of discrimination listed in Article 3, clause 1 of the Constitution.[122] On those facts, no question of constitutionality would arise, for submission to the Constitutional Court—unless one wished to impugn the rules of the Code, which in any case is silent on the freedom to make written rules of membership. Rather, the question would be one for submission to an ordinary judge, asking him to order that the clause in the rules of membership that contained a criterion of discrimination was null and void.

Another hypothetical question is whether discrimination may operate, not so much as against a person who already has the status of member, as against a potential member, that is, one who would like to belong to a society but does not possess the required characteristics, where these characteristics include discriminatory definitions that are condemned by the Constitution.

Here we see two values in conflict with each other. One is the right of the persons who are already members of a society freely to decide what rules are to govern the functioning of the life of their society (Article 18). The other is the principle of equality and, if you will, the principle of free development of the personality in the context of social groups (Article 2).[123] In practice, the problem can be resolved by admitting to the society only individuals who have been co-opted, that is who have been invited to become

[121] Judgment of 30 Dec 1997, no 443, in *Foro it* (1998) 697, note by Cosentino.

[122] 'All citizens have equal social dignity and are equal before the law, without distinction of sex, race, language, religion, political opinions [or] personal and social conditions'.

[123] 'The Republic recognizes and guarantees the inviolable rights of man, as an individual, and in the social groups where he expresses his personality, and demands the fulfilment of the intransgressible duties of political economic and social solidarity'.

members. But this solution cannot be said to be satisfactory: it evades the basic question rather than resolving it.

A society that excluded one of its members for reasons conflicting with Article 3 would be committing an unlawful act. It is a different story for a person wishing to become a member of a society, because a society cannot be compelled to accept everyone who wants to join.

The matter has been addressed only in doctrinal writings and does not appear to have been submitted to the Constitutional Court.

(ii) Human rights and the rights of the personality

As has happened in Germany and is happening in France, it is in the context of the rights of the personality that we see the highest incidence of application of the provisions of the Constitution. It is by applying these provisions that ordinary judges have created new rights, such as the right to privacy (Article 2 of the Constitution), the right to personal identity (Article 3 of the Constitution), the right to health (Article 32 of the Constitution),[124] and the right to enjoy a healthy environment (Articles 9[125] and 32 of the Constitution). The Constitution has been applied in the field of civil liability: the breach of those rights that are founded directly on the commands of the Constitution leads to the grant of remedies to prevent such breaches, or remedies in damages, and is actionable by one private person against another.

In recent years, many judgments of the Constitutional Court have defined and described these rights.

On the question of the right not to be deprived of one's name, there is an interesting judgment on the connection between Articles 22[126] and 2 of the Constitution. A person has a separately defined right to his name, which is a distinguishing means of assessing him. This right is linked to the right to personal identity (perceived as physical identity but also as an ideal or conceptual identity). The question considered by the Constitutional Court concerned Article 65 of the Royal Decree of 7 July 1939, no 1238. This was held to be unconstitutional as to the part which dealt with the possibility of rectification of the documents relating to civil status: there was no provision in the Decree for the right, held to be valid in the circumstances of the case, to retain a surname. A child had been given the surname of his

124 'The Republic safeguards health as a fundamental right of the individual and as a collective interest, and guarantees free medical care to the indigent.

No one may be obliged to undergo particular health treatment except under the provisions of the law. The law cannot under any circumstances violate the limits imposed by respect for the human persons.'

125 'The Republic promotes the development of culture and scientific and technical research. 'It safeguards the landscape and the historic and artistic heritage of the nation.'

126 'No one may be deprived, for political reasons, of legal status, citizenship or name.'

supposed father; a subsequent judgment found that the natural father was a different person; according to the Decree there was no option for the child to retain his original surname even though that surname had already become an autonomous distinguishing sign of his personal identity.

The Constitutional Court remarked that it is certainly true that among the rights irrevocably belonging to the person, Article 2 of the Constitution includes, recognizes and safeguards the right to personal identity. The Court defined this right as:

> the right to be oneself, which is the right to respect for one's image as a participant in social life, together with one's property of acquired ideas and experiences, and those ideological, religious, moral and social convictions, that differentiate and at the same time define the individual.
>
> Personal identity thus constitutes an asset in itself, irrespective of the personal and social circumstances of the person, or his virtues or defects, so that everyone is allowed to have the right to have his individuality preserved.
>
> Of the many forms it takes, the first and most immediate factor distinguishing a person's identity is obviously his name. It is separately stated to be an asset that is the subject of an autonomous right in the next article of the Constitution, Article 22. It takes on the character of a distinguishing and identifying sign of the person in his life of relationship with others.
>
> Now, since the legal rules governing names are a product of needs of both a public and of a private nature, the public interest in guaranteeing the accuracy of the register of births, marriages and deaths is satisfied when a document recognized to be untrue is rectified.
>
> Once a person's family relationships are ascertained and certain, it is of no consequence, for the purposes of the public interest, if he retains the name he previously bore, as does any other person of the same name.

Similarly on the question of rights in a name, the Constitutional Court has declared Article 262 of the Civil Code to be unconstitutional, because it did not allow for an illegitimate child to retain the name originally given to him by the official of the civil state, in circumstances where the (illegitimate) child had been subsequently recognized by his natural father and his original surname had become an autonomous distinguishing sign of his personal identity.[127]

On the question of *copyright*, the Constitutional Court has decided that the Italian Society of Authors and Publishers (SIAE) were not abusing a dominant position.[128] Article 180 of Law no 633 of 1941 grants to the SIAE exclusive management of the rights to make commercial use of the works protected by copyright. The judgment, which has been much criticized, found that the enormous circulation of imaginative works make the

[127] Judgment of 23 July 1996 no 297, in *Foro it* (1997), I, 11.
[128] Judgment of 15 May 1990, no 241 in *Foro it* (1990), I, 2401, with a note by Nivarra.

mediating and protective activity of the SIAE almost always indispensable in practice. This is especially true for foreign works, in respect of which permission for their commercial use can usually be obtained only through the SIAE, which is linked to the foreign Societies of Authors by mutual agency contracts. The fact that its mediation is virtually irreplaceable means that the SIAE, which is the exclusive owner of the right to mediate, exercises a virtual monopoly over the management of the rights to make commercial use of the works protected by copyright; because of this it enjoys the power of controlling the users and the market in a way proper to the holder of a monopoly. Moreover, since this is an exclusive right that is permitted by law, the Court stated that:

> the SIAE must be held to be under an obligation to contract, and prohibited from arbitrary discrimination, as confirmed by Article 2597 of the Civil Code, with the consequences set out by law. Likewise, the appointment of the SIAE complained of, must be construed in the light of Article 41 para 2 of the Constitution, as being intended to protect the user and the consumer against the abusive exercise of its power by the holder of the monopoly.

On the other hand, the judgment concludes,

> since the reason for allowing the SIAE to have this exclusive right consists, not only in the protection of the rights of its authors, but also in its function of promoting culture and in the dissemination of original works of a creative nature, there is no doubt that SIAE might fail to discharge its duties to the full, if it were not bound to contract with all users and to guarantee them equality of treatment in the like circumstances, not putting or allowing any of them to be in a position of advantage or disadvantage.

The Court has also considered the hire of compact discs. The particular case was about a complaint by authors, performers, and producers against distributors and hirers. It turned on the prohibition which could be construed from the Law on Copyright (rights of authors) but was then made plain in the Legislative Decree of 16 November 1994, no 985, which brought the Directive EC100/1992 into force in Italy.

> The competing interests in question were, on the one hand, the freedom of art and science, copyright in a work of the intellect, and the right] to development of the human personality under Article 2 and of culture under Article 9 of the Constitution, and on the other hand the right to engage in a private business enterprise and freedom of contract. The judgment of the Constitutional Court had to balance the two interests. The Constitutional Court found that the former outweighed the latter, and therefore held that it was constitutionally lawful to prevent the hiring of a copy of a compact disk that had been lawfully acquired by a private person.[129]

[129] Judgment of 6 Apr 1995, no 108, in *Foro it* (1995) I, 1724, with a note by Caso.

(iii) Biological damage (personal injuries) and the right to health

The concept of *biological damage* ('danno biologico') has been constructed on Articles 3 and 32 of the Constitution. It was already appearing in the judgments of judges on questions of fact from 1974 onwards and is now a deciding factor in the assessment of damage to the person. As there are no detailed rules either in the Civil Code or in special legislation, to guide the Judges' assessment, this is based on the principle of equitable evaluation [*equo apprezzamento*] (Article 2056 of the Civil Code). Recourse has therefore been had to the rules of the Constitution, in order to award compensation for damages arising from injury to the physical and psychological integrity of the person, independently of his capacity to earn and his capacity to work, whether general or specific. The application of the provisions of the Constitution (by the Constitutional argument) has become an essential means of justifying this new method of assessing personal injuries.[130]

The cases on biological damage constitute an interesting database of evidence, a sort of court laboratory providing the opportunity to engage in two types of, as it were, preliminary examination: of the use of the Constitutional argument and of the use of general principles in the reasoning of judgments. This examination makes it possible to document the developments in the case law on civil liability, which has combined the general provision of Article 2043 of the Civil Code with the provisions of the Constitution.

This combination of Articles 3 and 32 of the Constitution and Article 2043 of the Civil Code has enabled the judges to order payment of a head of damage caused by accidents resulting in disablement of the person, not merely to claimants who have been actually earning, but also to others. In

[130] An exhaustive and well-set-out bibliography on the subject of biological damage [personal injuries] is contained in Bargagna-Busnelli's book, *La valutazione del danno alla salute*, Cedam, 1988; this is a bibliography edited by Ponzanelli, divided into two parts of which the first deals with the period from 1974 to 1985 and the second with the period from 1985 to 1987. Each of the two parts is divided into three sections, dealing respectively with monographs, articles, and notes on judgments.

The following are particularly recommended: Alpa *Danno biologico* (Cedam 1987) and Busnelli-Breccia *La tutela della salute e il diritto privato* (Giuffré 1980), in addition to Bargagna-Busnelli, op cit.

Among the many commentaries on the judgment of the Constitutional Court no 184/1986, see those by Ponzanelli and Monateri, published in *Foro it* (1986) I, 2053 ff and 2976 respectively. Also see the note, signed AF, published in *Giur it* (1987) I, 1, 392. Finally see that of Alpa (1986) I, 546 ff.

On the subject of biological damage the following can be read: Cass 16 Jan 1985, no 102 (note by Giusti) and Cass 11 Feb 1985, no 1130 (note by AG), at 385 and 377 respectively; in part II, also 1985, see Busnelli, *Danno alla salute* (197); in part I of 1986 are Trib Verona [Judgment of the Court of Verona], 4 Mar 1986, with note by Alpa (525) and Cass, 14 July 1986, no 184, with note by Alpa (534); see finally in part I of 1987, Cass, 11 Nov 1986, no 6607, with note by Ferrando (343).

addition, it has led many courts to order payment of identical sums for identical personal injuries, without taking the victim's socio-economic category into account, but only his age and sex. A judgment of the Court of Cassation (the highest court of appeal in Italy) of 11 February 1985, no 1130, states the fundamental principle on the question: 'the right of every individual not to be physically or psychologically damaged is guaranteed and protected by our legal system as a primary and absolute right'. The Court proceeds, in an *obiter dictum*, to specify that damage wrongfully caused to the physical and psychological wholeness of the following must also be compensated: a new-born baby, an infant, a student, a housewife, a pensioner, a convicted prisoner, a person in hospital, a person without legal capacity, a person incapable of work, and so on. This is because from a biological point of view the damage constitutes an impairment of the physical and psychological wholeness of the person. The evaluation of the biological head of damage is separated, in financial terms, from that of the victim's former and potential future earnings.

In the first decade since 1974, this new trend, started with a judgment in the Court of First Instance of Genoa, excited a lively debate between those who insisted on equality and those who insisted on consideration of the surrounding circumstances as differentiating one victim from another. The Constitutional Court and the Court of Cassation have intervened several times in this field, with the result that the new method of evaluating damage has been upheld. Indeed the Constitutional Court took the opportunity, in its judgment of 27 October 1994, no 372, to specify that nervous shock is admissible as a head of damage in our legal system, subject to certain limitations:

> biological damage, like any other wrongful damage, is recoverable only as a wrong actually caused by an injury. Secondly, in the particular circumstances under discussion, a narrow interpretation of Article 2059 of the Civil Code in conjunction with Article 185 of the Penal Code does not pass the test of the practical argument that it would be irrational to make a decision distinguishing, among the consequences of the psychological shock suffered by the (victim's) relative, that which is merely subjective damage to his morale from that which affects his health, so as to allow compensation only for the first. Damage to health, in these circumstances, is the final stage of a pathogenic process that was originated by the same disturbance of psychological balance that is the evidence of damage to morale; and in people with a certain predisposition (such as a weak heart, weak nerves etc) rather than exhausting itself in a state of anxiety or obvious distress of mind, can degenerate into a permanent physical or psychological trauma, whose consequences must be measured in damages in terms of loss of personality and not simply as *pretium doloris* (the price of pain) in strict terms.

In the evaluation of the damage to the person, Articles 3 and 32 of the Constitution therefore serve to limit the boundaries of the area of damage for which compensation can be obtained.

On some occasions, however, the Constitutional Court has made use of Article 2 of the Constitution. This provision expresses the so-called personal principle. Our fundamental written Constitution chooses the person as the point of reference for its rules. In the context of the Constitution, the person is understood not so much as an individual whose right not to be physically injured must be protected in damages, but rather as a centre of interests and owner of rights, both as an individual and as a member of social groupings, which uphold and honour his personality, together with his political, economic, and social functions.

The Constitutional Court has used Article 2 to state that the provisions in the Laws on air transport, passed in ratification of the Warsaw Convention of 1929 as amended by the Hague Protocol of 1955 (Laws no 841 of 1932 and no 1832 of 1962) are in conflict with the Constitution. The case was about the quantitative limits to recovery of damages consequent on the liability of an air carrier.

The judgment is based on a comparative evaluation of the interests involved. In the opinion of the Court there must be a solution in legislation:

> [that is] apt to ensure a balanced satisfaction of the interests in question: and so, the [argument for the] limitation is supported on the one hand by the need not unduly to restrict the scope of the carrier's economic initiative, and on the other is constructed according to criteria that, for the purposes of attributing liability or deciding whether the limitation under discussion exists, include suitable and specific safeguards of the entitlement claimed by the person suffering the damage.

The Court states that the rules of the Convention are out of date. Where they limit recoverable damages they appear to have become inconsistent with the new system of values that has been introduced by the Constitution:

> in the terms in which it is put, the rule which in the face of personal injuries—and even, as here, in the face of the loss of human life—would exclude the possibility of complete reparation of the damage, does not have the assistance of an appropriate right. It therefore breaches the guarantee set up by Article 2 of the Constitution for the inviolable protection of the person.

The judgment was criticized in doctrinal writings. These pointed out that it was not right to make a comparative evaluation of the interests involved, in merely financial terms. They also noted that the judgment upset [flouted] the international law on air transport, whose economic effects the Court had completely ignored. In our legal system, they said, there was no right to *complete* compensation for victims; in other words it was not possible to identify in the system an absolute and unconditional right in the injured party to recovery of *any and every* damage to the person; still less was there a right to *total* compensation for the entire loss suffered, such that that right should be included among the inviolable rights of man. The Court's reasoning, which doubtless constituted the *ratio decidendi* of the entire judgment, would be understandable if the rule in the law ratifying the Warsaw Convention had *completely* excluded compensation for damages. Which it had not.

After considering the question of damage, the Court went on to consider the criteria for assigning liability:

> the general rule, for non-contractual as for contractual liability, is that only damage wrongfully caused through the fault of the person causing it is recoverable from him.

In the absence of fault, the loss or damage must be borne by the person suffering it. Without concerning itself with the opinion now held by doctrinal writers and by ordinary judges, that there are instances of strict liability, the Court observed that:

> it is certainly true . . . that the modern trend is in favour of undervaluing the requirement of fault, but this is happening exceptionally and with specific implications (such as the imposition of a quantitative limit on the amount of damages) and does not undermine the general principle of 'no liability without fault'.[131]

The Constitutional Court has also intervened on the subject of damages payable to people who were injured by allergic reactions to vaccinations against poliomyelitis (pursuant to the Law of 30 July 1959, no 695). The Law of 25 February 1992, no 210, which reformed the matter, did not provide for compensation in the cases where the damage had been inflicted while the former Law was still in force (Judgment no 27 of 1998);[132] thus it was unconstitutional. The Constitutional Court has returned to this argument several times (see Judgment no 258 of 1994[133] and also Judgment no 118 of 1996).[134]

On the question of the damage suffered by a passive smoker, it has been recognized that the infringement of his rights falls within the circumstances of Article 2043 of the Civil Code and gives rise to an obligation to pay compensation for the damage, including damage constituting a potential impediment to the activities by which the human person achieves self-realization. This pronouncement was made in the course of a judgment finding Article 1 of the Law of 11 November 1975 no 584 to be in accordance with the Constitution. Complaint had been made against the Article for not having provided that smoking should be prohibited not merely in hospital wards but in other areas of hospitals, as well as in the places where postal services were provided, and inside restaurants. In its Judgment of 7 May

131 Medina, *La dichiarazione di inconstituzionalità della limitazione di responsabilità del vettore aereo internazionale*, in *Dir mar*(1986), 2149.

132 In *Foro it* (1998), I 1370.

133 In *Foro it* (1995), I 1451.

134 In *Foro it* (1996), I 2326.

1991, no 202,[135] the Constitutional Court ruled that the Article was not unconstitutional. The ruling was based partly on the fact that the new legislation was not retroactive, and therefore did not make it possible to claim damages against smokers who had caused damage to passive-smoking victims before it came into force. Although it relates to an admittedly unlikely possibility, in this case also, the judgment contains several pronouncements on civil liability and shows how Article 2043 of the Civil Code is to be interpreted in the light of the principles of the Constitution. Thus, the Court had the means to specify that:

it must be considered that a person can be held liable in civil damages for his conduct only if at the time he engaged in that conduct, there was in existence a specific legal obligation, confirmed by a provision of legislation and ascertainable by him. In the judgment of this Court [*a quo*], there can only be a specific actionable wrong, consisting in failure to comply with a provision imposing a rule of conduct, if the provision was in force and ascertainable at the material time. Following the prevailing trend in decided cases and supposing liability to be founded on fault: even if a sufficient affirmation of the existence of that psychological element (fault) could be founded on the (mere) fact of failure to comply with a legislative provision, it must be necessary expressly to specify the relevant legislation, which must be in force at the time the event took place.

To justify its reasoning the Constitutional Court used the European Convention:

Even the European Convention on Human Rights (Articles 5, 6 and 7) is construed as meaning that for a court correctly to find that a (particular) breach of a general duty confirmed by a provision in legislation is actionable, it is essential that the provision should have been ascertainable at the material time. The citizen must know what behaviour the provision requires, especially if a restriction on one of his liberties is involved.

But the Judgment is important where it underlines that:

an infringement of the right to health (Article 32 of the Constitution) *is enough on its own* to found a claim in damages under Article 2043 of the Civil Code. Article 32 of the Constitution in conjunction with Article 2043 of the Civil Code imposes a primary, general prohibition against damaging health.

For the avoidance of doubt, the Court confirmed that the recognition of the right to health as a fundamental right of the person and as a primary asset, protected by the Constitution, *is fully operative even in the relationships governed by private law*. In the words of the judges of the Constitutional Court:

[135] In *Foro it* (1991) I, 2312, with notes by Pardolesi and Ponzanelli.

since it must be accepted that infringement of the personal right protected by Article 32 of the Constitution extends the circumstances [covered by] Article 2043 of the Civil Code, there can be no doubt as to the obligation to pay damages for infringement of that right. In other words, when Article 32 of the Constitution is combined with Article 2043 of the Civil Code as aforesaid, it follows that the wrong is unjust and consequently actionable in damages.

It should be noted that recoverable damages relate not only to damage to (material) assets but also to all the damage that potentially prevents the self-realising activities of the human person.

The individual is protected against himself by the Judgment no 180 of 1994, which makes the use of a helmet obligatory even for adults riding motorcycles.

Moreover, as regards experimental treatments, the Court has found that in the minimum content of the right to health, aspects must be also be included that must be satisfied when the interested parties are in disadvantaged financial circumstances.[136]

Article 32 of the Constitution has also been applied directly to work contracts, to allow a worker's state of health to be (compulsorily) ascertained with regard to the AIDS virus (Judgment no 218 of 1994). Here too, there are conflicting interests to be balanced: the interest of the infected employee in keeping his state of health confidential and thus protecting his privacy; and the interests of the persons who, in the course of the work he carries out, might come into direct contact with him. The law protecting AIDS sufferers gave precedence to privacy, but the Constitutional Court reversed this ranking of values, giving precedence to the health of third parties.

Still on the subject of direct application of the provisions of the Constitution relating to the person, in the course of research carried out a few years ago I was able to record instances of the use of the general terms, *dignity* of the person, and *solidarity* as well as the use of the yardstick of *social conscience* to measure the relationship between the individual and the group.[137]

(iv) Legal relationships involving obligations

Legal relationships involving obligations, which are governed by Articles 1173 ff of the Civil Code, are not directly covered by the Constitution. The Constitutional Court has indicated in several judgments that freedom of contract does not receive direct protection from the Constitution, because

[136] Judgment of 26 May 1998, no 185, in *Foro it* (1998) I, 1713, with note by Izzo.
[137] Alpa, *L'arte di giudicare* (Roma-Bari 1997).

it is merely instrumental in exercising the economic freedom governed by the Constitution in Article 41[138] (Judgment no 7 of 1962).

A complex picture of the limits to individual autonomy emerges from the case law of the Constitutional Court: the quest for profit is legitimate and therefore although price regulation is permissible the law must not be used to restrict economic initiative (Judgment no 144 of 1972); limitations to economic initiative can only be imposed by laws (Judgment no 4 of 1962) and this does not mean that all such laws will be constitutionally legitimate. It is legitimate for the State to intervene to suppress private monopolies (Judgment no 59 of 1960); its intervention aimed at suppressing the obstacles to free competition can take the form of imposition of a public monopoly (Judgment no 255 of 1974); the public interest may be expressed in declarations of (State) planning but the plans must not be too rigid or arbitrary (Judgment no 46 of 1963); agreements in restraint of competition may be suppressed in order to safeguard the public (collective) interest (Judgment no 223 of 1982).

One of the first judicial statements made by the Constitutional Court of the general principles of legal relationships involving obligations was made on 1 April 1992, in its Judgment no 149.[139] The question before it related to the legislation governing property lettings (the Law of 25 November 1987, no 478), Article 2 of which provided that the tenant was exempt from liability in damages to the landlord for delay in giving up possession, but made no provision for the landlord or the court to verify whether the tenant actually had any difficulty in finding suitable alternative accommodation. The provision had been enacted in derogation from the rule set out in Article 1591 of the Civil Code, which though it allows the possibility of damages being payable in addition to sums equivalent to the rent, during the period of delay in vacating, does not make any distinction as to the tenant's circumstances, or mention the question whether he can find alternative accommodation.

The Constitutional Court had previously stated that the provision for temporary exemption from liability did not conflict with the principles of the Constitution.[140] However, in Judgment no 149, the Court changed direction, on the basis of the following reasoning:

[138] Private economic initiative is free.

It cannot be conducted in conflict with the public interest or in such a manner as to damage safety, liberty and human dignity.

The law determines appropriate planning and controls so that public and private economic activity is given direction and coordinated to social objectives'.

[139] In *Foro it* (1992), I, 1329.

[140] Especially with Art 42 para 2 of the Constitution; see the Judgment of 24 Jan 1989, no 22, in *Foro it* (1989) I, 959, with note by Piombo. Subsequently the Constitutional Court found the said provision to be lawful, in numerous Judgments: see the note in *Foro it* (1992) I, 1329 referred to above.

the limits of constitutional legitimacy are a consequence . . . of the nature' (of the provision under discussion). [It is] 'a rule [provision of legislation] expressing a value judgment based on the balancing of two conflicting interests, both of which given importance by the Constitution. It is characteristic of the constitutional values (or principles) to be weighed against each other that it is impossible to predetermine once and for all which one should be placed above the other. The precedence given to one over the other, where the task of balancing them is not presented to the judge on a case-by-case basis, but is to be operated by the law in the form of an abstract rule, must be made to depend on certain typical conditions, as having a legal effect in the particular circumstances. In the absence of such conditions, the outcome of the comparative evaluation cannot be the same.

The Court goes on to state that a rule of this type will be unconstitutional:

to the extent that it does not reserve the right for the person, whose interest has been postponed, to prove that, in the particular case, the conditions are not fulfilled which alone would justify the precedence given to the opposing party's interests, in the balancing carried out pursuant to the rule. The rule complained of [Article 2 of the above Law] in fact precludes the landlord from offering any evidence to the contrary, without taking account of the fact that his rights can lawfully be restricted, only to the extent actually necessary for the purposes of supporting the tenant's economic activity [business], where the tenant needs a period of time in which to find another suitable property for the exercise of his business. If these conditions are not fulfilled, that is, if and as soon as the tenant gains possession of another property or could have done so with reasonable diligence, the denial to the landlord [of his right to] payment of damages for [any] further delay in vacating the premises constitutes a breach of the protection of the right to ownership provided by the Constitution.

On the question of the duration of a letting contract and inheritance of it on the death of the tenant, the Constitutional Court has, in an extremely courageous judgment, extended the right to inherit a residential tenancy even to cohabitees living as husband and wife when the cohabitation can be defined as stable.[141] The basic premise of the judicial reasoning is consideration for the family the cohabitees have established:

in 1975 the legislator wished to protect not only the nuclear family or the family of relatives but [also] the group of cohabitees living together in an extended group including non-relatives (since heirs can include non-relatives), relatives no matter how distant, and even relations by marriage. It is clear that the legislator wishes to make itself the interpreter of that duty of social solidarity that consists in preventing anyone from being homeless and that announces itself here in the regulation of the inheritance of letting contracts, the aim of which is, to avoid making homeless, immediately after the death of a tenant, as many categories of person [as possible], even outside the circle of the legitimate family, provided they were habitually living with [the deceased at the time of his death].

[141] Judgment of 7 Mar 1988, no 404, in *Foro it* (1988) I, 2515, with note by Piombo.

The Court took account, in its examination of the matter, of the actual (albeit not legitimate) family as a grouping in which the personality of the individual finds expression (Article 2) and of the fundamental need for a home (the so-called *right to a home*).

The Constitutional Court had a field day criticizing the decisions made by the legislator when regulating housing, which ignored the actual (albeit not legitimate) family, despite the wishes expressed in doctrinal writings, which had relied not so much on the protection of the family as on Article 2 of the Constitution and the right to a home as an absolute right of the person. In analysing the earlier court judgments, the Constitutional Court remarked that:

> at the beginning of the eighties there was a trend in doctrinal writings and in court judgments for perceiving the right to a home as an absolute right of the person, which was always bound to make the position of the tenant take precedence over that of the landlord. It was suggested that the example of French and German law be followed, so as to enable residential tenancies [to continue] for an indefinite time, subject to termination by the landlord only for a legitimate reason.

This represents a departure from the Constitutional Court's previous position. This had been that the stability of a residential situation did not constitute independent and unfailing grounds for exercising inviolable rights under Article 2 of the Constitution, even though the Court recognized the home as a primary asset to be adequately and effectively protected, because of its fundamental importance in the life of the individual.

However, the right to a home does not have unlimited protection.

The Constitutional Court considered the matter afresh[142] in relation to the constitutionality of the legislative provisions inflicting forfeiture of the right to an allocation of cooperative housing and concomitant loss of credit benefits in the event that the person to whom the housing had been allocated did not at once proceed to occupy it (Article 98 of the Consolidated Law of 28 April 1938, no 1165, and the Law of the Province of Bolzano, of 2 April 1962, no 4). Here, however, the Court declared that the Law was in accordance with the Constitution; provided the principle was respected that *performance cannot be compelled*, which principle has constitutional status. In other words, forfeiture and revocation do not operate if the person concerned is temporarily in difficulties. As a general principle, the Court specified that:

> the interest of the creditor (or obligor) in the performance of the duties argued to be an obligation must be placed, in the order of precedence which the provisions of the Constitution, or of ordinary law, give to the values that govern the matter before us.

[142] With its judgment of 3 Feb 1994, no 19 in *Cons Stato* (1994) II, 150.

And when, in respect of a particular performance, the rights or interests of the creditor [obligor] come into conflict with a right or interest of the debtor [obligee] that is protected by the legislation, or actually by the Constitution as a pre-eminently meritorious right [*merito*] or one which is in any case superior to the one that is advanced in support of the creditor's claim, then [debtor's] non-performance, to the extent strictly necessary for the satisfaction of the interest whose merit is pre-eminent, appears to be legally justified.

This principle that *performance cannot be compelled* finds confirmation by the highest courts, both ordinary and administrative.

Having set out this principle, the Court continues, remarking that:

there is no doubt that [if] a person cannot fulfil the legal requirement for continuing to benefit from the public contribution to [his] home loan, which requirement is actual, continuous and stable occupation of his home by him, [and if he cannot fulfil it] because he needs to be with and to help his father, who is seriously ill and incapable of an independent existence, in another city, [then] that [person's] case fulfils the conditions for mitigation by the higher duty of social solidarity. [This higher duty] is defined in Articles 2 and 29 of the Constitution as not subject to derogation and [it] is capable of amounting to reasonable justification for non-fulfilment of the aforesaid requirement. The application of this principle is not restricted to the context of the State's legislation. As it involves categories [definitions] and meritorious rights that are of Constitutional importance and as it is a general principle concerning the obligations involved in legal relationships as such, it is universally applicable in the [entire system of] legislation and therefore must not be ignored, even in the interpretation of the regional or provincial laws.

The Constitutional Court has several times stated its position on *long-term work contracts*, in its Judgments nos 311 of 1995, 822 of 1988, 349, and 36 of 1985 and more recently, in its Judgment of 31 May 1996 no 179[143] relating to a question concerning the insurance of work and against work-related illnesses. On this subject, it has confirmed that:

in our constitutional system the legislator is not debarred from making enactments that unfavourably modify the rules on long-term [work] contracts.

But it specified that:

the said enactments, however, like any other precept [command] in legislation, must not go to extremes so as to make an irrational ruling, or arbitrarily affect the fundamental [legal] situation created by earlier laws, so as to betray the citizen's trust in that stability of the legal system that is a fundamental and indispensable feature of the legal State.

On the question of *prescription* (statutory extinction of rights by lapse of time), the Court, examining Article 2941 item 7) of the Civil Code, specified that the principle of the suspension of prescription [time ceasing to run]

143 In *Giur cost* (1996) 1660.

operates in favour of anyone who finds himself in circumstances that prevent him from exercising his rights and so justify his failure to do so.[144]

The Constitutional Court has considered the question of the *surrogation* of the INPS (the government body in charge of social insurance against invalidity, etc for private, non-state employees) to the rights of the assisted person, where he is entitled to payment of damages derived from the civil liability of a private person for a road traffic accident. In its Judgment of 6 June 1989, no 319,[145] the Court declared Article 28 paras 2,3, and 4 of the Law of 24 December 1969, no 990 unconstitutional. This was because the Law purported to entitle the INPS to obtain reimbursement of expenses incurred by it for services rendered to the injured party as a consequence of such an accident. In the event of insufficiency of the sum insured through the INPS, to cover the damages caused by the accident, the INPS would demand reimbursement of the shortfall, from the civil liability insurer to itself, to be withheld or deducted from the sums paid to the insured, thereby limiting the victim's right to payment of the damages owing to him. Since, the Court observes, 'in our legal system the right of a person not to be injured can be described as a:

> fundamental right of the individual' which the Republic is enjoined to protect (Article 32 of the Constitution), in the event of injury 'the particular definition of, and protection afforded by, this right impose on the legislator the duty to legislate for suitable measures to ensure the fullest [possible] compensation [in the event of its infringement].

A similar decision was made about Article 1916 of the Civil Code, which relates to private insurance, and Article 10 paragraphs 6 and 7 and Article 11 paragraphs 1 and 2 of the Decree of the President of the Republic no 1124 of 1965 which relate to public insurance. The decision dealt with the passages in these items of legislation which allowed an insurer to claim from the person liable in damages, the amount of the shortfall between the amount it had paid out in damages for biological damage (personal injuries), and the amount covered by its own insurance, thus depriving the victim of that amount.[146]

On the subject of *insurance cover for liability for damages arising from road traffic*, the Court anticipated the bringing into force of the EC Directive of 30 December 1983, no 84/5 on the question of insurance cover including members of the insured's family. In its Judgment no 188 of 1991,[147] the Court declared that Article 4 letter b of the Law no 990 of

[144] Judgment of 24 July 1998, no 322, in *Foro it* (1998) I, 2617.
[145] In *Foro it* (1989) I, 2695.
[146] Judgment of 18 July 1991, no 356, in *Foro it* (1991) 2967 and judgment of 27 Dec 1991, no 485, in *Giur it* (1994) I, 162.
[147] In *Foro it* (1991) I, 1981.

1969 was unconstitutional, insofar as it purported to exclude from compulsory insurance cover for his personal injuries, the insured's spouse, his legitimate, natural and adopted ascendants and descendants, and his adopted relations, relatives and relations by marriage to the third degree, if living with the insured or maintained by him.

In its judgment no 301 of 1996, the Constitutional Court, this time applying the Law no 142 of 1992 with which the legislator brought the said Directive into force, found that Article 4 letter a of the said Law was not unconstitutional, to the extent that it only excluded the driver from cover. The Court's finding was based not only on the necessity to bring the domestic legislation into line with EC legislation, but also on the provisions of Article 32 of the Constitution. The Court stated that:

> the decision made by the legislator in 1992, [which was] grounded in the necessity to comply with the EC source of the law, forms part of this development and should be viewed positively, as reinforcing the protection of health that is guaranteed by Article 32 of the Constitution. This protection has, on the question under consideration, been undergoing a gradual process of accommodation [into the legal system] which [process] has come to completion in the new formulation of Article 4 of the Law no 990 of 1969. But precisely because of this, it [the decision] cannot act as a *tertium comparationis* [third element for comparison] for the purposes of deciding whether the legal provision previously in force and which has been impugned, was constitutional. That provision had its own, appropriate grounding in the connection already stated, based on Article 2054 para 3 of the Civil Code, between exclusion from cover and the class of persons who were nevertheless liable in any event for road traffic accidents. This is enough to hold it immune from the alleged vices of unconstitutionality. Nor is any negative reflection cast on its reasonableness by the context of legislation that has been created since the reform of the law relating to families, [although] the referring [judge] seeks to rely upon that, underlining in particular [the] favour with which the legislator has treated the institution of joint ownership of assets [*comunione dei beni*] as the legal property regime of the family. Indeed it is obvious that once such a regime has been established [ie joint ownership], the spouses cannot escape the legal consequences that the law connects to co-ownership of each asset, whatever the source of its establishment; and liability under Article 2054 para 3 of the Civil Code is indeed one of these consequences.

To continue with these examples of the application of the Constitution to legal relations between private persons: the Constitutional Court has frequently emphasized that the freedom of private persons to contract receives *indirect* protection from the Constitution, because that freedom is *an instrument intended for the achievement of economic initiative*. That is why the legislation on the forced administrative winding-up (*liquidazione coatta amministrativa*: a special form of winding-up for companies of particular public significance) of insurance companies by the court has been declared by the Constitutional Court) to be in conformity with the Constitution; the legislation provides that only the insurance company taking over the obligations of the one in liquidation has the right to withdraw from the insurance contract and prevents the insured from doing so for a period of two years.[148] The matter turned upon Article 2 paragraph 1 of the Legislative Decree of 26 September 1978 no 576, which was converted into the Law of 24 November 1978 no 738. The judgment of the Court goes beyond the boundaries of the limited question before it to consider the limitations to the protection given by the Constitution to private autonomy [freedoms].

The arguments are many and various.

First of all, the principle of equality is not considered to have been breached in any way:

not in relation to the position of those who are insured with other [insurance] companies'—the Court said—'because their position is wholly different and cannot be compared with the position of those who have had the bad luck or bad judgment to insure themselves with companies that were insufficiently capitalised or improperly managed and which in the end went into forced administrative winding-up. On the contrary, the law in question has the effect of putting the insured, in terms of risk cover, in the position he would have been in had he taken out insurance with a *solvent* insurance company. [Nor is the principle of equality breached] in the legal relations between the insured and the company [that has taken over the obligations of the insurer], because the derogation from the principle of formal equality between the parties to a contract in terms of the liberty to terminate it, allowing the company to retain [that liberty] and depriving the insured of it for a two-year period, is justified: first, because the company should not be deprived of the means of restoring the business to health by abandoning non-economic contracts and those that are out of keeping with legal requirements (for example, contracts with huge premium discounts, agreed in the context of tariff dumping); and secondly, because it is necessary to ensure, without an excessive sacrifice of the insured's liberty to contract, preservation of the assets of the business for the purposes of the public interest in production and job-saving.

The Court did not consider that Article 41 paragraph 1 of the Constitution had been breached (either):

particularly because this rule of the Constitution is designed to protect productive business, which is usually exercised in the form of a company, so that freedom of contract *per se* has only indirect protection, as being an instrument of economic initiative. Secondly, [this is so] because, even if one admits the possibility of construing an implied general principle from Articles 41 and 42, to the effect that the Constitution protects private autonomy, the reasons of public interest set out above are sufficient, according to a criterion repeatedly affirmed by this Court.[149] to justify the extraordinary and temporary restriction imposed by Article 2 of the Legislative Decree no 576 of 1978 upon the insured's freedom of contract, in terms of his liberty to terminate the contract.

[148] Judgment of 11 Feb 1998, no 159, in *Foro it* (1988) I, 1445.
[149] Cf finally, the Judgment of 23 Apr 1986, no 108, in *Foro it* (1988) I, 1145.

1.3.3. Concluding remarks

With regard to the Italian model for applying the rules of the Constitution to legal relations between private persons, the foregoing analysis of the case law relating to the Constitution does not bring to light any particular anomalies or reasons for criticism. Leaving aside the French model, whose construction is still in progress, and comparing the Italian with the German model, one finds similarities in the use of governing principles, general categories, general terms and general clauses. There is a greater volume of case law in Italy on the law of personality, and thus a *direct creation* of individual rights of the person. On freedom of contract, in both models application of the Constitution is *indirect*, in the German model it is more invasive; the Constitutional Court makes a connection between fundamental rights and the autonomy of the individual which is still not permitted in the Italian system. The prohibition against connecting them has been justified in Italy on the grounds that the legislator should not interfere in contracts (more or less) freely agreed by private persons except where this is essential for the protection of the public interest, or the health, safety or dignity of the person. But analysis in the decided cases has confined itself to justifying the powers of the legislator over the reasonable use of the liberty to contract, which includes liberty for the stronger party to impose his terms on the weaker one.

The picture that we have drawn shows the complexity of the debate on the relationship between constitutional and private law. The complexity of this debate makes it impossible to draw definitive conclusions; but it prompts reflection on the promising changes that have marked the two disciplines of constitutional and private law over the last few decades, the models on which their respective legislation is based, the ways in which they affect each other and their boundaries. Just as the dichotomy between private and administrative has been resolved, in several important areas the dichotomy between private and constitutional law has been overcome also. In the present situation, the invasiveness of the constitutional legislation, the *Drittwirkung* of the rules of the Constitution upon legal relations between private persons, the *Drittwirkung* of the (super-national) rules defining fundamental rights, the renunciation of sovereignty in matters that come within the competence of EC law, the spread of EC law into the domestic legal system, and the globalization of the markets, make it necessary to redefine the meanings of the expressions 'constitutional law' and 'private law' and thus to redraw their boundaries.

Looked at from this point of view, constitutional law in the traditional sense should now have the task only of organizing the State: economic and social relationships should be split between constitutional and EC law; private law in the traditional sense should have the task of dealing with the (technical) legal rules of detail in the law relating to property, and with bringing EC legislation into force in the domestic system, as well as those matters that are not within EC competence, such as family, inheritance, and property law.

The areas concerning personal meritorious rights, the rights of the personality, and relationships between the individual and the group, form a collection of matters in which the traditional distinction between constitutional law, EC law, and private law has lost its meaning, since the distinctions between them are no longer dictated by differences in the objects or subject matter of the legislation, so much as by the *order of precedence* or *competition* between different sources of law.

This result can be arrived at by a variety of different routes: the formal route, concerned with the identification of the applicable legislation; the hermeneutic one, concerned with the methods of interpretation to apply, and the consequent operations, the 'results' obtained; the methodological one, concerned with the reference rights and values, the legislative models for comparison and the identification of the factors both internal and external to the legislation that have a bearing on it and are the driving force behind the evolution of the forms of the law.

But even a merely descriptive account of these active phenomena reveals how reductive is an analysis that is restricted only to their legal aspects, and how illusory—and therefore misleading—it is to break them down into an analysis, sector by sector, of uncoordinated material. Obviously a more complete account would have to deal with the policies of the law enacted by the legislator and the other institutional agents, as well as with the domestic, EC, and international economic situations, and with the development of social structures. The horizons end in this way only to extend themselves further, affecting the very concept of law and of the role of the legal analyst as currently known to us.

1.4. JUDGE-MADE RULES IN A CODIFIED SYSTEM: THE CASE OF THE RIGHT OF PRIVACY

1.4.1. Terminology

The use, in the Italian legal vocabulary, of words which have their origin in legal developments in other countries, is becoming more and more widespread. Such words are used in the creation of legal doctrine, in the reasoning of judgments, on occasion in judicial decisions, and even in the wording of legislation. This may flow from the national 'xenophilia' that is the hallmark of the Italian culture and national character, or it may be the result of the impossibility of rendering concisely in Italian a particular phenomenon, institution or concept. Other explanations could be found but it would serve no purpose to list them here. For the fact remains that imported words such as 'leasing', 'factoring', 'franchising', and 'project financing' are now in common use in Italy. There has been no sign of any negative or resentful attitude to these words that would have ensured their immediate conversion into Italian, on the lines of what has happened in France. There is no prohibition in Italian law of the use of foreign words; indeed any such prohibition would be unthinkable.

This was what happened with the word 'privacy,' which has always been used in Italy in its English version. To be sure, there has been no shortage of Italian translations of the term such as *diritto alla riservatezza* (the right to privacy), *diritto al riserbo* (the right to be treated with discretion or, to privacy), *diritto al segreto della vita privata* (the right keep one's private life secret) and *diritto ad essere lasciati soli* (the right to be left alone). Yet it does not take much to realize that some of these terms are literal translations: *riservatezza and riserbo* are translations of privacy'; and *diritto ad essere lasciati soli* is equivalent to 'the right to be left alone'. In any event, none of these literal translations has undermined the widespread and uncontested use of the word 'privacy.' This phenomenon is of interest not only for students of Italian linguistic usage and the Italian language, but also for lawyers. Terminology in the law is never a matter of chance. It is manifestly the result of tradition, or of practice (especially commercial or contractual practice), or of its own foreign origins. In the development of Italian law, the right to 'privacy', in the modern sense of the word, is the result of an importation from the world of common law. The legal meaning has been imported together with the linguistic usage. What we are looking at, therefore, is a real transplant—a phenomenon attentively studied by comparative lawyers—with all the modifications required by the peculiarities of the legal system into which the transplant has been made.

1.4.2. The transplant and its formative elements

It is interesting to enquire how this transplant has come about: in other words, what formative elements have enabled its insertion into Italian law and its subsequent development. Two such elements have played a major part in this operation: legal doctrine; and (academic) commentary on case law. Legal doctrine has assisted, accompanied, and consolidated the creation of the right to privacy. Italian legal scholars, always curious to know what is happening abroad, and especially about the most important legal developments, have attempted to describe the right as having originated in the United States at the end of the last century, in the writings of Warren and Brandeis;[150] they have tried to find a basis for the right in the

150 Rodotà, *Tecnologie e diritti* (Bologna 1996), in which the fundamental themes of the right to privacy are dealt with. The history of Italian legal doctrine and, first of all, German

scanty provisions of international, constitutional, and ordinary law, in order formally to place it in our legal system;[151] and they have traced the course of various developments abroad. They have examined these first, where the right to privacy has been the subject of case law, as in the common law systems; second, where it has received the recognition of general legislation, as in France, where the French Civil Code has been 'renewed' by the introduction of Article 9; and thirdly, where legal provisions have been enacted relating to single specific branches of the law, as in the numerous statutes on the collection of personal data on computer.[152] Academic commentary on decided cases has been the deciding factor, as a formative element, because the right to privacy in the Italian experience has been, and still is, specifically derived from such legal activity. Actual legislation has so far had little influence, with the exception of a few provisions contained in the Workers' Statute designed to protect the privacy of employees, and of some provisions contained in the legislation on criminal records and on the treatment of members of the armed forces. In Italy, until a few weeks ago, there was thus still no general legislation on data-banks. The draft law, dating back to the beginning of the 1980s, had had a long and tormented legislative life. I, myself, was a member of the Commission, whose chairman was the President of the Court of Cassation, Professor Giuseppe Mirabelli, which was given the task of producing the first draft. The absence of any general legislation on personal databases had been preventing Italy from signing the Schengen Agreement. Despite difficulties, the law was finally passed by Parliament on December 1996.

Article 1 of the law mentions the right to privacy (*riservatezza*) and the right to *identità personale:* the right to have one's personality protected from false representations in the public eye. It goes on to explain that the new law is to 'ensure that in the handling of personal data, the rights, the fundamental liberties and the dignity of natural persons are respected, with particular reference to the rights to privacy and the right to have one's personality protected from false representations in the public eye'.

legal doctrine is offered by Ferrara-Santamaria, *Il diritto alla illesa intimita privata*, in *Riv. dir priv.* (1937), 17, 1. After the war, among the first unfavourable contributions see Pugliese, 'Il preteso diritto alla riservatezza e le indiscrezioni cinematografiche', in *Foro it* (1954) I, 115 and Ondei, 'Esiste un diritto alla riservezza?' in *Rass dir cinematografico* (1955) 66; among the favourable contribuitons see Musatti 'Appunti sul diritto alla riservatezza', in *Foro it* (1954) IV, 184; De Cupis *I diritti della personalità* (Milan 1959) 47 ff.

[151] eg, Giacobbe 'Il diritto alla riservatezza in Italia' in Dir. e società (1974) 687; Frosini 'L'informazione pubblica e la riservatezza privata', in Riv trib (1973), 5.

[152] On this point see Alpa, Bessone, and Zeno-Zencovich; *I fatti illeciti*, vol 14 of the *Trattato di dir. priv.* edited by P Rescigno (Turin, 1996).

Obviously, the text of this law was not the place to offer a complete regulation of the right to privacy as a whole; arguably that is unnecessary, since the right is already regulated by 'case law.' Nevertheless, it is important that the right has been mentioned in the wording of an enactment, because this can be seen as a definitive recognition of the right, giving it the legislative seal of approval.

A fundamental characteristic of the right to privacy in the Italian legal system may now be stated. It is a right which, apart from the creations of legal theory (which though necessary, are not conclusive), has been able to come into being and to develop as a result of judicial activism. Of course, there remain differences of style. The formalistic method, which generally prevails in Italy, may tempt observers to focus on differences with the common law. Yet notwithstanding this, it is arguable that our present experience in this particular branch of the law, though a continental one in character and flavour, has come close to that of common law, especially in so far as it shows that this right has its origins in decisional law. It can also be seen as an example of the phenomenon which Professor Markesinis has described as 'the gradual convergence' of the European legal systems.

Still on an introductory note, it may be useful to point out that, in terms of the references found for it in existing legislation, the right to privacy in Italy has gone through several phases as far as its legal basis is concerned. During the first phase, its basis was found in Article 8 of the European Convention on Human Rights. In the second phase, the right was based on Article 10 of the Civil Code, which governs one's rights over one's image (that is, the right to prevent the use of visual images of oneself and one's family being used in such a way as to damage one's own, or one's family's, dignity or reputation). In the third phase, the basis was seen to he in Article 2 of the Constitution, which protects the individual, both as a single person and in the social groupings in which his personality is active; and in the last and present phase, the right is justified by reference to the general principle of protection of the person, as acknowledged and guaranteed by the Constitution as well as the EU.

1.4.3. *The conceptual forms of the right to privacy and its applications*

The legal transplant to which I have alluded, has not been merely mechanical. For one thing, it has needed the modifications dictated by the existing legal system and by the new needs occasioned by the computer society in which we now live. For another, it has grown and divided itself into categories.

The contemporary situation is more complex, than will appear from these short notes; and there are several reasons for this complexity.

The first reason that—even in the context of a general right of personality—

several forms of right can be discerned which resemble, assist or are actually intertwined with the right to privacy. I refer to the following:

(1) The rights of a human being over his image, which relate to the use made by third parties of the visual representation of a person, whether for the purpose of information or publication or for financial purposes in the narrowest sense (in the latter case, we refer, using English words, to the 'right of publicity');
(2) The rights of a person to his identity, that is, to the identity he knows in himself, which consists of the wealth of ethical values and political, economic, social, and sexual persuasions that belong to an individual and that must not be misrepresented or distorted in their presentation to the public;
(3) The rights of a person to his name, perceived not merely as the means of identifying him but also as an expression of the individual's personal history, his way of being and presenting himself;
(4) The right to a person's genetic identity;
(5) The rights of a sick person when his illness is related to his behaviour (his pleasures, his sex life, and so on); and
(6) The ways that these rights or, more specifically, these forms of the single, all-embracing right of the personality, conflict with the right of reporting, which belongs to journalists working in the press, radio, and television networks, and with the right of artistic expression.

The right to privacy also affects activities which, because of developments in technology, make the person more vulnerable, such as the creation of personal databases on computer, phone-tapping, and the transmission of information and images via the Internet.

Following the earliest recognitions of the right to privacy by judges in decided cases, awareness of this new right spread not only to legal scholars but also to the rest of society; and the (rather imaginatively so-called) 'social conscience' has assimilated the concept of the right to privacy, taking it to mean that the freedom of the individual must be protected within the social structure. Privacy is regarded as a 'civil right' and ranks as one of the so-called third-generation rights (after political rights and social rights). Proceedings relating to the right to privacy have been quite a growth industry; and the records of decided cases for the last 15 years offer a very rich selection of applications of the right: in the collections of judgments from 1980 until today, there are more than 500 recorded decisions of courts of all instances; and this does not include decisions which have not been published in journals. Given the huge and growing volume of civil litigation, this may not be an enormous figure; but it may indicate that the number of suits brought and settled is even higher.

The application of the right to privacy first lapped the edges of and then invaded distinct branches of the law which are quite remote from each other. Merely to obtain an outline and approximate idea of the phenomenon, one should think of questions such as: the right to privacy and the voting powers of an administrative committee;[153] the sanction of suspending a driving licence;[154] the dismissal of a local government employee during his probationary period;[155] the use in the course of a criminal trial, of recordings made illicitly;[156] the theft of company documents by an employee;[157] the negative effect upon communal living of the cessation of the legal extension of the lease;[158] the question whether balconies and roof terraces may be built;[159] whether it is lawful for an employee to present a false medical certificate to his employer because he does not want to reveal that he is, or has been in custody;[160] the publication of information relating to the payment of taxes;[161] the entrusting of the children to the other, separated spouse if the spouse to whom they had been entrusted has abandoned all discretion by publicly revealing his relationship with another person;[162] searches of the property of persons in custody;[163] a divorced woman's use of her ex-husband's surname;[164] the installation, by the joint owners, of a security camera in the hall and staircases of a block of flats;[165] and so on.

The majority of cases relate to the protection of the privacy of employees (which is outside the scope of this work) and the protection of privacy as it affects the publication of news, caricatures, and physical and conceptual images of persons in the mass media.

This branch of the law has been beset from the beginning by the problem of the protection of 'famous' people, that is those people who because of their family, their profession, their role in politics, or the events of their lives, are already known to the public, so that there is a public interest of some kind in publication.

In this area of the law, the use of comparative case law—a practice inaugurated in Italy by that great master, Gino Gorla[166] and particularly developed

[153] *Cons Stato*, VI, 2 May 1983 no 300, in *Cons Stato* (1983) I, 556.

[154] TAR [Tribunale Amministrativo Regionale] Abruzzi, sez L'Aquila 24 Mar 1982, no 150, in *Rivista della Circolazione dei Trasporti* 1982, 156, 346.

[155] TAR [Tribunale Amministrativo Regionale] Lombardia, sez Milano 26 Oct 1982, in *TAR* (1982) I, 3384.

[156] *Cass pen* (1983) 684.

[157] *Trib Lodi* 16 Mar 1982, in *Orient giur lav* (1982) 1280.

[158] *Cass civ* 16 Sept 1983, no 5604.

[159] *Cass Civ* 8 Nov 1983, no 6594.

[160] *Cass civ sez civ*(29 Nov 1982) no 6494.

[161] *TAR* Liguria, 26 June 1980 no 371, in *Foro amm* (1980) I, 2171.

[162] *App L'Aquila* Corte d'appello 31 Dec 1976 in *Giurisprudenza di merito* (1979) 625.

[163] *Corte assise Torino* 12 Nov 1987, in *Giur cost* (1988) 221.

[164] *App Roma* 18 May 1987, in *Foro It* (1987) I, 3143.

[165] *Trib Milano* 6 Apr 1992, in *Arch locazioni* (1992) 823.

[166] Gorla *Il contratto* vol II (Milan 1955).

in the United Kingdom by Basil Markesinis[167]—is an interesting subject for analysts. It has hitherto been very unusual for Italian judges to refer to foreign judgments as precedents; they have preferred to refer to domestic *precedents* but in order to lighten the difficult task of balancing the interests involved and strengthening the right to privacy, it is probable that in future this method of comparing commentary on decided cases will find favour even with our judges. There are some interesting signs that this may already be happening in your own system; but that is not for me to comment upon.

1.4.4. The method and the logical reasoning

The steps in the formal reasoning, of both academic and practising lawyers, are as follows. If an interest is to be protected it must be raised to the level of a subjective right (in this case, an absolute subjective right) that is protected *erga omnes;* that subjective right must be founded upon a reference to it in legislation. Such reference is 'found' (using the practice *of Rechtsfindung*, or 'finding the law') in legal provisions already in existence; once the right has been so established, it must be coordinated with any other rights that are in conflict with it; and any conflict is resolved by comparing the respective rights' legal validity and the relative interests in their protection, having regard to the current state of the legislation.

In a case of breach of privacy, the reasoning is therefore as follows. The facts fall within the ambit of civil liability, which requires the application of Article 2043 of the Civil Code, the general provision on liability. The case is about 'unjust' (or, unlawful) damage, caused by the infringement of an absolute subjective right, the general right of personality. At present, this right is 'found' by directly applying Article 2 of the Constitution. According to this reasoning, the right to privacy is placed in a defined category: the type of damage is categorized as a tort; and the type of interest infringed is categorized as one of the rights of the personality; some aspects of it are covered by constitutional law, and some also by the criminal law, when the infringement is accompanied by damage to assets that are protected by the criminal law.

Clearly, there are techniques, or fictions, at the heart of this reasoning. The fiction lies in the 'discovery' of the legal provision and thus in the notion that the judge cannot create, but can only find, a rule that applies to the case, in the existing legal system. Another fiction lies in the comparison (or weighing) of interests, which is made as if the text of the provision or provisions referred to were so clear as to dictate to the judge what the outcome of the case should be.

[167] Markesinis, *The German Law of Torts* (3rd edn Oxford 1994).

In reality, an analysis of the facts and the 'living law' reveals the truth to be the opposite of these fictions. Where there is no specific provision covering the facts under consideration (as there would be, by contrast in France, under Article 9 of its Civil Code) the 'finding' is the result of interpretation, extending the application of the necessary rule, to cases it was not intended to cover, or applying it by analogy, or retrieving fragments of rules and putting them together in a sort of mosaic, from which the form of the right can be described. Moreover, the construction of the right is driven by the additions the interpreter of the law makes to it from the values in which he believes and which he is interpreting, probably also praying 'social conscience' in aid. These techniques of judicial procedure are an interesting aspect of the study of the right to privacy.

The majority of the judgments on the matter pertain to the interlocutory stage of proceedings: whether because of the urgency with which an order is needed, to terminate the abuse complained of and limit the damage, or whether because of the long time required in the Italian legal system to reach a judgment on the merits. In addition, since the damage is non-material, even though sometimes the damages are significant in economic terms, compensation may be required to take a specific form (eg rectification) or to take a different form (eg the payment of appropriate pecuniary damages).

1.4.5. The founding cases relating to prominent persons' rights to privacy and the reasoning in their judgments

Since, as has been underlined above, the right to privacy has its origins in legal doctrine and in commentary on decided cases, it has taken shape as a result of the process carried out by theoreticians and judges, often in opposition to each other, of refining the models of judgments. The theoreticians sketch the ideal models of judgments. The judges set out the actual models. The history of the protection of privacy in Italy is an instructive example of the following: the way in which model judgments evolve; the extension of private law by commentary on decided cases; and the growing sensibility of public opinion, of academic lawyers, and of judges, about the protection of the rights of the person. The most difficult problems are posed by the protection of the privacy of famous people; rather, the first cases relating to breaches of privacy relate to famous people or members of famous families. It is even possible to say—though I have never found the distinction very convincing—that the right to privacy in Italy has been formed from 'hard cases'. Certainly it has had a difficult evolution.

The earliest judgments deny the existence of any right to privacy (*riservatezza*) in our legal system and consequently either they refuse to award compensation to the plaintiff, or they award it by protecting related rights, such as the right to one's name (and not to have it falsely used), to one's dignity and reputation, and one's rights over one's image. In the first 20 or 30 years, a straight contradiction grew up between the lower courts (where matters are decided on the merits of their evidence) and the Court of Cassation. The former were more inclined to admit the existence of new rights, partly because they were and are more sensitive to the facts of a case. The latter was more inclined to apply the provisions of law strictly, since its duty was and is to supervise the correctness of judicial reasoning.

The earliest cases, both favourable and unfavourable, began to appear in the 1950s. It is difficult to determine whether the timing is merely fortuitous (as it often is in other tort cases), since these are dependent on the accidental occurrence of a damage-causing event; or whether the importance accorded by the law to these matters at that time was increased by the socio-political circumstances prevailing after the war. The Fascist regime had ended; the press was more free to publish news, and to criticize the behaviour of individuals and especially of famous people; people were reading more books, and the improvement in living standards favoured their circulation; the radio, though it was owned by state, state, was no longer gagged as it had been before; and television, likewise publicly owned, was taking its' first steps at free reporting, and gaining popularity among viewers (especially those who belonged to the less fortunate social classes) who had to congregate in bars and cinemas to watch the most engaging programmes.

It was in this new climate that the earliest judgments were handed down, in the *Caruso* case and in the case of *Petacci*.

A. *The* Caruso *Case*

The judgments given in the case of *Caruso* differed at first, seconds, and third instance. The case was about the making of the film 'Legend of a Voice'. The film was about the great tenor, Enrico Caruso; and events from his private life were portrayed in it in a romanticized way, some of them with no foundation in fact. The singer's heirs claimed that this was damaging to his memory, his dignity, and his right to privacy. They sued the film company accordingly. There were, for example, episodes in the film which depicted the humble environment in which the tenor had lived in his youth, and showed his disputes with tax inspectors, his tendency to get drunk, his quarrels with colleagues and even his attempted suicide. The judges at first instance affirmed the existence of the right to privacy and found for the plaintiffs. Even in their argued judgment[168] all the questions are addressed

[168] Trib Roma, 14 Sept 1953, in *Foro it*, 1954, I, 115.

that were to be discussed in the years that followed and that even today constitute the main elements of the problem of privacy. The judgment is also exemplary in its logical structure which takes the form of a series of syllogisms—because it proceeds, after describing the applicable legislation, to describe the facts, and returns to the facts again in its statement of the law.

As for the foundation for its findings in existing legislation, the judgment states that:

our legal system although there is no explicit provision on the point, does recognize the existence of a right to privacy (*riservatezza or privatezza*). This is expressed in the prohibition against any interference by strangers in a person's private life and against any disclosure, by third parties, of facts or personal behaviour which, not being by nature public, are not intended by the persons to whom they relate, to be made public. This right represents a fundamental need of the personality and the construction of the right and the rules relating to it must be sought, in the absence of specific legislation on the point, in the legislation relating to a person's rights over his image. The fact that these are protected by the law is a sign that the privacy of the person is also protected.[169]

As for the fact—that it was a famous person whose rights to privacy were being infringed, the judges at first instance affirmed that in such a case there were derogation's from the rule:

The public interest in knowing about the facts of these people's lives and about their behaviour, has the same weight and is as worthy of protection, as is the [public] interest in being acquainted with their visual images. Nevertheless, the invasion of the private life of another person even when it is lawful, must be seen to be justified . . . in other words it must be proportionate to the said public interest. It is in the public interest that everything should be known that may have contributed to the famous person's development or that is necessary for the public to evaluate him. It cannot be said, however, that it is in the public interest that disclosures should be made about the private life of the person, which are not justified by these purposes but merely satisfy the public's reprehensible inquisitiveness or taste for gossip. The limitation that fame imposes on the famous person's enjoyment of his right to privacy demands that the public interest be fairly balanced against the individual interest, so that the former does not cause the total, and unjustified, sacrifice of the latter.

We do not know whether the words *'riservatezza ' and 'privatezza'* were used in the advocates' written pleadings, or whether the judges of the Court of Rome used them on their own initiative; but the fact remains that since that decision the term and the concept have come into use. Since, however, it was necessary, for formal reasons, to discover a provision of legislation on which to base the protection of the interest under discussion the judges

169 Ibid c 128.

made use, by analogy, of an interpretation of Article 10 of the Civil Code. They did not consider the rules of the Constitution, because at that time the provisions of the Constitution were not regarded as applicable to relationships between private individuals but were seen as being relevant only to the relations between state and private persons. We should also take account of the fact that one of the most distinguished scholars of Roman law and comparative law, the late Professor Giovanni Pugliese, severely criticized the judgment. In his view, the right to privacy (*riservatezza*) had no legal foundation in our system.[170] He held this opinion in spite of being fully aware of the efforts made in that direction by the creators of Italian doctrine, the Italian comparative law scholars, and by German and Anglo-American legal commentary. Indeed, he cited some of them with his customary precision, referring to Ferrara-Santamaria, Kohler, and Ravà (all writing before the Second World War). He referred also to the writers of treatises and text books such as De Cupis and Santoro-Passarelli. He disposed of their efforts without mercy. He thus stated that the sweeping statements in these writings and pronouncements are not balanced by any persuasive demonstration using the inductive arguments of positive law; instead, moral and social axioms are repeated, which would serve at best for an argument *de lege ferenda.*[171]

The model of the reasoning of the judgment, itself, was maintained on appeal but the judges' opinion differed as to legal doctrine. They questioned whether a right to privacy existed in our legal system. The model of the judgment came to grief in the judgment of legitimacy (ie at the Court of Cassation).[172]

The Highest Court—Court of Cassation—asked itself the question whether there should be protection for a general right to *riservatezza* or *privatezza* as defined in Anglo-American case law as the 'right of privacy'. Its reply was in the negative:

> No provision of law authorizes us to hold, as a general principle, that absolute respect for the privacy (*intimità*) of a person's private life has been sanctioned by legislation; still less, has it been so sanctioned as a restriction upon artistic licence; the mere desire for privacy (*riserbo*) has not been considered by the legislature to be a protectable interest. No one who has failed, or who has not wished, to keep the facts of his own life a secret, is allowed by the law to claim that the secret should be kept by other people's discretion. Curiosity and harmless gossip, though they are not one of the highest manifestations of the human spirit, do not, of themselves, give rise to a legal wrong. Still less, is it possible to speak of a right to privacy (*riservatezza*) when, as in the present case, the facts narrated do not belong to the real life of the character but have been drawn from the film director's imagination about the

[170] 'Il prieteso diritto alla riservatezza e le indiscrezioni cinematografiche', in *Foro it* (1954) I, c 117.

[171] Ibid.

[172] *App Roma* 14 Sept 1955, in Foro it (1956) I, c 796.

subject of the film, in order to make the narrative more lively and interesting and more expressive and significant as a creative work of the imagination.

In defence of this judgment, it would be possible to admire the unusual citation from foreign case law; but this is actually quite generic, since no reference is made either to a decided case or to the court making the decision; and one suspects that the judges of the Court of Cassation had mistaken for English law, a development that had taken place in the law of the United States! Moreover, there is a certain narrowness of vision as to the possibility of applying the rules of existing legislation—if rules were needed; and there is a very noticeably moralising tone in the judgment particularly where it is claimed that the individual, if he does not wish to be assailed by the curiosity of the public, should live as if he were subject to the rules of a *monastero,* or actually become agoraphobic (as did the mysterious Greta Garbo).

It is interesting to follow the course, not only of the debate carried on by the creators of legal doctrine, which accompanies the developments in commentary on decided cases, but also of the invective exchanged between the courts of appeal (especially the Court of Appeal of Milan and the Court of Appeal of Naples) and the Court of Cassation, which is a strange and altogether unusual occurrence, when seen in the context and climate of the time. At the end of the 1950s, and then at the beginning of the 1960s, the cultural climate of study and practice in the law was changing. The formal method was still *de rigeur* and *Rechtsfindung* still regarded as essential, as was the notion, dating from the Napoleonic era, that the judge is the *bouche de la loi* (mouthpiece of the law). The attitude of the judges on the merits in all courts below the Court of Cassation was loyal in following the direction of the Highest Court, as if in observance of an unwritten law (since the judgments of the Court of Cassation do not constitute binding precedents). These judges adopted this attitude perhaps because they had a certain fondness for rules, or because of the prestige of the judges of the Court of Cassation. Less noble reasons may also have played a part since the reversal by the Court of Cassation of judgments given in the courts below is commonly taken as a negative evaluation of the professional abilities of the relevant judges when it comes to their promotion. But the picture was beginning to change: the provisions of the Constitution were coming to the fore in the reasoning given in judgments; the diversity of reference values regarded as available was being extended; and the protection of the person (even if famous) was becoming an important point of reference.

B. The Petacci *Case*

The model judgment, which reaffirmed the existence in our legislation of the right to privacy, is still that of the Court of Appeal of Milan in the *Petacci* case.[173] By this time the trend was quite clear (the first instance judgment is not recorded).

The case related to the publication of a book in which the author reconstructed the personality of Mussollini's mistress, Claretta Petacci, who was executed with him at the end of the war. The book made assertions about her, and made them in a way that Claretta's family considered offensive and damaging to the privacy not only to herself, but also of members of her family. The reasoning in the judgment is at once simple, concise and conclusive:

> The right to privacy (*riservatezza*) has, in this case, been breached. It is one of the fundamental rights of the personality, taking its place in that varied field of rights, alongside the right to one's name, over visual images of oneself, the author's moral rights, and so on. The right to privacy (*riserbo*) is the legal liberty to exclude any invasion made by strangers into the realm of one's personal and family privacy (*intimità*). This right requires that the person must be respected, and it must be applied fully, in its own right and absolutely, and must not be limited save by the restrictions which appear to be imposed on it for reasons of the public order or because of the higher interests of society.

In this judgment, in contrast to earlier ones, the right to privacy (*riservatezza*) was presented as a right of the personality that is so wide in its scope as to embrace the other aspects of it that are expressly protected by the law, such as the right to one's name, one's rights over visual images of himself, and the confidentiality of documents etc.

Rechtsfindung is saved by the reference which the Milanese judges copied from the written pleadings of the parties—to the European Convention on Human Rights. This states in Article 8 that: '*toute personne a droit au respect de sa vie privée et familiale, de son domicile et de sa correspondance.*' As for the question whether a person's fame makes any difference, no derogation is admitted: this is because the right of reporting cannot be justified in the absence of the presupposition of public interest. The judges determinedly underline this clearly when they say: 'even when it is a question of people belonging to the public life of a country, the secret of their private (intimate) life must be respected: there is no place, even in such a case, for the disclosures and interferences of public curiosity.'[174]

The dispute finally reached the Court of Cassation.[175] This time the Highest Court had difficulty. It did not wish to alter its own case law, so it persisted in excluding the possibility of the existence in our legal system of

[173] *Cass* 22 Dec 1956 n 4487, in *Foro it* (1957) I, 877.
[174] *App Milano*, 26 Aug 1960, in *Foro it.*
[175] Judgment given on 20 Apr 1963 n 990, in *Foro it* (1963) I, 877.

a right to privacy (*riservatezza*); but its embarrassment is evident, for it also held that there had been a breach of the absolute right of the personality. In other words, the judicial form of the question was changed; but this time the underlying interest was recognized and protected. The Court held that the specific and piecemeal protection of individual rights of the personality, as provided in the Civil Code or in ordinary special laws, did indicate that there was a general right of the personality in our legal system.

The duty of *Rechtsfindung* is, likewise, discharged, though this time the judges did not rely on Article 8 of the European Convention on Human Rights. The Court held that Article as superfluous, since it expresses a principle that is already present and protected in our legal system. It relied, instead, on Article 2 of the Constitution, which provides: 'The Republic recognizes and guarantees the inviolable rights of man both as an individual and in the social formations where his personality is active, and requires the fulfilment of the binding duties of political, economic and social solidarity.' This is an admission of the right to free self-determination in the development of the personality within the limitations we have discussed above, which are imposed by fife in the community.

This recognition by such a high authority, sounding as it does more like a '*non obstat*' than a '*place*' paved the way for the fuller protection of privacy in our legal system. Legal doctrine almost unanimously continued the trend, and the judges of fact, who courageously pre-empted the decision of the Court of Cassation, were duly rewarded. Indeed if we were called upon now, to identify the 'leading precedent' we should be embarrassed: the decision of the Court of Cassation precedes in time, and culturally takes precedence over, the decisions of the judges on the merits; they are 'precedents', in every sense of the word; they are not however 'leading' because they appeared as courageous acts of anticipation rather than as models to be followed.

1.4.6. The case of Esfandiari *as 'leading precedent'*

Rather than adopting the reasoning used by the courts below the Court of Cassation prefers to construct its own model. At the beginning of the 1960s the model judgments of the courts of fact could be regarded as isolated decisions, in which the reasoning depends more on the particular circumstances of each case than on any consciousness of introducing a new right into the list of fundamental rights. That is why legal doctrine[176] has preferred to treat one of the later decisions of the Court of Cassation as the leading precedent. It is the judgment in the case of the Princess Soraya

[176] Visintini *Trattato breve sulla responsabilità civile* (Padua 1996) 82.

Esfandiari.[177] The 'precedent' in Italian legal practice and development does not have the same significance or role as in the common law jurisdictions. This makes it possible to say that the Italian right to privacy has quite a long history and that its origin can be found at the beginning of the 1950s. If, however, we wish to point to the first decision in which the Highest Court unhesitatingly recognized the right to privacy, we find it in the middle of the 1960s.

The case of Soraya is extremely simple. A news weekly devoted specifically to events in the lives of royal families, and consequently circulating among a wide public, had photographs—taken with a telephoto lens—prepared for publication (but had not yet been published). They showed the Princess Soraya behaving affectionately with an actor, inside her Roman villa. At that time the princess, who had formerly been the Czarina of Persia, was living in exile, having been abandoned by her husband because of her inability to conceive children. It was also known that she had been granted an annuity, subject to the condition that she led a chaste and exemplary life. This was what gave rise to the princess's claim, both for breach of her rights over her visual image and for breach of her right to privacy and for trespass in her home.

At first instance, the Court of Milan allowed her claim. In the judgment given on appeal, the Court of Cassation—though until that time it had maintained an unfavourable attitude to the right to privacy—changed its opinion (we do not know whether this was to comply with the previous trend set by the Court of Cassation or whether it was because of a change in the committee of judges) and partly reversed the judgment given at first instance. It did, however, stress that the public interest in information about a famous person is not to be confused with the public's morbid curiosity about facts relating to that person's private life.

There are several reasons why this case is interesting. First of all, the case involved the combined protection of a person's visual image and reputation with the protection of her privacy. Second, it showed that it is necessary to adjust the right of reporting (and of the public to information) to the rights of the person. Finally, the case related to a famous person and can be connected with recent events concerning members of reigning families.

The logical steps in the reasoned judgment of the Court of Cassation are also interesting. The Court ran through the history of judgments on the matter, from the earliest cases in which the right to privacy was affirmed, to the cases which revealed conflicts between judicial opinions (already alluded to above), to a consideration of the opinions formulated in legal doctrine.

177 Cass 27 May (1975) n 2129, in *Foro It* (1976) I, 2895.

With regard to rights over one's visual image, the Court stated that the commercial purposes inherent in the publication of visual images of other people must be considered in the fight of Article 41, clause 2 of the Constitution. This Article grants individual liberty to engage in commercial initiatives provided they do not damage human dignity. This means that the liberty to exploit commercially the visual image of another person is conditional upon obtaining the interested party's consent which, in the circumstances of this case, had certainly not been given.

With regard to the liberty to express one's thoughts from which the freedom of information derives (under Article 21 of the Constitution), the Court specified that these liberties must be exercised within the limitations construed from 'case law'. These are, that the facts that are made public must not only be true, but must also be consonant with an appreciable public interest; and that respect must be maintained for the *privacy* (*riservatezza*) and dignity (*onorabilità*) of the person, to which even well-known people have the right.

The outcome of the case followed from this. It was that sequestration of the weekly would not be granted, because neither the ordinary nor the constitutional legislation relating to the press enabled such an injunctive measure to be taken for breach of the rights of the person. Instead, the Court ordered the payment of damages.

As a matter of method, the Court specified that 'the time has not yet come when it would be right to hold that the national conception has been superseded, of subjective rights as the defining category of those subjective legal situations that are particularly important in our legal system, inasmuch as the court grants them the protection of immediate remedy [in their own right and not by analogy with other rights].'

The judges proposed therefore to carry out a *Rechtsfindung*, that is, to identify the provisions of law in force that, without listing privacy (*riservatezza*) among the rights so immediately protected, can nevertheless can be used in order to afford it some protection. First of all, however, the Court of Cassation noted the need to define the meaning of the right which has by then come to be called in Italian: '*riservatezza*'. They identified three different meanings which are as follows (starting from the narrowest meaning): (a) domestic privacy (*intimità*), which is linked to the protection of the home, to which the Court says that perhaps the Anglo-American 'right to be let alone' is equivalent; (b) the realm of individual and family life, and certain forms of illicit, inter-personal intimacy in relationships, including outside the home and in correspondence; (c) *riserbo*, or the right to require other people's discretion about one's private life, or privacy. Applying the 'general principles of the legal system' the Court held that the fast definition was too restrictive, the second more 'reasonable,' and the third too wide and general.

The list of the provisions referred to in order to found the right to privacy as described above in section (ii) is by now far wider than it was in the past; even though specific provisions relate to specific situations, the Court recalled the passage in Celsus: '*Scire leges non est verba carum tenere, sed vim ac potestatem*'.[178] In addition, many provisions in the Constitution are used as means of affirming that the preservation of privacy is not implicit but explicit in the legislation (Articles 2, 3, 14, 15, 27, 29, and 41 of the Constitution); and use is also made of international provisions, from the United Nations Declaration on Human Rights to the United Nations Resolution of 16 December 1966 no 2200, to the European Convention of Human Rights, to the Resolution no 428 of 1970 of the Assembly of the Council of Europe.

The Court also specified that a rigid definition of privacy (*riservatezza*) is not appropriate, since it needs 'flexibility as to its precise content' in order for it to be adapted 'to the needs of [different] environments, places and times'. A definition is, however, proposed in the following terms:

> this right is a right of protection for those situations and events that are strictly personal and relating to the family and which, even if they take place outside the domestic residence, do not have an appreciable public or social interest for third parties. It is a right to be protected from such interference even if it is affected by lawful means, for purposes that are not exclusively speculative and that involve no offence against dignity, reputation, or propriety, as is not justified by an overriding public interest.

As for famous people, the Court reaffirmed that there need only be an exception to the rule in respect of them, if there is 'a real social interest or an overriding public interest'.

The judgment has been greeted by the creators of legal doctrine with favourable commentary. In it, the conception of privacy (*riservatezza*) *as* having to do with ownership, is superseded; restrictions are imposed on the tight of reporting; and it is admitted that even well-known people have a right to protection.

1.4.7. *The current debate around the limits of the right to privacy*

Notwithstanding its recognition by the Court of Cassation and the favour it has found in legal doctrine, the right to privacy is still under discussion. There is no longer any doubt as to its naturalization into our legal system, but in defining its limitations, its scope remains uncertain. These limitations can be summarized as set out below.

[178] L 17 Dig De leg ('Knowing the law is not a matter of knowing the letter of the law but its force and its power').

(i) The status of the interested party

There remains a grey area relating to famous people insofar as they carry on a political or institutional activity. Does the public interest justify the invasion of their private lives? Legal doctrine is divided on this point. A person proposing himself to the public for election to Parliament is not bound to lead a blameless life in the behaviour prompted by his affections; we Italians have always considered the reactions of American public opinion to the 'escapades' of presidents or presidential candidates to be excessive, moralistic and puritan at the same time; American smear campaigns have appeared to us more like the methods of political competition at its lowest level than the means of alerting the public to unbecoming and therefore unpromising traits of character or behaviour. It is as if the contenders had only those arguments available to them to beat their opponents. On the other hand, it has been thought that breaches of privacy were permissible, where the facts of a person's private life, his friends, and those he is intimate with, might affect not only his sexual, but also his political morals.

The question remains open; and judgments are recorded, even from the criminal section of the Court of Cassation, specifying that 'the right of reporting is limited by the right to privacy because facts relating to the intimate relationships and private life of a citizen are not matters of interest to society even if he is in public office'.[179] Contrariwise, other judgments are recorded, which take a different line and specify that 'the right to privacy may be sacrificed to the right of reporting, provided that a balance has been struck between the two rights: not an absolute, but a relative [balance], on the boss of a consideration of the subjective characteristics of the interested party'.[180]

(ii) The subordination of privacy to other rights

Commentary on decided cases draws a distinction of degree between the rights (or between the forms) of the personality. The right to dignity and reputation has in many cases been considered more important than the right to privacy, so that the right to dignity and reputation appears to prevail—even when the right to privacy would have to yield to the right of reporting. The judge of the lower court of Rome, for example, says that 'the right to privacy [*riservatezza*] and the rights over one's visual image may be reduced if the person belongs to current events, to history or to the news;

[179] *Cass pen* [see n 7] 9 Feb 1979, in *Riv pen* (1979) 1041 ff, *Pret Roma* 15 July 1986, in *Dir informatica* (1986) 926; *Pret Roma* 13 July 1987, in *Dir informatica* (1987) 1005.
[180] *Pret Roma* [see n 29] 7 Nov 1986, in Giur Merito [see n 13] (1987) 1190.

but in such a case the prohibition against causing damage to that person's reputation and dignity still stands'.[181]

(iii) Conflict with, and adjustment to, other rights: artistic expression

Commentary on decided cases also draws distinctions between the different ways in which privacy is breached. Artistic, photographic, romantic and satirical creations are protected even in the Constitution, as well as being manifestations of thought and words. The case of Claretta Petacci again comes to the fore. Her love affair became the subject of a television screenplay *The Duce and I*. This time, however, the court found against her (plaintiff) family because the judge considered that there was no obligation to respect historical truth in imaginative works of narrative literature or cinema, provided that the person was not presented in a pejorative way and the author did not evince a denigratory intent.[182] However, if the publication of photographs in a magazine results in a negative and insulting image of the person portrayed in them, the publisher and the editor of the paper are ordered to pay damages.[183] It is added also that what must be preserved in this case is privacy, dignity, and reputation, but not the image the individual has of himself.[184] Satire is looked upon with favour because it acts as a social monitor of the behaviour of famous people. Indeed, one reads in a judgment of the *Tribunale of Rome*[185] that satire has the standing of a subjective right and has constitutional importance; the boundaries within which it is permitted cannot be modelled on those of the right of reporting; and, indeed, satire does not answer a need for information, it does not have any necessary or obvious connection with factual truth, and it need not comply with canons of balanced expression, so that its only limitations consist in:

> an internal limitation, inasmuch as its legitimate exercise is dependent upon the fame of the person against whom it is aimed, the person, precisely because he has chosen fame as a dimension of his life and actions, is presumed to have renounced that part of his right to privacy that directly relates to his public dimension; and various external limitations, pertaining to each of the media by which the satire is published, and to the content of the satirical message, such as [a restriction against] the attribution of offensive facts, the disclosure of confidential information or the ironic representation of a person's private life.

In any case, satire [should], according to the Roman judges, fulfil the function of 'restraining the powerful, debunking and humanizing the famous,

181 Judgment of 6 May 1983, in Giur Merito [see n 13] (1984) 550.
182 *Pret Roma* [see n 29, 25 May 1985, in Dir Autore (1986) 181.
183 *Tri. Milano* 16 Apr 1984, in *Rass dir civ* (1985) 1107.
184 *App Roma* 11 Feb 1991, in *Giust civ* (1992) I, 223 and 2859.
185 Of 13 Feb 1992, in *Dir Famiglia* (1993) 1119.

and humbling the proud', thus limiting the excesses of power, reducing social tensions and upholding the virtue of tolerance.

(iv) The right of reporting

The most important moral values that are in conflict with the right to privacy are still the liberty to make one's thoughts known, the freedom of opinion and the freedom of the press. These are protected in the Constitution among the fundamental moral values in Article 21. In Italy this is a moral value which, since being trampled upon for the entire period of the fascist regime, has kept an aura of sanctity, so that every restriction placed upon it is rigorously examined, and often breaches of those rights that are in opposition to it are looked upon with indulgence. This makes it difficult to draw a line between the area in which the journalist's right of reporting can expand and the area which must be kept intact because it relates to the person; and even more difficult when the question concerns famous people, those in public office and those who belong, by birth or acquisition, to the most visible classes of society.

The distinction to be drawn is between the use of information, data, and images for an informative purpose and the use made of them for commercial gain; in the latter case the interests of a person who has not given his consent to their use certainly prevail.[186] In the former case, the relationship between the right of reporting and the right to privacy has had alternating fortunes: at the beginning, the right of reporting prevailed; in the latter part of the 1980s the right to privacy prevailed; and now it seems that the right of reporting is again in the ascendant. It is difficult to say whether this pendulum effect is due to changes in the mentality of the judges, or to changes in social consciousness, or to external factors, which mean that sometimes more attention is paid to the right to know than to the right to be left alone; the secrets and the underground relationships that have been a distinguishing feature of the last few years and have led to a real political and institutional revolution in Italy, have reasserted the public's right to know, and especially to know about famous (or notorious) people.

One case that has caused a good deal of controversy was decided by the Court of Cassation on 18 October 1984, no 5259.[187] It is the case which has gone down in history as 'the journalists' ten commandments', because in it the judges 'codified' the conditions upon which the press can be said to have freedom to publish news and comment (the case was about a financial transaction which was criticized in a specialist journal).

[186] See *Cass* [see (24)] 16 Apr 1991, n 4031 in *Nuova giur civ comm* (1992) I, 45.

[187] *In Nuova giur civ comm* (1985) I 84, with a favourable comment from myself, at p 214 and a critical comment from V Roppo, on p 326.

The conditions relate to the usefulness of the information to society, the objective truth of the facts disclosed and whether the facts are reported in a civilized manner. The controversy sparked by the judgment extended not only to journalists' organizations, who were seeing rules for the conduct of their activities imposed on them by the judges, but also to legal commentators. What many people disliked was not the inclusion of the first two conditions, which in any case had been repeated in many other judgments, but the inclusion in the list of the third, which relates properly to the way in which an article is written: the means, even the literary means, of its expression. The judges (justly, in my opinion) censured the use of knowing implications, suggestive juxtapositions, scandalized tones, innuendoes, and so on.

As for privacy (or confidentiality) of information the new law (mentioned at the beginning of this work) introduces restrictions on the use of data made by journalists: Article 13 really introduces a privilege for journalists, because the consent of the interested party is not required when the information is gathered in the exercise of the journalist's profession, provided that the data are gathered for professional purposes; but the privilege ends there, inasmuch as personal data may only be disclosed and published, pursuant to Article 20 Clause 1 letter d): 'within the restrictions that have been placed upon the right of reporting for the purpose of protecting privacy.' These limits are posed by the question whether the information is necessary as a matter of public interest and the question whether the journalists' code of ethics is being respected. In any case, pursuant to Article 22, sensitive data may neither be collected nor published. These are data on person's racial and ethnic origin, his religious, philosophical or other convictions, his political opinions, his membership of parties, trade unions, associations or organizations of a religious, philosophical, political or trade-union nature, or personal details apt to reveal a person's state of health and sex life.

(v) The type of damage

The ethical value (or right) of the person is treated as having not only a moral value, but also a value in pecuniary terms. These matters have been briefly dealt with. It is also worth mentioning another judgment in which a further kind of damage was highlighted, to add to those already mentioned: biological damage. It can happen, indeed, that the breach of privacy involves damage not only to a moral right, in that information which should have been kept private has been made public, but that it also involves physical and psychological damage to the victim. That is why damages have been awarded under this heading also.[188]

[188] *App Trieste* 13 Jan 1993, in *Giur it* commenting on decided cases (1994) 1, 2358.

It is interesting to note, on the question of civil liability for breach of privacy (*riservatezza*) in respect of personal details collected in data banks, that the new law provides, at Article 18, that Article 2050 of the Civil Code shall apply. This relates to liability for carrying on dangerous activities. Legal doctrine and commentary on decided cases have interpreted this provision as heralding the presumption of not merely subjective, but objective liability. In any event, the reference to Article 2050 reverses the burden of proof, so that it falls upon the author of the wrongful act.

1.4.8. Conclusion

The history of the right to privacy in the Italian legal system is symbolic. It demonstrates that the differences between codified and non codified legal systems are really only stereotypes, which may be useful for teaching purposes but do not always accurately represent the reality of living law. It also demonstrates that when it is necessary to fill gaps in the legislation, our judges do intervene (even if they are not directly empowered to act as legislators) and prepare the way for the intervention of the legislators, provided that they consider it necessary. Really, the right to privacy needs to have a chapter devoted to it in an entire book dealing solely with those elements of Italian private law that have actually been constructed and developed from case law.[189]

1.5. THE USE OF FOREIGN LAW BY JUDGES

1.5.1. 'Foreign law' in the Italian legal culture. Trends and models from the nineteenth century to the present

In the Italian legal culture, the expression 'foreign law' has a quite restricted meaning, inasmuch as it refers to the law in force in other countries necessarily applied by the Courts by virtue of the rules on the conflict of laws, or to the law chosen by agreement of the parties to govern the relationship installed between them.[190] However, the expression may be used in a wider

[189] I am grateful to Ann Thompson for producing the first (and crucial) version of the translation of my Italian text.

[190] The same perspective is adopted by U Drobnig, 'The Use of Comparative Law by Courts, General Report', in U Drobnig and S van Erp (eds), *The Use of Comparative Law by Courts, XIVth International Congress of Comparative Law* (Athens, 1997) (London 1999) at 6.

But what is striking is the use of foreign models to solve domestic cases: see B Markesinis, '*Reading Through a Foreign Judgment*', in P Cane and J Stapleton (eds) *Essays in Celebration of John Fleming* (Oxford 1998) 261 ff.

meaning, which regards not only the statutory rules applied, but also the other 'legal formants', namely 'doctrine' (legal literature) and case law, according to the teachings of one of the most eminent Italian scholars of comparative law, Rodolfo Sacco.[191] From this perspective, we are to take into consideration the cultural models, the legal institutes, the judgments coming from foreign experiences and which are used by individuals or by the courts in the solution of domestic legal problems.

In this wider meaning, the use of foreign law in Italy is the subject of a very rich history, still awaiting its narrator.[192] Summarily, this history can be sub-divided into five periods: (a) the first period comprises the whole of the 19th century, (b) the second the first half of the 20th, (c) the third, the period which spans roughly two decades (from 1950 to 1970), (d) the fourth regards the following two decades (from 1970 to 1990), and (e) the fifth, the last years of the 20th century. Each sub-division into periods is arbitrary and each period cannot be assumed as a monolith in which a sole and consistent approach took hold; however, taking a bird's-eye view of the formation of law in Italy, certain hues—which correspond to the periods previously mentioned—appear prevalent, thereby lending scientific credit to this temporal sub-division.[193]

(a) The first period records a preponderant influence of French law, which reverberates over all the formants of our legal system, the statutory formant, legal literature, and the decisions of the courts.

As regards the statutory formant, the *Code Napoléon* constituted at first the law imposed by the General's armies in the provinces conquered from the Piedmontese, from the Austrians, the Lorraines, and the Bourbons; after the fall of Napoleon, his model of Civil Code is transplanted in several of the States into which Italy was divided (the Civil Code of the Kingdom of Two Sicilies, the Civil Code of the Duchy of Parma; the Civil Code of the Kingdom of Sardinia or 'Albertine

[191] R Sacco and A Gambaro, *Sistemi giuridici comparati* (Turin 1996) at 6 ff; G Alpa (ed) *Corso di sistemi giuridici comparati* (Turin) at 10.

[192] G Gorla had studied the use of *lex alii loci* in the Middle ages (*ius commune Europeum*): see ID, *Il ricorso alla legge di un 'luogo vicino' nell'ambito del diritto comune europeo,* in *Foro italiano* (1973) V, 89 ff. For further details see P Grossi, '*L'ordine giuridico medievale*' (Rome and Bari 1998) *passim.*

Roman Law is still mentioned in Italian decisions, but only *exornatione gratia* (G Micali, '*Il diritto romano nella giurisprudenza della Corte suprema di cassazione*', in *Giurisprudenza italiana* (1993) IV, 489 ff), while, according to the Spanish Civil Code, Roman Law is the basis for interpreting the law through general principles.

[193] Unfortunately the literature in English language about this proceeding is very poor: see, among others, M Bellomo, *The Common Legal Past of Europe (1000–1800)* (Washington, 1995); for new comments see P Grossi, *La scienza giuridica in Italia nell'Ottocento* (Milan 2000); G Alpa, '*La cultura delle regole. Storia del diritto civile italiano*' in Rome and Bari (2000).

Code') and is subsequently chosen as the model for the first Civil Code of unified Italy, which is born in 1865.

As for the legal literature formant, the *Ecole de l'Exégèse* becomes the method for analysis and application of universal law, so much so that the majority of the treatises and manuals of French law are first translated and then imitated by Italian legal writers. More than 600 of these works were translated over the whole century, which sees the coming into being of the Italian 'scuola dell'Esegesi' (School of Exegesis—Interpretation), which holds that law is only the statutory state-enacted law, and the legal writer's work is limited to an analytical commentary of the provisions of the same.

With reference to the case law formant, given the closeness of French Law and Italian law, the judgments of the *Cour de Cassation* and of the French tribunals are quoted by the legal writers and employed by the judges with largesse, without regard for the fact that they have been rendered by foreign judges: French law is not considered by Italian jurists as a 'foreign' law, belonging to a *ius alienum*, that is to the system of a different state, and applied by judges belonging to the administration of a foreign state.

(b) The second period records a repudiation of the '*Scuola dell'Esegesi*' (the school of interpretation), and the triumph of the Pandectist model, the historical School of Germanic origin, introduced in Italy by the scholars of Roman law. Even Roman law was not considered then, as it is not today, a 'foreign' law in a proper sense: it is not only the primary source of the Italian legal language, but also of many of the institutes governing natural persons, property, contracts, torts, and the remedies thereto. Roman law is so widely diffused among the roots of our own legal culture that it constitutes, to this very day a fundamental subject matter of study for the formation of lawyers, is often quoted in decisions of the courts and is studied in a 'current' dimension, almost as if it were not a body of rules and principles to be historically placed in the context of its bi-millennium evolution, but as a *corpus* of rules still in force.

The choice of moving from the French culture to the Pandectist culture was not only the product of a fashion, but rather born of a requirement that at the end of the 19th century and the beginning of the 20th was perceived as necessary: the intent was to dogmatically reconstruct Italian civil law, and consequently the method for studying the same. Savigny, Arndts, Dernburg, Windscheid, among others, peep out from the bookshelves of lawyers, are top of the list in the courses of civil law, constitute the staple diet of jurists and therefore of judges, who, having received a Pandectist training, flaunt the same in their judgments. So much so, that a jurist of those times, Biagio Brugi, a famed author, a veritable scholar of Roman and private law, and editor of one of the manuals of Institutions of Private Law most widely studied by generations of students,[194] could well state, in a lecture held in 1919, that 'no efficacy ever perhaps was had in Italy by foreign scientists, which can be comparable to that of the Germans in our day and age'. His was not a simple reckoning: it was a *cri de coeur*, aimed at fostering the awareness in Italian jurists of the bi-millennium history to which they were heirs, and which he now saw as being flattened in the books copied from the German jurists, and an attempt to recover these studies to the originality of the Italian model. It was also an invitation not to disregard the other aids of foreign legal science: the Italians—he suggested—'may indeed look as farther afield as to the English *common law* (in which often our own authors are still quoted) and to the decisions of North American Courts, in certain points inimitable'.[195]

Brugi's invitation was to remain unheeded: the influence of German culture was to remain unaltered up to the formulation of the new Civil Code in 1942, and further still for several more decades. However, due to the vagaries of legal history, at the end of the 1920s, an extraordinary event was recorded, thanks to the cosmopolitan climate which pervaded Continental Europe during that period. In 1927 a bilateral commission officially installed by Italy and France drafted a uniform Code of Obligations. This initiative is due to another great jurist, a scholar of Roman law and private law, Vittorio Scialoja, and to the Frenchman, François Larnaude. Jurists from other countries, such as Belgium, Rumania, Greece, and Canada took part in the initiative at the beginning, but the same was finally restricted to the two founding nations.[196]

The purpose of the *Projet de Code des Obligations et des Contrats*, consisting of 739 articles, drafted in the two languages by the scholars of the 'sister Nations', was to 'create, with the consensus of all their strengths united, a body of laws which, within each of the two States, would represent that most perfect regime of law which legal science wished for and legal practice required'.

With the changing political balances, at the end of the 1930s, the German influence makes itself felt again; but the scholars of comparative law continue to study also the models of *common law*, taking into account not only institutes unheard of in Italy, such as *trusts*, but also company law.

[194] B Brugi, *Istituzioni di diritto civile* (Milano 1915).

[195] B Brugi, 'I danni dell'imitazione straniera nella nostra giurisprudenza', in Atti della R Accademia Lucchese di Scienze, *Lettere ed Arti*, vol XXXVI (1919) at 7.

[196] *Commissione Réale per la Riforma dei Codici/Commission Fancaise d'Etudes de l'Union Legislative entre les Nations Alieés et Amiés*, *Progetto di Codice delle Obbligazioni e dei Contratti*, Testo definitivo approvato a Parigi nell'Ottobre 1927–Anno VI (Rome 1928).

(c) After the introduction of the new Civil Code, which incorporates also commercial law in a unified whole, from the 1950s onwards, we record a sort of closure, on the part of Italian jurists, towards foreign experiences: everyone is busy understanding, commenting, interpreting the new text, and references to comparison or to foreign laws are quite rare, both in legal literature and in Court rulings.[197]

The most notable exception is that of Gino Gorla who, already in 1955, published a prodigious treatise on contracts in which, in addition to the historical perspective, a comparative approach is also adopted, by reliance on cases: reference to cases, then as today, becomes a way to seek in other experiences, in particular in common law, the similarities, the convergences, the more useful practical solutions.[198] We too can pride ourselves, as nowadays also the United Kingdom can pride itself, thanks to the works of Basil Markesinis, on scholars who are concerned in studying what unites us, more than what constitutes division, 'convergences' more than 'divergences', the formulas adaptable to the practical cases, rather than erudite musings which are an end unto themselves: scholars, in other words, animated by the longing for research, not to produce a sterile form of culture, but with the aim of seeking immediately functional, practical solutions.[199]

(d) The fourth period is the most lively, and to this we shall devote more time: it includes the influences recorded in decisions of the courts, from cases and from the other sources of foreign law, the influences of legal practice from other countries, in particular from the United States, and the deployment of remedies derived from those experiences.

(e) The current period records, in addition to the tendencies which developed during the fourth period, above all the incidence of the law of the EU and therefore the necessary circulation of the models of the Member States of the EU, which are merged in the regulations, in the directives, in the very language used by the European legislator and by the European Court of Justice.

1.5.2. Examples of foreign models used by Italian courts

The models of foreign judgments (or legal rules) used by Italian judges are still rare. Usually it is the lawyers who use these foreign elements in their defences and the judges, if they take them into account, make use of them in their motivations. But the recourse to foreign models is not only left to

197 G Alpa *La cultura delle regole*, above at n 4.

198 G Gorla, *Il contratto* (Milano 1955).

199 This is the leitmotiv through the essays collected by B Markesinis (ed), *The Gradual Convergence. Foreign Ideas, Foreign Influences, and English Law on the Eve of the 21st Century* (Oxford 1994).

the culture of the lawyer or the judge, but also to the extent the quotation may be instrumental in bringing about the favourable decision of a dispute. However, it cannot be said that the use of comparative law is a usual and normal working for the Italian lawyer. Furthermore, many cases have been decided taking foreign models into account, but the judge does not reveal the sources of his reasoning, nor does he expressly quote them. Scrutiny of these cases, however, reveals the influence of foreign experiences. Here are some examples.

(i) Privacy

One of the first Italian cases in which the problem arose of the safeguarding in our system of the right to privacy[200] regards the tenor Caruso, whose family life during childhood had been depicted in the film *Leggenda di una voce* (Legend of a voice). Certain sequences showed scenes of violence committed by his father, and Caruso himself had been portrayed as a short-tempered, heavy-drinking man, of dubious morality. To uphold the right of Caruso to obtain compensation on the basis of *tort law*, the judges put the question whether there should be protection for a general right 'to confidentiality or privacy', qualified in Anglo-Saxon Court rulings as a 'right of privacy'. The judges' reply—we are in the mid-1950s—is negative: the reasoning is formalistic, because in seeking a provision of the law aimed at protecting this specific right, and the judge having found only rules aimed at safeguarding the use of a person's name or image, or the person's decorum or reputation, but not privacy *per se,* the research is fruitless, and gives a negative result. Therefore, the judges conclude that 'in our legal system there is no right to privacy, but only individual subjective rights of the person are acknowledged and protected, in different ways; therefore, it is not forbidden to communicate, either privately or publicly, events, especially if imaginary, of another person's life, when knowledge of the same has not been obtained by means unlawful in themselves, or which impose an obligation of secrecy'.[201]

Gradually, however, the right of privacy charts its way through the Italian courts: this time, through the utilization of the 'European Convention on human rights and fundamental liberties', signed in Rome on 4 November 1950 and ratified in Italy with Statute no 848 of 4 August 1955. The Convention—whose Article 8 sets forth that '*toute persone a droit au respect de sa vie privée et familiale, de son domicile et de sa correspondance*' (every person has the right to the respect of his/her private and

[200] G Alpa, 'The protection of privacy in Italian Law', in B Markesinis (ed), *Protecting Privacy* (Oxford 1999) 105 ff.

[201] Tribunale di Roma, 14 Sept 1953, in *Foro italiano* (1954) I, 115.

family life, home, and correspondence) is quoted as the basis for the decision which upheld, both on appeal, and in the Court of Cassation, the right of the family of Claretta Petacci, the unfortunate lover of Benito Mussolini, who had been executed alongside him, trying to shield him with her own body, to obtain damages. In this case, it was a book, in which Claretta Petacci's personality was described with scornful and discrediting phrases, which had prompted the family to claim their right of privacy, and the judges upheld the same, despite the fact that the injured party was deceased.[202]

(ii) Taking

Although no cases were expressly mentioned, nor was the legal theory of German origin relating to the subject matter, the Constitutional Court, in a landmark decision regarding the regulation of ownership, held that the legislator cannot, without compensation, compress the powers of the owner on a thing beyond the limits 'naturally attached to the right of ownership' such as they are acknowledged at the current time. The case regarded certain owners of land situated in the centre of the town of Palermo, land which was under a zoning ordinance which excluded the possibility of building on the same; the town plan was compliant with the zoning law, which envisaged no compensation for zoning ordinances or encumbrances which limited or compressed the rights of the owners. The Court applied—as was immediately pointed out by the scholars of the subject matter—the German concept of '*Einzelakttheorie*', according to which the individual right, the right of ownership in particular, must be considered as a sphere, on the surface of which the legislator can carve, that is, can impose restrictions on the owner without compensation; but when restrictions carve onto the essential nucleus, and reach into the 'vital core' of the right, the sacrifice imposed on the owner must be compensated.[203]

(iii) Leasing

Leasing contracts made their appearance in an Italian court—according to the records—only in 1972. A small tribunal in the province of Pavia, which is full of small businesses lead by able and tireless entrepreneurs, had to solve the question of whether the machinery given by the lessor to the lessee for the manufacture of shoes should be considered the property of the lessor or of the lessee. The contract utilized was a leasing contract, unknown until then in the Italian experience, where according to tradition, use of a thing

[202] Corte di Cassazione, 22 Dec 1956, n 4487, *ibi* (1957) I, 877.
[203] Corte costituzionale, 29 May 1968, n 55, *ibi* (1968) I, 1365.

can be the subject of a contract of rental or of a contract of sale, or of a contract creating property rights. The Tribunal instead referred to commercial practice—without however quoting the experience from which this type of contract had been imported—to acknowledge right of citizenship of the same in our own system, by virtue of the principle of freedom of contract.[204]

(iv) *Liability for prospectuses*

Even for the presentation to the public of financial products, in the absence of statutes which would be enacted only in 1983, and then more widely in 1991, the judges—in this case the judges of the Tribunal and of the Appeals Court of the town of Milan, which is the main financial centre of the country—relied on foreign experience, in particular the English and US experience. They did not take care to mention any cases, but simply proceeded to follow the reasoning of the same. On that occasion there was a prospectus prepared by the issuer to favour the underwriting of debenture securities by investors; the issuer was the client of a bank, American Express Bank, subsequently American Service Bank spa, which was in charge of placement of the securities on the Italian market; it had invited its clients to underwrite the debentures and assured them that the issuer was in an economically sound position; the investment, however, proved disastrous, because a few months later the issuer went bankrupt. In the first instance the bank was not held liable, because the judge ascertained that there was no contract of guarantee with clients;[205] in the appeal, instead, the bank was held liable in tort, because it had spread groundless information on the economic soundness of the issuer. In defining the limits of liability, the judges refer to liability for (misrepresentation in) prospectuses, well known to common lawyers.

(v) *Nervous shock*

In the Italian legal system, there has been great discussion as to the extent and qualification of personal injury. In addition to physical injury and so-called moral injury (which corresponds to the 'pain and suffering' of common law) a different type of injury, consisting of injury to health (so-called 'biological damage') has been ascertained. The purely psychic damage, due to the nervous shock produced by an accident, had never been taken into consideration as a legally relevant injury. However, the Constitutional Court, taking into account the English experience, specified as *obiter dictum*, in a case in which the issue was whether compensation

[204] Tribunale di Vigevano, 14 Dec 1972, in *Banca e borsa* (1973) II, 287.
[205] Tribunale di Milano, 11 Jan 1988, in *Giurisprudenza commerciale* (1988) II, 585.

was due to the relatives of the victim, that such psychic injury, if caused by fault (negligence) or wilful damage, gives rise to compensation. The writer of the judgment was one of the most noteworthy scholars of private law, Luigi Mengoni, a former Professor at the Catholic University in Milan, subsequently appointed to the Court. The judgment sets forth that liability for nervous shock must be tied to fault, it cannot be strict liability; on the other hand, the English courts which admit this principle, in order to avoid arbitrariness, and so as not to burden the risk of the insurance companies with an overly high number of claims, make the distinction of whether the claimant suffered shock as an occasional onlooker at the time of the accident, or if he was told of the event removed from the scene of the accident, upholding the claim in the first instance, but rejecting it in the second.[206]

(vi) Italian trust

The last example regards trusts, a typical institute of *equity*, originally only available in the systems of English descent, and subsequently introduced, with different legal configurations, and on the basis of special statutes, also in countries of different legal traditions. Trusts were the subject of the Hague Convention of 1 July 1985, rendered executive in Italy by Statute no 364 of 16 October 1989, which entered into force on 1 January 1992. The Convention deals with the applicable law, but contains certain provisions which give the definition of 'Trust', for the purpose of extending the rules to all the types of this category, in the various forms in which the signing countries acknowledge the existence of the same. It is without doubt, in the Italian legal system, that a trust established abroad with a foreign trustee, relating to property located in Italy, is valid, even if the settlor is an Italian citizen. Italian citizens who intend to set up a trust mostly use foreign legal systems, mainly the rules applicable in Jersey, but also those applicable in Ireland. This choice is preferable for succession purposes, for fiscal reasons, for reasons of confidentiality, but also because the purposes achieved through the establishment of a trust are not equally available using the institutes of civil law, such as fiduciary contracts, fiduciary nomination or registration, etc. Usually the following transaction takes place: the property is registered in the name of an Italian company, whose quotas or shares are in turn registered in the name of a foreign trustee.

After the approval, ratification and entering into force even in Italy of the Hague Convention, the problem arose as to whether it was possible to set up a trust, obviously governed by a foreign law, with an Italian trustee. This because the Convention, as it contained provisions on the definition of 'trusts', introduced in Italy rules of substantive law; trusts (in their structure

206 Corte costituzionale, 27 Oct 1994, n 372 in *Foro italiano* (1994) I, 3297.

at equity) governed by a foreign law, would now be fully compatible with Italian law, but only under condition that the trustee be a foreigner.

Decisions of the courts, extremely rare, are divided.

The first case regarded compulsory purchases, promoted in Sardinia, in the 1950s, in order to enact the agrarian reform. The land subject to compulsory purchase had been set up in trust by an English national, by will and testament; the expropriating body, had instituted proceedings against the surviving spouse, designated as the trustee, and not against their children designated in the will as 'beneficiaries'. The Tribunal of Oristano, a town on the island, had acknowledged the validity of a trust set up abroad on property located abroad, but had deemed incompatible with Italian law (in particular with the principles of so-called 'public policy') the institute of trust, when the same consisted of property located in Italy, as this would have been in contrast with the so-called 'numerus clausus' of property rights. The basic point of the ruling was the idea that in trust, ownership is split between *cestui que trust* and the trustee, and that this gives rise, therefore, to a form of property right which is not compatible with the wholeness of the right of ownership envisaged in the Italian Civil Code. For the judges, therefore, the alternative was between considering as owners either the surviving spouse or the children. By holding that the surviving spouse, as trustee, had only apparent title to the property, with powers to dispose of the same, but only in accordance with the aims of the trust, the Tribunal decided that the children had right of ownership, and therefore they should have been the recipients of the expropriation procedures, which, thus, had not been effected properly.[207]

The second case regarded a trust set up by an English national on property situated in Italy; the executor trustee had applied to the Italian judge (of the Tribunal of Casale Monferrato, a small town in the northern region of Piedmont) for an authorization to sell the property; the judge, maintaining that the trust in question was similar to a fiduciary agreement '*cum amico*' under civil law, refused authorization, and held that the same was not necessary, as the fiduciary agent was already the owner of the property, albeit on a fiduciary basis.[208]

The third case regarded a trust set up in Jersey by Italian nationals. The trustee was the settlor's wife, an Italian citizen, who held the property (that is the shares in two companies) in the interest of the beneficiaries, her children and her husband, the settlor himself. Having deposited the shares to take part in the Annual General Meetings of the two companies, the direc-

[207] Tribunale di Oristano, 15 Mar 1956, *ibi* (1956) I, 1020.

[208] Tribunale di Casale Monferrato, 13 Apr 1984 (decree), in *Giurisprudenza italiana* (1984) I, 2, 754.

tors of the companies then refused to return them to her. She had therefore acted to reacquire possession of the shares; the directors had objected, claiming that 'trusts' were not recognized in our own legal system, and that the trustee (who had been replaced in the meantime) could not claim any right to the shares. The judge instead ruled in favour of the plaintiff, without however discussion of the nature of 'trusts' and their compatibility with the Italian legal system (which, according to the majority of authors, in the case at hand should have been ruled out, as the trustee was Italian); the judge based his ruling on the provisions relating to actions for recovery, which exist regardless of the title to the property, but are based on the factual relationship with the property, such as possession.[209]

1.5.3. Use of Anstalt *from Lichtenstein*

For the purpose of tax savings, to invest capital abroad, for reasons of confidentiality, wide use has been made of the institute of *Anstalt*, a typical device of the law of Lichtenstein. It is similar to a foundation, set up by a sole subject; it has legal personality and is considered by the Italian judges as a legal person existing under foreign law, recognized in Italy in the same way as our legal system recognizes other foreign legal entities. Under the laws of Lichtenstein, the necessary officers of the company are the founder and the administrator, while the Assembly and the Statutory Auditors are not strictly required. The administrator may dispose of the estate and may promote actions to safeguard the same. The general provisions of law (Article 16) and the Bruxelles Convention of 28 February 1968 (Article 1) are applied.

The first doubts that had been expressed by the Italian judges (in particular the Tribunal of Milan),[210] have been settled, and the Court of Cassation has upheld the legitimacy of *Anstalts* even if set up by founders who remain secret.[211]

1.5.4. The foreign models utilized in Italian contractual practice

In Italian contractual practice it is rare for the parties, if they are both Italian, to choose a foreign law to govern the contract. On the other hand there are numerous institutes, types of contracts, negotiating practices, and remedies which have been imported from foreign experiences, especially from English or US common law, to govern economic relations. Here are a few examples.

[209] Pretura di Roma, 8 July 1999 (order), unpublished.
[210] Tribunale di Milano, 11 Jan 1979, in *Rivista di diritto internazionale* (1980) 523.
[211] Corte di Cassazione, 21 Jan 1985, n 198.

Many types of contract have been accepted in our legal system, by virtue of the principle of freedom of contract. These—as opposed to what occurred in other countries, such as France—have retained their original names: for instance, leasing contracts, factoring, franchising, merchandising, project financing, joint ventures, contracts regarding the use of information and data transmission technologies, and so forth. As with all contracts defined as 'atypical', because they are not comprised among the types regulated by the Civil Code or by statutes, they are governed by the contractual clauses negotiated between the parties. The judge's control is twofold: on the one hand he verifies if they are worthy of protection under the Italian legal system, that is if the interests and the objectives they pursue are lawful and economically useful; on the other hand, in the event that a contract should fail to make adequate provisions for all the eventualities that may come about, the judge proceeds to qualify the same, taking into account the reference legal types. For instance, in the case of a leasing contract, reference is made either to the conditional sale agreements (with retention of title), or to rental contracts; for joint ventures, reference is made to association in participation, etc.

As for negotiating practices, the use of side-letters is frequent, and so is the use of letters of intent, letters of guarantee. Above all, for certain complex economic transactions, such as the sale of share holdings, the technique adopted in the United States is followed: a due diligence research is made, a first agreement is reached (closing) and then the parties proceed to the definitive contract.

Even as regards remedies, reference has been made to the experiences of common law, to better attain the interests of the parties: after some hesitation, the so-called 'autonomous contract of guarantee' has been accepted (configured at common law as bid bonds, etc).

But it should be specified that often even among Italian parties, the use of US Standard Contract forms, drafted in English, is preferred.

Even if the contracts are complex, and therefore more articulate than the average contract utilized in Italy, we never arrive at the detailed regulation of US contracts, consisting often of weighty files, in which every conceivable event is taken into account and provided for.

1.5.5. Lex Mercatoria *and Unidroit principles of International Commercial Contracts*

In international commercial contracts the Italian parties, when with a foreign counterparty they do not choose a foreign law, they normally refer to the principles of *Lex Mercatoria*, or to the principles developed by the Institute for the Unification of Law (Unidroit), with Head Office in Rome.

(a) Lex Mercatoria

Even for the *lex mercatoria*—to which the Italian merchants of medieval times set great store[212]—we can make the same observations as were made in relation to Roman Law: it was not considered as a sort of foreign law, as in the history of our experience (not national but cultural) it is considered part of the history of Italian law. In any event, while the Italian judges have no difficulty in acknowledging it as 'a body of rules of conduct appraisable as widely used in the mercantile societas', the problems that may arise regard the possibility of making arbitration awards based on the same. The question is intertwined with the issue of international arbitration, which is not the subject of this work.

It is worth recalling one of the few instances in which Italian judges have dealt with the matter.

The case regarded a contract entered into between an Italian company and a German one, containing an arbitration clause which referred the settlement of disputes to the Refined Sugar Association of London, which applies the principles of the *lex mercatoria*. The award was not motivated, in accordance with the practices of the Association. As the parties were citizens of two countries (Germany and Italy) which had signed the Geneva Convention of 21 April 1961 on International Commercial Arbitration, the Italian party (non-prevailing) claimed that the award was null and void, on the basis of the fact that the Convention envisages that where either party requests that the award be motivated, prior to the rendering of the decision, the award must be so motivated (Article 8). The German company had defended itself claiming that the Association belonged to a country (the United Kingdom), which had not signed the Convention, and therefore the award was valid.

The Court of Cassation issued a very elaborate ruling in which it upheld the claim of the Italian party. The motivation for this sets off from the notion of *lex mercatoria* previously mentioned; it went on to specify that *lex mercatoria* lacks sovereignty, because the mercantile 'societas' has no boundaries, but it does not have the enforceability of sovereign systems. Having therefore to refer to a legal system in order to render the arbitrators' decisions enforceable, the Court of Cassation deemed it appropriate to apply the Geneva Convention, claiming that the same has a more modern approach than that of New York. The choice is motivated in the sense that being the parties citizens of countries which are signatories of this Convention, this Convention 'must be considered as recalled by implied reference in the contractual stipulations between entrepreneurs belonging to ratifying States of the same'.[213]

212 P Grossi, *L'ordine giuridico medievale,* above at n 3.
213 Corte di Cassazione, 8 Feb 1982, n 722, in *Foro italiano* (1982) I, 2285.

(b) The principles of Unidroit

The principles of Unidroit represent a veritable melting-pot of the models from the most varied experiences, but above all represent a fortunate attempt to merge the principles of civil law, of common law and of the *lex mercatoria*.[214] They move from the upholding of freedom of contract and they propose clear and simple rules which regard the binding force of contracts, the principle of good faith and reasonableness, the formation, interpretation, and execution of the contract, in addition to rules on non-performance and damages. From the viewpoint of the Italian experience, of particular relevance is the envisaging of rules relating to situations of hardship.

In all systems, rules are established, expressly or construed from judicial or legal theory interpretation, regarding the eventuality that performance may become frustrated. In the Italian experience we can point out two occurrences: that in which frustration was extraordinary and unforeseeable, which bears with it the consequence of termination of the contract (Article 1467); and that in which the frustrating circumstances were foreseeable, but not actually envisaged by the parties. In this case, one has to ascertain the possibility of applying the theory of so-called 'pre-supposition' which, connected with the *bona fide* clause, with 'Causa' of the contract, with the negotiating basis (that is with the assignment of advantages and risks) may entail the termination of the contract.

In international trade there is a trend, as underlined many times, toward keeping to the contract. Therefore, the general rule is that the parties are compelled to carry out their respective obligations, even if performance of the same has become more onerous (Article 6.2.1.). This rule is tempered by the institute of 'hardship'.

The features of this institute are outlined in Article 6.2, where they are indicated as follows: frustration must be dependent on a risk not accepted in the contract, on external circumstances, which must not be ascribable to the party which invokes the same, and must have supervened or, if precedent, must not have been known or recognizable by the party who invokes them.

The effect of 'hardship' clauses is directed at maintaining the relationship alive. Therefore, the possibility is given to the party invoking the same to reopen negotiations without hindrance and without suspension of the performance due under the agreement.

Should negotiations fail, the interested party may apply to the judge (in our case to the arbitrator).

Here lies another scope for intervention, which in countries of codified

[214] J Bonell, *An International Restatement of Contract Law. The Unidroit Principles of International Commercial Contracts* (Irvington, NY 1994).

law is totally ignored, indeed it is strenuously opposed: the judge, in fact, may—beyond the ruling of termination of the Contract, which is the customary conclusion—'adapt the contract with the aim of re-establishing the balance between performances' (Article 6.2.3).

What is really extraordinary for civil lawyers is to admit the power of the judge to 're-write the contract' on behalf of the parties, in contrast with the principle of 'sanctity of Contract'. But the aim of the principles is precisely to save the economic transaction and to render it feasible in accordance with the supervening risks.

1.5.6. The rules of the common market of the European Union

Community law cannot be considered a 'foreign law', because it is one of the sources of the legal systems of the Member States. However, both Regulations and Directives tend to create uniform rules for the internal market; these rules are created originally by the organs of the Community, but can be traced back to the models coming from the individual countries of the Community; these rules are effective in the 'strong' models (the French, German, and English models) which are often adapted to the new exigencies; to those stronger models the weaker models (from a political, numerical, economic viewpoint) adapt.[215] Thus it was, for instance, for the Directive on Unfair Clauses in Consumer Contracts, for the Directive on Consumer Credit, for the Directives on Banks and Insurance Companies and, above all, for the rules on competition.

It is important to underline that from the complex of directives on the subject matter of contracts, special rules can be singled out which tend to become general: let us think of the use of the form of contract to protect the weaker party, to the ban on the abuse of bargaining (contracting) power; to the rules on prior and subsequent information in the stipulation of contracts, to the principle of good faith which is now at the basis of any type of contract.

1.6. THE USE OF GENERAL CLAUSES: *GOOD FAITH* AND PRECONTRACTUAL LIABILITY

1.6.1. The provisions of the Civil Code concerning 'precontractual liability' and the general rules of torts

Precontractual liability is recognized in the Italian jurisdiction as a subject

[215] B Markesinis, '*Learning from Europe and Learning in Europe*, in id, *Foreign Law and Comparative Methodology. A Subject and a Thesis*' (Oxford 1997) 163 ff and id, *Our Debt to Europe: Past, Present and Future*, in *The Clifford chance Millennium Lectures. The Coming Together of the Common Law and the Civil Law* (Oxford 2000) p 37 ff.

into itself, its terminology reflecting its past history. In Italy, the institute owes its beginnings to the popularity of German academic theory at the end of the last century, in particular that of Rudolf Von Jhering,[216] giving rise to *culpa in contrahendo* liability: an expression which is still used in current legal terminology to indicate precontractual liability in general.

Philologically speaking—the term *culpa in contrahendo* was and is still—today used by Italian authors to define a specific hypothesis of precontractual liability: failure to disclose the voidness, illegality or similar of a contract to the other party during the negotiating phase.

The term '*responsabilità nelle trattative*' or negotiation liability is also used to refer to the stage at which liability comes into being; '*responsabilità da recesso*' or liability for breaking-off negotiation is applied in other precontractual situations.

The correct term, however, in both the theoretical and the textual context, is 'responsabilità precontrattuale' or 'precontractual liability'.

The Italian Civil Code of 1942 includes several provisions dealing expressly with precontractual liability and others from which the authors derive precontractual liability.

(1) Article 1337, concerned with the contract in general terms, is entitled: 'Negotiations and precontractual liability' and reads as follows:

> The parties, in the conduct of negotiations and the formation of the contract, shall conduct themselves according to good faith.

(2) Article 1338 of the Civil Code then refers to the original hypothesis, as derived from Jhering, regarding the 'Knowledge of reasons' for invalidity:

> A party who knows or should know the existence of a reason for invalidity of the contract and does not give notice to the other party is bound to compensate for the damage suffered by the latter in relying, without fault, on the validity of the contract.

(3) Article 1398 of the Civil Code is one among a number of other provisions dealing with this subject, the text reading as follows:

> Representation without power.
>
> One who has contracted as a representative without having the power to do so, or in excess of the authority conferred on him, is liable for the damage which the third person suffers as a result of having fault, relied on the validity of the contract.

[216] '*Culpa in contrahendo*' *oder Schadenersatz bei nichtigen oder nicht zur Perfektion gegelangten Verträgen*, in *jahrbücher für die Dogmatik*, 4 (1861) 1 ff).

(4) Finally, in the special contracts sector focusing on insurance, provision is made for the hypothesis whereby the insured party has failed to provide the insurer with complete information, has misrepresented the facts, or has in some way presented his particular situation as other than it is. In this case, though moving into the realm of a typical precontractual liability hypothesis, the consequences are not limited to compensation for damages but also involve the rescission of the contract. Articles 1892 and 1893 of the Civil Code lay down as follows:

> Misrepresentation or fraudulent or, grossly; negligent to disclose.
>
> If the contracting party, fraudulently or through gross negligence misrepresents or fails to disclose circumstances which, if known to the insurer would have caused him to withhold his consent on the same conditions, the insurer can annul the contract.
>
> The insurer forfeits his right to attack the contract if, within three months from the day on which he had knowledge of the falsity of the representation or of the failure to disclose, he fails to notify the contracting party of this intention to attack the contract.
>
> The insurer is entitled to the premiums covering the period of insurance running at the time when he petitioned for annulment of the contract, and in all cases to the premiums agreed upon the first year. If the accident occurs before the expiration of the period indicated in the preceding paragraph, the insurer is not bound to pay the amount of the insurance.
>
> If the insurance concerns more than one person or thing, the contract is valid with respect to such persons or such things as are not affected by the misrepresentation or the failure to disclose.
>
> False representation or withholding of information without fraud or gross negligence.
>
> If the contracting party has acted without fraud or gross negligence, misrepresentation or failure to disclose are not grounds for annulment of the contract, but the insurer can withdraw from the contract by means of a declaration to be made to the insured within three months from the day on which the insurer had knowledge of the falsity of the representation or the failure to disclose.
>
> If the accident occurs before the insurer has knowledge of the falsity of the representation or of the failure to disclose, or before he has notified the insured of his intention to withdraw from the contract, the amount due by him is reduced in proportion to the difference between the premium agreed upon and the premium which would have applied if the true situation had been known.

Only hypotheses (1), (2), and (3) are relevant, however, to the general concept of precontractual liability.

This gives rise to the question why the legislators felt the need to introduce two new provisions dealing with this problem. The answer is provided in the '*Relazione al Re del Ministro Guardasigilli*' (the Minister of Justice's report to the King) (no 163): it was considered necessary to give formal expression to the obligation to act in good faith during negotiations and contract formation. This principle was already provided for in the 1865 Civil Code as regards the performance of contract but gave rise to doubts regarding its extension to the stages preceding performance.

It is clear, therefore, that these provisions concern the phase previous to the making of the contract, after which any act not in good faith, any concealment or misrepresentation no longer entails 'pre'-contractual liability but actual contractual liability which is bound by a different set of regulations.

The term 'negotiation' is understood in its widest sense of any 'contract' between the parties aiming at making the contract.

The term 'good faith' is understood in its objective acceptation of honest and fair behaviour.

At what point, however, does the negotiation stage become the performance of the contract?

This must depend on the material circumstances. Case law adopts abstract rules, *dicta and rationes decidendi, ex*pressed as follows: 'to establish contractual obligation, agreement must have been reached on all the terms and clauses of the contract in that the said agreement must cover all the obligations deriving from the transaction; completion of the negotiating phase and performance of the said contract must not, therefore, depend on the agreement only on essential points, since the contract is binding only when agreement has been reached on all points whether principle, secondary or accessory.'[217]

1.6.2. Judicial interpretation and extension of the rules provided by the Civil Code

The existence of a written code has not obviated the need for intense activity by the courts and the courts and the growth of ample case law for specific and, precise interpretation of code provisions. The provisions quoted above are in fact sufficiently generic to permit of wide interpretation.

The code does not define precisely the nature of precontractual liability and the choice of which liability regulations to apply and the extent of the compensation for damages depend on this very definition.

This problem will be discussed further below.

As regards the first point, the authors sustain that breach of good faith during negotiations gives rise to:

(a) civil liability in that the parties are linked simply by social contact and not bound by a contract which has yet to be formulated; in this case the

[217] Cass Sez Un, 24 Apr 1970, n 1179, in *Foro it* (1970) I, 1566.

general principle of *alterum non laedere* applies of which Articles 1337 and 1338 are a specification;

(b) contractual liability, both because the behaviour of those involved is directed towards the making of the contract and because they are contracting parties and not third parties. It has been established by the Court of Cassation, however, that where only one subject has taken part in negotiations which were supposed to involve more than one, only that subject which has in fact taken part is answerable for the damage suffered by the opposite party; and[218]

(c) *a tertium genus* liability, given its particular physiognomy.

The Court of Cassation has recently stated that 'precontractual liability' fails within the 'civil liability' genus and hence the brief term of limitation is applicable, ie five years, see Article 2947 of the Civil Code.[219]

Some authors, on the other hand, have fallen, back on the thesis of the contractual nature of *culpa in contrahendo* on the grounds that the obligations expressed in the general clause of good faith tend to protect the other party's future interests (ie to make the contract).[220]

Ever-increasing interest is being shown in precontractual liability; even simple handbooks are focusing more attention on the subject. In case law the number of cases of precontractual liability is on the increase, indicating the existence of more litigation in this sector. Usual business procedures rely on having 'given one's word'; traders know that fairness is indispensable both with other traders and with customers, even though these latter are generally contractually weaker. It is difficult to say, however, whether the introduction of the new provisions in the 1942 Code has had the hoped for effect of 'moralization' of the market and, therefore, of negotiations.

1.6.3. *Bargaining in 'good faith' and remedies of the damaged party*

Since the discipline of precontractual liability is summed up in the general clause of good faith, the authors and case law have approached 'bargaining in good faith' as they have other general clauses, ie by defining the principle in detail and indicating recurring hypotheses of application, with due warning that the term 'good faith' be understood objectively: 'it is not necessary, therefore, to ascertain the presence of subjective bad faith, determined, that is, by the intention to damage the opposite party'.[221]

218 28 Oct 1983, n 6386, in *Resp civ and prev* (1984) 368 ff.
219 18 June 1987, n 5371, in *Foro it* (1988) I, 181.
220 See, eg, Benatti, '*Culpa in contrahendo*' in *Contratto e impresa* (Cedam 1987) 287 ff; against: Alpa and Bessone *I fatti illeciti* Rescigno, Utet (eds) (Torino 1984) 212.
221 Cass, 27 Oct 1961, n 2425.

The sub-regulations lay down as follows:

(a) the duty, during formation of an agreement, not to dispute points already agreed upon;[222]
(b) the duty not to violate mutual concessions, specifically requested conduct, programmes specified in a letter of intention;[223]
(c) the duty, not to begin negotiation unless there exists the serious will to negotiate;
(d) the duty to stand by the line of behaviour promised during the negotiating stage and not, therefore, to start parallel negotiations with other parties or to fail to inform the opposite party concerning the opening of parallel negotiations with other parties;
(e) the duty not to extend negotiations *sine die*, by continual modification of the initial position, requesting further benefits or imposing new obligations on the opposite party;
(f) the duty not to present oneself under false name or title or authority;
(g) the duty not to break off negotiations without just cause;
(h) the duty of secrecy regarding personal or proprietary matters concerning the opposite party; and
(i) the duty of disclosure.

Concerning this last point the authors and case law further specify:

- the questions put by the opposite party need not always be answered, as when, for instance, the apposite party is obliged to be acquainted with the circumstances or matters concerning which he has requested information;
- in all other circumstances the questions put by the opposite party must be answered fully and correctly;
- latent (but non patent) defects in the property sold must be disclosed;
- ties inhibiting enjoyment and availability of the property sold must be disclosed unless this information is contained in public records and the opposite party at fault if uninformed;
- information regarding the expediency of the transaction need not be given;
- circumstances regarding the fulfilment or otherwise of a condition need not be disclosed; and
- there is an obligation to disclose information with regard to contract flaws.

The remedies which may be claimed by a: party which has suffered violation of fairness of negotiation, breaking off negotiation, or which has not been provided with full information, cannot under any circumstances

[222] Cass, 19 May 1961, n 1195.
[223] Trib Roma, in *Nuova giur civ comm* (1987) I, 411; Cass 11 July 1988, n 4750.

include the obligation to conclude the negotiation or to make the contract.

This remedy is possible only where on completion of the negotiating stage, the parties have made a contract defined the '*contratto preliminare*' or the so-called contract to make a contract, by which they are bound to make a new contract. This, however, is a different hypothesis to that considered previously concerning the negotiating phase.

The sole remedy consists, therefore, in compensation for damages. This does not, however, signify the entire damage (*damnum emergens, lucrum cessans*), but only the '*interesse negativo*' or other business lost. In other words, the injured party is not acknowledged the right to make up for his anticipated profits had the contract come to a successful conclusion, only his expenses and loss of earning from other business or other lost opportunities.[224] Moreover, precontractual liability cannot be invoked to make good damages or inconvenience which would otherwise have been avoided.[225]

No precedent exists with regard to the possibility of the contracting parties regulating the negotiation process. Rules can certainly be established, as can penalties for receding from the negotiations, but in this case the court can reduce the penalty to render it fair where it is considered excessive. In other words, the freedom to make or not to make the contract must remain inviolate. If the penalty is excessive, the party intending to recede from the contract could be induced not to do so for fear of incurring heavy sanctions. The parties may also make a gentlemen's agreement or sign a letter of intent. In case of breach of the gentlemen's agreement or of the intent expressed by the letter a difficult problem arises: is this behaviour sanctionable by law? The answer depends on the circumstances regarding, for instance, the expectations of the other party of whether the wrongdoer was in bad faith.

Previous dealings between the parties may help to persuade the court as to the violation of the obligation of good faith if, for instance, the same party had already previously violated this obligation.

While obligation to renegotiate a contract is not so frequent in internal contracts as it is in international contracts, and a hardship clause is usual.

1.6.4. *Precontractual liability of administrative bodies*

Traditionally, given the acknowledged privileged position and presumed correct conduct of the public administration—and to avoid limiting its discretionary powers—it was not possible to sustain precontractual liability for negotiations opened by government bodies even though acting as any private body.

[224] Cass, 20 Aug 1980, n 4942.

[225] Cass, 20 May 1977, n 2083.

However, the last few years have seen the public administration, acting *jure privatorum,* considered more as any private body; consequently, the public administration can also be ordered to redress a damage subsequent to failure to disclose, violation of good faith, unjustified breaking off of negotiation, and so on.

Precontractual liability of government bodies can apply in all cases in which the body has, in negotiations and relations with third parties, performed actions or fallen into omissions in contrast with the principles of fairness and good faith, with which the public administration is also obligated to comply within the limits of observance of the primary obligations guaranteed by the principles of *alterum non laedere* (Article 2043 cc). Consequently, it is up to the Civil Court to ascertain, exercising extreme caution, the existence of the above-mentioned liability should the public administration, through its conduct, have engendered in the third party, even though unintentionally, a reasonable reliance subsequently disappointed with regard to the making of the contract. Verification of the good faith of the public administration, this being the expression of an obligation extraneous to the contract, is actually beyond the cognizance of the controlling body, being the jurisdiction of the Civil Court.[226]

Precontractual liability for violation of the principle of good faith (from Article 1337 of the Civil Code) depends also in the case of the public administration, on the existence of a simple contract, the administrative process by which a future contracting party is chosen in relation to the expectations of award on the side of the private party cannot, therefore, be considered as injurious conduct. Such is the case of a government body inviting tenders: the contracting parties referred to in Article 1337 cc do not exist, nor is there a recognizable private relationship between government body and competing bidders which may give rise to an obligation of good faith on the part of the authorities, given that the individual bidders know their own tender but not that of the others and, therefore, cannot express an estimative assessment concerning the favourable outcome nor appeal for reasonable reliance on the conclusion of the contract. In this case, therefore, the government body is not subject to precontractual liability even following the jurisdictional annulment of the acts for the suppression of the tender and leading to the drawing up of a privately negotiated contract with another firm, in that the executive decision of annulment does not materially alter the subjective situation as inferred in judgment, it remaining unchanged as a legitimate interest.[227]

As regards private and public procurement contracts, the principle in

[226] Cass, 10 Dec 1987, n 9129.
[227] Cass, 29 July 1987, n 6545, in *Foro it* (1988) I, 460.

force is that anticipated breach, which allows only the contracting party to withdraw from the contractual obligation when the reason which had given rise to the contract no longer apply.[228]

Should the government body succeed in obtaining from the owner the detention on sufferance of a building during sale negotiations but then not take steps to release it, even though the negotiation be suspended and the contract not stipulated, the owner has the right to take legal steps to attain official release of the same, even when in the meantime the building has been dedicated (as a post office, for instance) and providing no official order has been given, due to the purely private nature of the detention effected by the public administration.[229]

Owing to the specific discipline as laid down in the civil code and the nature sui generis of precontractual liability, this institute does not lend itself to the doctrinal processing involved in tort versus contract considerations. The authors are currently attempting to derive from case law a set of guidelines for traders (and their legal representatives) for the effective application of the general clause of good faith.

228 TAR Lazio s I, 12 May 1987, n 1020, in *Trib amm reg* (1987) I, 1674.
229 Cass, 26 Feb 1987, n 2047, for further clarification see AM Marini *Nota* in *Foro it* (1982) I, 2013.

2. THE IMPACT OF EC LAW

2.1. UNFAIR CONTRACT TERMS (EEC DIRECTIVE NO 93/13) AND THE MODIFICATION OF THE CIVIL CODE

2.1.1. Introduction

The Directive on unfair contract terms in consumer contracts, being the first EC measure which goes 'to the heart of contract law', has been regarded 'as a valuable step towards Europeanisation of contract law'.[1] Its importance has been widely recognized by the academic world and much attention has been devoted to its implementation by the Member States of the EC.[2]

After a long delay, the Directive on unfair contract terms was recently implemented in Italy. In the following pages we have the opportunity to give a short outline of the new Italian legislation which transposed the Directive. Then, we will try to compare the new Italian law with the implementing measures in other Member States. In particular we will analyse the laws enacted in the United Kingdom and in France.

By describing and comparing in a nutshell the laws of Italy, United Kingdom, and France, we will try to address the question whether the measures implementing the EC Directive on unfair contract terms in different Member States really tend towards harmonization and Europeanization of contract law, or else whether they do not bring any substantial contribution to the creation of a new European common law, which still remains the unfulfilled dream of pro-European lawyers.[3]

2.1.2. The implementation in Italy

(i) The implementing measure

EC Directive 93/13 on unfair terms in consumer contracts[4] was finally

[1] EH Hondius, EC Directive on Unfair Contract Terms, in 'Consumer contracts: towards a European law of Contract' *Journal of Contract Law* (1994) 7 35.

[2] CM Bianca and G Alpa (eds) *Le clausole abusive nei contratti stipulati con i consumatori. L'attuazione della direttiva comunitaria del 5 aprile 1993* (Padova 1996) European Review of Private Law, 1995, issue n 2 on 'The impact of European integration on private law: the case of the Directive on unfair terms in consumer contracts'.

[3] O Lando, *Principles of European Contract Law. An Alternative or a Precursor of European Legisiation?* (Rabels Zeitschrift 1992) 261.

[4] G Alpa and P Zatti (eds), *Commentario breve al codice civile. Leggi complementari* (Padova) 2909.

transposed into Italian law by Article 25 of the 1994 Community Act. Instead of commenting on the new law article by article and comparing it with the text of the Directive, it seems more useful to focus on the choices the legislator made in drafting the implementing measure and on the prospects of application of the new law.

Light and shadow are cast on the present and future of the text of implementation of the Directive. Legislative choices and prospects of the new regulation will raise a great deal of discussion. Some of the most relevant points will be outlined in the following pages.

(ii) The implementation technique

There are no great substantial differences between the text of the Directive and the text of its implementation. In a way, this is a bad sign, given that when the Directive was issued many commentators pointed out the poverty and lack of precision of its terminology and of the legal concepts it contained. Furthermore, due to the fact that the new measure needed to be approved by both chambers of Parliament and was shifted from one to the other, a few amendments were inserted in the original proposal of implementation, which made its text more complex and difficult to read and understand.

On the other hand, it was a good choice to insert the new regulation on unfair contract terms in Book IV of the Italian Civil Code, where after Chapter XIV, a new Chapter XIV *bis* was introduced with the title 'Consumer contracts'. This means that the legislator adopted the theory which considers the new rules on consumer contracts as rules affecting contract law in general, and introduced into Italian law a new category of contracts. Besides banking contracts and stock exchange contracts now we have also consumer contracts. This new category is characterized by the quality (or status) of the contracting parties: the businessman (or professional) and the consumer.[5]

Eventually the new regulation on unfair contract terms was therefore introduced in Book IV of the Civil Code concerning the law of obligations, and not in Book V concerning company and labour law, as it had been, mistakenly, proposed by the Minister of Industry on the assumption that the regulation of unfair terms was closely connected with the policy of enterprises.

(iii) Problems which have been solved

Among the interpretative problems solved by the implementation of the

[5] G Alpa, *Il diritto dei consumatori* (Roma-Bari 1995).

Directive we can count the following ones. In the first place, the scope of application of the new regulation was clarified: it must be applied only to individual consumers as such, who are physical persons. Small businessmen, associations, charities, and legal persons in general are not considered consumers. Second, it was clarified that when a contract term is declared unfair, it becomes ineffective, but its ineffectiveness does not affect the 'rest of the contract'. The court can declare a term unfair *ex officio,* without any express request of the parties. Some terms are deemed unfair *per se,* even when they are the outcome of negotiations between the parties (Article 1469 *quinquies*, section 2, nn 1, 2, 3). When a term is declared unfair and, as a consequence, the seller suffers a damage, he himself has been given a right of redress against his supplier. Given that the law expressly states that 'the rest of the contract' is not affected by the ineffectiveness of its unfair terms, the Court cannot evaluate whether the contract 'can survive without the unfair terms' it contained, which was prescribed, instead, by Article 6, section 1, of the 93/13 Directive. In this respect, Article 1419 of the Italian Civil Code on partial nullity (which states that the whole contract is void when some terms of a contract are void and the parties would not have concluded the contract without those terms) cannot be applied in the case of unfair contract terms, because the new implementing legislation expressly refers to 'ineffectiveness' of the contract terms and not to 'nullity'. It seems therefore that the new regulation is meant to give consumers a stronger protection, which strengthens the 'minimal protection' ensured by other Directives.

(iv) Problems which have not yet been solved

Despite what we so far have written, the implementing legislation failed to solve some problems that academic scholars pointed out in their comments on the Directive. One of these problems concerns the phrase 'despite good faith' contained in Article 1469 *bis,* which reproduces the official Italian version of the Directive. This phrase should mean that a term may be declared unfair even when there is good faith. Good faith, therefore, should not be one of the criteria to take into account when evaluating the lack of balance between parties' rights and obligations arising out of the contract. Good faith, in this respect, seems to mean 'objective good faith'. Some interpreters, however, think that the phrase refers, instead, to the inner attitude of the parties, and especially to that of the business party. A more precise drafting of the original legislation and of its implementation should have solved these problems of interpretation, which will continue to puzzle lawyers for a while.

Another problem regards the effectiveness of arbitration clauses contained in consumer contracts. The Annex to the Directive on unfair contract terms (letter q) does not clarify whether arbitration or other methods of alternative dispute resolution are allowed or not. A proposal by the European Union suggested to promote alternative dispute resolution systems in the Member States so as to offer consumers an alternative to ordinary justice. According to Article 1469 *bis* section 3, no 18 the term which 'prescribes' an exception to the jurisdiction of the ordinary courts is deemed unfair. However, the drafting of this rule is wider than the original rule contained in the Directive, which was aimed at protecting consumers against alternative dispute resolution systems not regulated by objective rules. This means that out-of-court voluntary conciliation, and conciliation and arbitration proceedings promoted by the local Chambers of Commerce will have to be based on specific agreements rather than on terms contained in consumer contracts.

Another problem concerns the way contract terms should be drafted, the implementing measure states they should be 'clear and understandable' (Article 1469 *quater*). The criterion of reference will be represented by the average consumer, considering also the nature of the contract concerned.

Eventually, the implementing legislation does not establish the criteria according to which the associations, empowered to apply to the ordinary courts for an injunction on the basis of Article 1469 *sexies,* should be selected and given *locus standi.*

(v) Problems of coordination

One of the major defects of the new regulation on unfair contract terms, is the lack of coordination with the existing legislation in the matter of package tours, consumer credit, banking contracts, insurance contracts, investment contracts (also regulated by 1994 Community Act), public utilities contracts, 'authorities', etc.

In particular it is not sure whether the specific measures, just mentioned, should be considered specific sectoral regulations, which are to be regarded as exceptions to the general legislation on consumer contract terms. Or, else, whether the general legislation on consumer contract terms should prevail over the more specific sectoral measures.

(vi) Partial implementation of the Directive

The implementing legislation takes into account only one of the systems of control on unfair contract terms envisaged by the Directive, ie judicial control, and neglects completely the system of administrative control, which might be exercised either *ex ante* or *ex post.*

There are a few possible solutions to amend this partial implementation of the Directive: (a) to introduce a specific board with the task to control unfair contract terms; (b) to refer to the control exercised by the Bank of Italy, Consob and Isvap (ie the authorities controlling banking, stock exchange, and insurance sectors);[6] (c) to attribute this task either to the antitrust authority or to the chambers of commerce.[7]

In any case the problem requires a solution urgently. In this respect one may wonder whether the partial implementation of the Directive does not constitute a good argument to start enforcement proceedings against Italy, on the basis of Article 169 of the Treaty of Rome, for 'partial' implementation of the Directive.

(vii) Future prospects

Future prospects of the implementing measure are uncertain: will enterprises comply with the new law on their own initiative? Or will it be necessary either an activity of moral suasion carried out by chambers of commerce, or a more assertive request by consumers, users and savers associations? As one can see, the 'new citizenship', ie the new status of individuals in (ex) wealthy societies, to which the European Union Commissioner Emma Bonino referred in the context of her consumer protection programmes, is still quite far.

2.2. A COMPARISON WITH THE ENGLISH AND FRENCH IMPLEMENTATION

2.2.1. The implementation in the United Kingdom

(i) The implementing measure

The EC Directive on unfair contract terms in consumer contracts was implemented in the United Kingdom by the Unfair Term in Consumer Contracts Regulation 1994 (UTCCR) approved on 8 December 1994. Implementation was inspired by the basic idea of enacting the Directive in its minimal content and enacting the already existing Unfair Contract Terms Act 1977 (UCTA) unchanged. However, even this 'minimal' implementation, as we will try to show in the following paragraphs, will cause many problems of interpretation.

[6] G Alpa (ed), *Investimento finanziario e contratti dei consumatori. Il controllo delle clausole abusive* (Milano 1995).

[7] G Alpa and Del Re-P Gaggero, *Le camere di commercio e la regolazione del mercato* (CCIAA Milano 1995).

(ii) The implementation technique

Two implementation techniques could be used in the UK to implement the EC Directive. The first alternative was to enact an Act of Parliament, with all the possible problems and delays that enacting a piece of primary legislation involves. The second alternative was to enact a regulation, ie a piece of secondary legislation, on the basis of section 2.2 of the European Communities Act 1972, thus speeding up the process of implementation.

The British Government, in order to implement the Directive before the expiry of the deadline set by the Directive itself (31 December 1994), chose to follow the second option, and on 8 December 1994, just in time before the expiry date, the Secretary of State for Trade and Industry issued the new UTCCR. The Regulation entered into force only on 1 July 1995.

(iii) Problems of coordination

It is important to underline that the new Regulation on unfair contract terms partly impinges in an area already regulated by UCTA 1977. So that currently two different bodies of rules, each with a different scope and a different test of what is acceptable apply to the same general issues of consumer protection.[8]

As far as the *scope of application* is concerned, UCTA 1977 has a wider scope than the Directive and its implementing measure. Whereas the Directive and UTCR apply only to consumer contracts where the consumer is a physical person, UCTA applies to consumer contracts where the consumer is 'someone who does not make the contract in the course of a business and who deals with someone who does' (section 12), which means that under, UCTA even a company can be a consumer.

Furthermore, the Directive and UTCR apply to contract terms which have not been individually negotiated, whereas UCTA applies also to contract terms which are the outcome of negotiations between the parties.

However, as for the *contract terms* concerned by the two measures, it is worth mentioning that UCTA applies only to exclusion and limitation clauses, whereas the Directive and UTCR apply to all unfair contract terms in consumer contracts for supply of goods and services, not individually negotiated.

In addition, UCTA automatically outlaws certain terms (such as, for example, those regarding exclusion or limitation of liability in respect of death or personal injury caused by negligence) and subjects the others to the *test* of 'reasonableness'.

[8] A Downes 'The Directive on Unfair Terms in Consumer Contracts', paper presented at the Conference organised by The Academy of Trier, Rome, 21 Apr 1995.

On the other hand, the Directive and UTCR, without *prima facie* blacklisting any term, subject all the contract terms, to the test of 'fairness' and establish an indicative 'grey list' of terms which may be regarded as unfair.

It is worth underlining that the test of 'reasonableness' under UCTA and the test of 'fairness' under UTCR are different, though they might sometimes lead to the same result.

1. According to UCTA (schedule 2) the test of 'reasonableness' implies evaluation of the following elements: the strength of the bargaining positions of the parties *relative* to each other, taking into account alternative means by which the customer's requirements could have been met.
2. Whether the customer received an inducement to agree to the term, or in accepting it had an opportunity of entering into a similar contract with other persons, but without having to accept a similar term.
3. Whether the customer knew or reasonably ought to have known of the existence and extent of the term (having regard, among other things, to any custom of the trade and any previous course of dealing between the parties).
4. Where the term excludes or restricts any relevant liability if some condition is not complied with. Whether it was reasonable at the time of the contract to expect that compliance with that condition would be practicable.
5. Whether the goods were manufactured, processed or adapted to the special order of the customer.[9]

According to UTCR, the test of 'fairness' has to be carried out by looking at two requirements:

1. the requirement of good faith; and
2. the presence of a significant imbalance in the parties rights and obligations.

In order to assess good faith UTCR recommends to take into account: (a) the strength of the bargaining positions of the parties, (b) whether the consumer had an inducement to agree to the term, (c) whether the goods or services were sold or supplied to the special order of the consumer, and (d) the extent to which the seller or supplier has dealt fairly and equitably with the consumer.

On the other hand, in order to assess the imbalance of the parties' rights and obligations one should take into account all the circumstances leading to the conclusion of the contract, including the nature of the goods and services and the other terms of the contract (but not including the consideration).[10]

[9] C Wiliett 'Directive on unfair contract terms in consumer contracts' (1994) *Consumer Law Journal* 114.

[10] R Kemp, 'Suppliers beware: implementation of the unfair contract terms Directive in Europe' The Computer Law Association Bulletin (1995) vol 10, 16

As we said before, though in most cases the two tests of 'fairness' and 'reasonableness' would lead to the same result, they are different and they cannot be treated as equivalent. Especially given that, by applying the criteria just described, there are terms contrary to good faith which may be reasonable, and terms not contrary to good faith which may be unreasonable.[11] As an author said, it seems that 'under the influence of the EC harmonization programme, UK contract law will eventually be pushed towards a fundamental division between consumer contracts and business contracts with radically different regimes applicable to both'.[12]

(iv) Problems still to be solved

One of the major problems caused by the Directive and by its implementation was the introduction of a genera] principle of good faith in English law, which before, was alien to the common law of contract. In fact, though in some fields elements of a doctrine of good faith could be implied (let us think, for example, of the rules regarding duress and misrepresentation in the process of the making of contracts), there was no general principle of good faith as such.[13]

Now, instead, in order to assess whether a term is unfair or not, according to UTCR, the judge will have to consider whether, *contrary to good faith*, the term creates a significant imbalance in the rights and obligations of the parties. As we already said, Schedule 2 of the UTCR gives directions on how to make this assessment of good faith, and in particular it says that one should have regard to: (a) the strength of the bargaining positions of the parties, (b) whether the consumer had an inducement to agree to the term, (c) whether the goods or services were sold or supplied to the special order of the consumer, and (d) the extent to which the seller or supplier has dealt fairly and equitably with the consumer.[14]

To the best of our knowledge, so far, there is no evidence of the application of the new principle of good faith in English case law. However, an author suggested that English law might have fewer difficulties embracing the new principles introduced by the Directive than assimilating those parts of the Directive which overlap with existing law which was not repealed. This is also because, in the end, in order to apply the principle of good faith,

[11] M Dean 'Consolidation or confusion?' [1995] *New Law Journal* 28.

[12] H Collins, 'Good faith in European contract law' Oxford Journal of Legal Studies [1994] 229.

[13] A de Moor, 'Common law and civil law conceptions of contract and a European law of contract: the case of the Directive on Unfair Terms in Consumer Contracts' in [1995] *European Review of Private Law* 257; La trasposizione nel diritto inglese della direttiva sulle clausole abusive nei contratti con i consumatori, in: Bianca-Alpa, op cit, 103.

[14] R Kemp, op cit.

English courts will probably draw inspiration from the traditional sources developed by the courts of equity throughout the centuries.[15]

To conclude on this point, it is interesting to report the words of another author who commented that it may be that eventually 'the assimilation of social values embodied in the European Directive will lead the common law of contract, which Kahn-Freund once described aptly as 'designed for a nation of shopkeepers', to succumb to a more communitarian ideal which balances the interests of consumers against those of 'shopkeepers'.[16]

(v) Partial implementation of the Directive

Like Italy, also the United Kingdom did not fully implement the Directive. To be more specific Article 7 of the Directive was not implemented properly.

The view of the Department of Trade and Industry was that the doctrine of precedent could well ensure that once a term had been judged unfair, traders would know that they would not be able to rely on it in the future. However this approach has been criticized because precedents cannot constitute what Article 7 demands which is that 'adequate and effective means exist to prevent the continued use of unfair terms in contracts'. As an author said: 'There is in fact nothing in UK law to deter a trader, from continuing to use an unfair term, and then to rely upon consumer ignorance and inertia for its effectiveness'.[17]

As a consequence of the 'minimal' approach just described, no legal action by consumers' associations to challenge unfair contract terms before the courts, was introduced in the United Kingdom by UTCR. Despite the provision of the Directive (Article 7.2), which seem to favour the introduction of class action, or representative action, class action is and still remains a concept alien to English law.

However, as a partial implementation of the Directive, the UTCR (section 8) introduced a system of administrative control exercised by the Director General of Fair Trading who was given the authority to deal with complaints about unfair contract terms, and *locus standi* to apply, where appropriate, to the court for an injunction preventing traders from using such unfair terms in their contracts.

It has been argued that, though restricting the right of action to the Director General, section 8 of UTCR somehow implements Article 7.2 of the Directive which, strictly speaking requires that 'persons' or organizations, having a 'legitimate interest under national taw in protecting consumers' are given the right of action. In fact, though it is undisputable that many other persons and organizations may have an 'interest' in

[15] A Downes, op cit.
[16] H Collins op cit.
[17] Ibid. op cit.

protecting consumers, national law may well recognize a 'legitimate' interest only to one of them, namely to the Director General of Fair Trading.[18]

2.2.2. *The implementation in France*

(i) The implementing measure

In France the EC Directive on Unfair Contract Terms was implemented by Act 95–96 of 1 February 1995 which amended the Consumer Code.

(ii) The implementation technique

The Directive on Unfair Terms in Consumer Contracts was implemented through enactment of primary legislation. As we said, a new Act which amended the already existing Consumer Code was issued.

The new Act was presented by the Ministry of Finance, and the preparatory works were mostly carried out by the Committee for Economic Affairs in the Senate, and by the Committee of Production and Exchanges in the National Assembly. This caused criticism for the lack of legal precision of the text of the Act, whose drafting it seems should have been committed to the Ministry of Justice and to the Law Committees.[19]

Furthermore, the new Act was criticized for its 'omnibus approach'. Besides '*clauses abusives et presentation des contrats*' which represent its 'core' and are regulated in title n 1, the Act regulates also other various matters, thus gaining the denomination of '*melange legislatif*'.[20] To give but a flavour, these other matters, tackled by Act 95–96, include: *demarchage et activités ambulantes, tit 2; marquage communautaire de conformité, tit 3; cautionnement relatif aux marchés de travaux privès, tit 4; pratique commerciales illicites, tit 5; disposition concernant les règles de concurrence et le droit des contrats pour l'activité de transport routier*.

Eventually, the new provisions dealing with unfair contract terms were also inserted also in the Consumer Code (Code de la Consommation L 93–949 of 26 July 1993) and replaced the old ones which dated back to the Scrivener Consumer Act 78–23 of 10 January 1978.

[18] R Brownsword and G Howells 'The implementation of the EC Directive on Unfair Contract Terms in Consumer Contracts—some unresolved questions' [1995] *Business Law* 243.

[19] C Jamin, Legislation française et conimunautaire en matiere de droit privé: contrats et obligations: clauses abusives, *Revue trimestrielle de droit civil*, n 2(1995) 437.

[20] C Jamin, op cit.

(iii) Problems of coordination

It is important to point out that when the EC Directive was issued, the legislation on unfair contract terms, already in force in France, had a wider scope than the Directive. Therefore, given that according to Article 8 of the Directive, Member States could adopt or keep stricter provisions than the Directive, and give consumer a higher level of protection, the Act implementing the Directive in France did not introduce significant changes in the existing legislation.[21]

In view of the above, French regulation on unfair contract terms still applies to: (a) contracts between 'professionals' and 'non professionals or consumers', which means that not only physical persons but also legal persons and small businessmen dealing as consumers, outside their field of business, are offered protection; (b) contracts whose terms have been negotiated by the parties, which means that the law does not apply only to adhesion contracts, as required by the Directive.

A change introduced by the new Act is the definition of unfair contract terms, as, according to the previous law a term was Unfair if two requirements were presents, ie (a) '*abus de puissance economique*' and (b) '*avantage excessif*' of the business party. The new definition (Article L 132-1), (avoiding any reference to good faith unlike its Italian and English counterparts), requires only the 'significant imbalance in the rights and obligations of the parties' ('*desequilibre significatif*'). However, it is not sure whether the new definition really implies a substantial change,[22] given that, even before, an '*avantage excessif*' was necessarily the result of an abuse of bargaining power, and that an '*avantage excessif*' of the business party leads by necessary implication to a significant imbalance in the parties' rights and obligations.

The criteria prescribed by Article L 132–1 to evaluate the 'significant imbalance' are the French translation of those contained in Article 4 of the Directive.

The *Conseil d'Etat*, as was prescribed by the previous law, remains competent for the primary control over unfair contract terms. An indicative and non exhaustive 'grey' list of terms which might be considered 'unfair', corresponding to the Annex to the Directive, was introduced in the Consumer Code by the new Act, but the new Article L 132-1 specifies that,

[21] J Ghestin Marchessaux, L'elimination des clauses abusives en droit français, à l'epreuve du droit communautaire, Revue europeenne de droit de la consommation (1993) n 2 67; E Petit, Clause abusives, presentation et interpretation des contrats—transposition de la Directive communautaire: la loi du 1 février 1995, *Revue europeenne de droit de la consommation* (1995) n 2 p 59.

[22] R Davo 'Clause abusive: bref apercu de la loi du I février 1995 transposant la directive 93/13', *Revue européene de droit de la consomniations* (1995) 217.

in case of litigation, the consumer is not relieved from the burden of proving the unfairness of the term under dispute. This, in a way, devoids the list of its purpose and diminishes its effect.

As a consequence of what we just said, the new amendments to the Consumer Code implicitly confirmed the power of ordinary judges to declare unfair (and therefore not binding) a contract term, even when no prior Decree declaring the same term unfair was issued by the *Conseil d'Etat*. This, in a way, had already been established by the *Cour de cassation* in its decisions.

In addition, given that the rules contained in the new Article L 132–1 are expressly defined as '*disposition d'ordre public*' any judge can *ex officio* challenge the validity of an unfair term contained in a contract which is under his examination.[23]

In line with the previous law, unfair terms are considered '*non écrites*' and in line with the Directive it is prescribed that their invalidity does not affect the rest of the contract which remains in force.

The Act implementing the Directive in France did not deal in depth with other aspects regulated by the Directive itself, such as for example representative actions by consumer associations, because they were already dealt with by other French laws (in particular l 88–14 of 5 January 1988), and inserted in the Consumer Code.

2.3. CONCLUSIONS

After giving a short outline of the implementation of the EC Directive on unfair contract terms in three different Member States, it is interesting to point out the three different approaches to implementation: whereas Italy inserted new articles in the Civil Code, France chose to amend the already existing legislation, however, without introducing substantial changes, finally, the UK decided to adopt a new Regulation, ie a piece of secondary legislation, parallel to the already existing UCTA 1977.

As far as the timing of implementation is concerned, considering the deadline established by the Directive (31 December 94), it seems that only the UK, who chose the quickest way of implementation made it on time, (though it postponed the entry into force of the measure for six months after enactment). France had only one month delay, whereas Italy more than a year.

Besides the problems in meeting the deadline for implementation caused by the complexity of the process itself, from the short outline given above

[23] A Giampieri 'L'attuazione della Direttiva sulle Clausole abusive negli Stati dell'Unione Europea' [1995] *Riv Dir Civ* 551.

it seems that harmonization of European contract law may create new legal problems without even properly solving the problems it aims to solve.

Especially when EC legislation addresses areas already covered by domestic statute and case law its impact seems to be quite low, because the resistance of the domestic measures already in force against the new changes imposed from an outside legislator is stronger.

The EC Directive on Unfair Contract Terms offers a good example of the difficulties encountered in the process of harmonization of European law, which entail, especially, problems of coordination with other domestic measures already in force and introduction of legal concepts and institutions which are only familiar to some legal systems and totally unknown to others.[24]

In addition, as we can especially see from the Italian and English examples, it seems that the current trend of implementation of European Directives favours: (a) mere reproduction of the text of the Directive into national legislation, with the least possible number of variations from the original text and (b) non-implementation of parts of the Directive which would be controversial or time-consuming because they require the introduction of new legal institutions or authorities, alien to domestic law (see for instance class actions in UK and administrative control of unfair terms in Italy).

On the one hand the described approach minimizes the problems of compliance of the implementing measures with the Directive itself and makes it relatively easy to apply any future interpretation of the Directive by the European Court of Justice to the national measure of implementation. On the other hand it exposes the Member States to possible enforcement proceedings brought by the Commission under Article 169 of the Treaty of Rome, for partial implementation of the Directive.

However, though the just described 'literal yet partial' approach to implementation seems to be the quickest and easiest way to implement a Directive, it is not the best one. In this way, the domestic legislator without even fully complying with EC obligations, sometimes neglects his domestic law-making function.

Implementation of the EC Directives in the Member States often fails to insert the new measures into the domestic legal systems properly. It reproduces and gives force to an alien body of law which, sooner or later, more or less awkwardly, lawyers, traders and the public at large will have somehow to deal with.

By failing to adapt and coordinate the new measure with those already existing in his legal system (which may be overlapping, parallel, or even conflicting with the new law), the domestic legislator leaves his difficult

[24] A Giamperi, op cit.

task to occasional interventions by the courts activated by occasional public awareness and initiative.

Besides the objective legal problems of implementation just outlined, the task of harmonization of European law is made more difficult by rather more trivial issues, such as the translation of the Directives into the different languages of the Member States. From the analysis we made in paragraphs 2.4 and 3.4 it appears that the different official translations of Article 3 of the Directive caused different requirements to be needed in English law and in Italian law in order to establish the unfairness of a contract term. Therefore, following the implementation of the Directive, according to Italian law a term is unfair if 'despite good faith, it causes a significant imbalance in the parties' rights and obligations', whereas according to English law a term is unfair if 'contrary to the requirement of good faith, it causes a significant imbalance in the parties rights and obligations'. This is a small but significant example of how harmonization can be easily frustrated.

To conclude, it seems to us that substantial harmonization and Europeanization of contract law still needs a lot of work, which goes beyond drafting Directives and 'literally yet partially' translating them into the different languages of the Member States. However, it is now left to lawyers and courts in the different Member States, the difficult task to interpret and apply the different implementing measures in the light of the spirit of harmonization which is embodied in the European Directive.

3. CONTRACT LAW IN A CHANGING SOCIETY

3.1. ACCORDANCE AND UNIFICATION OF CONTRACT LAW

3.1.1. Underlying principles

Traditionally, the common roots of contract law in the various legal systems have been identified in Roman (Justinian) law.[1] As is often the case with tradition, this belief corresponds only partially to historical fact. It is without doubt that much of the terminology and many of the concepts employed have their origin in Roman sources; for example, the word *contract* (from the Latin *contractus*, in Italian *contratto* and than in French *contrat*, and in Spanish *contrato*), or the words obligation or debt and their derivations. But these are mostly cases of homophony since words originating from the same root often do not stand for the same concept. If one surveys the legal discipline, some curiosities are immediately evident: eg the discipline of contracts in common law is closer to Roman law than to continental law, which is instead based on rational rules and practices formulated by Domat and Pothier, later collected in the Napoleonic Code. It is well known that the general theory of contracts has developed above all from Pandectism which has reached far beyond Roman sources in constructing the general categories of 'legal relations', of juristic act (*Rechtsgeschaft*), of 'declaration' and 'legal transaction'. These were then absorbed into the German, Italian, Spanish, and Austrian legal cultures while the French, instead, elaborated the concept of '*acte juridique*'.[2] Logical–geometric (or ideological) constructions of this sort did not catch on in common law where the more generalized notion of 'promise' emerged. The situation was further complicated when general theories were adapted to the provisions contained in the codes, leading to a kind of schizophrenia in which notions were hermeneutically superimposed on written rules. Emblematic examples can be found in Italy where the legal doctrine and the judges still speak in terms of '*negozio giuridico*' (juristic act), even though this notion is not expressly regulated in the Civil Code.

In Austria the theorization of legal negotiation has been superimposed on codified notions a century after the introduction of the Civil Code

[1] See, eg, E Hondius 'Towards a European contract law', introductory paper at the Scheveningen meeting (1997) 2.

[2] An insightful analysis of the importance and present role of legal negotiation is carried out by Galgano *Il negozio giuridico* (Milan, 1988) VII 6ff.

(ABGB) due to the expansive and persuasive strength of the Pandectism and the German BGB in Austrian legal culture. It is not a mere coincidence if these differences can be felt even in the translation of terms such as *Rechtsgeschaft* (generally translated with no danger of misunderstanding in Italian and Spanish), translated in English as *juristic act, legal act, transaction*, and in French as *acte juridique*. These translations, however, do not correspond to the original meaning: for example, the English *transaction* entails a consensus and a plurality of parties who are involved in a category of operations traceable to 'declaration of willingness' which, however, may be unilateral; *acte juridique*, instead, suggests an act that does not have, as in certain continental legal systems, the value of negotiation, as is the case with *traditio*.

It is commonly believed that the discipline of contracts in the different legal orders is founded on 'common values'.[3] Here the same considerations may be made as those cited above concerning Roman sources. It is evident that, if *contract* is intended generically as an 'economic operation', common values can be identified which serve to emphasize the 'consensus,' and thus the willingness of the signer, the 'freedom to contract', and the need to 'preserve' the operation for reasons of economy and stability of the business relations as well as for purposes of development of trade and commerce. But it is equally evident that in some cases certain values are emphasized, such as, for example, that of the 'person', which are not otherwise protected in contractual law. The German experience is emblematic in this sense, where the Constitutional Court has recently considered value of the person as having an effect on the validity of the contract when he or she expresses values in conflict with those stipulated in the contract. Similarly, in Italy, considerable discussion has taken place regarding the importance of the values of the person in this context.[4] On the other hand, a survey of the possible objects or contents of contracts reveals the values and limitations contemplated in the different single legal systems. The legal value of family agreements, the legal validity of agreements for surrogate motherhood or for the transplant of human organs, are all indicators of the differing conceptions of values that effect the notion and the discipline of contracts.

Thus it is evident that the process of convergence and unification in the discipline of contracts can not be based on presumed common roots, nor on

[3] Thus P Stein and Shand (Ital trans, Milan, 1980); see also G Alpa *I principi generali* (Milan 1993).

[4] Bundesverfassungsgericht, 19 Oct 1993, in *Nuova giur civ comm* (1995) I, 202, with a note by A Barenghi. As to the relationship between 'persona' and 'contratto' see, eg, L Mengoni, 'Autonomia privata e costituzione', in *Banca, borsa, tit cred* (1996) I, 1; Irti, 'Persona e mercato' in *Riv dir civ* (1995) I, 289; N Lipari, 'Spirito di liberalità' e 'spirito di solidarietà' in *Riv trim dir proc civ* (1997) 1; P Rescigno *Manuale del diritto privato italiano* (Naples 1994).

a fictitious definition of a common value system, but must instead reflect the empirical and economic intentions binding the parties in an attempt to facilitate the exchange of goods, services and capitals. In other words, the economic substratum is the connective tissue in this process; it is the conception of contract as the 'juridic garb' of an economic operation that unifies texts which are planned to achieve a common language, an authentic terminological *koiné*, both conceptual and normative.

As happens in all *koinés*, the results attained have a functional rather than an aesthetic or philological value. The terms are simplified, the concepts are diluted, the uniqueness or originality is attenuated until it disappears altogether. There is a kind of collective surrender imposed on those who come bearing their own culture and traditions, their individual convictions and customs, in the attempt to achieve common objectives which prevail over the individual. The goal is not that of imposing one model or one conception over all the others, but rather that of creating unequivocal terminological, conceptual, and normative instruments. A functional conception of law and its instruments must prevail over historical, philological, and national conceptions. The individualistic ambitions of those who wish to uphold both past and present must be abandoned in order to look towards and plan for the future, even if this surrender implies sacrifices and requires adaptation, imagination and simplification. When all is said and done, the desire to preserve the existing terminology and conceptual and normative structures conflicts with the natural *convergence* of systems.[5] This desire is substantially anti-historical because it proposes the perpetuation of tradition in the face of juridic–economic demands dictated by new complexities or by 'modernity.'

A European Community can not be constructed without a common legal system at its base; economic relations can not be promoted if the barriers of separate tongues, different or opposing conceptual categories, different or conflicting legal rules are maintained. In order to construct a common juristic culture, there must be a mutual willingness to talk and the desire to find a common ground for discussion. In order to achieve this, we must abandon criticism of the attempts to draft a European code of principles regulating contracts, as well as criticism of the proposal to establish general principles regulating international trade.

The present reality invites us to look at these initiatives benevolently, without prejudice. This reality, as often happens in the province of law, is in opposition with older models, with pre-dating rules, and new ones must be drawn up which are more appropriate to the times and to the vocation of a united Europe. This reality is the energizing force at the heart of economic relations, and it is not a mirage but is actually coming to fruition.

[5] B Markesinis *The Gradual Convergence* (Oxford 1996).

Opposition to this process would be waging war against the windmills.[6] This fact must be acknowledged while a concerted effort is made to achieve the desired goals as efficiently as possible.[7]

3.1.2. The procedure

The process of harmonization of contract law is not a new one, but has its roots in a fascinating and complex multi-layered historical context. Comparative studies, economic analyses of law, and hermeneutic analyses must all be considered.

(1) The best-informed scholars have thoroughly examined the question of the circulation of national models, both insofar as concerns the codification of underlying general principles, as well as the question of statutes and that of conceptual models.[8]

(2) Law and economics studies have introduced uniform conceptual instruments for the evaluation of the economic effects of legal rules.[9] The construction of an economic analysis of law is a common topic of discussion among scholars of different origins and diverse formation, as they seek to weigh the various instruments and techniques, and to compare problems and solutions. The variety of theories and the different approaches and ideological premises have been no hindrance to the circulation of texts, manuals and essays, along with their discussion and evaluation. The legal realists have accustomed us to the idea that legal phenomena must be understood not only in *form* but also in *substance*. Behind, or rather, within any given law there are concrete and real interests that must be evaluated, balanced out, and recomposed. The attitudes of scholars should not be considered as an invari-

[6] P Legrand 'Sens et non-sens d'un Code civil européen', in *Rev inter dr comp* (1996) 779 ff.

[7] Superficial or simplistic attitudes must be avoided: the warnings to this effect made by certain French scholars should be heeded, in particular C Spinosi and B Oppetit (see the proceedings of the seminar organized at the University of Florence by A De Vita during the 1996/97 academic year). Equally significant are the suggestions made over 40 years ago by R Sacco in an essay published in the *Nuova Riv dir comm* (1953, II, 49 ff) and now reprinted in *I Contratti* (1995) 1, 73ff under the title 'I problemi dell'unificazione del diritto in Europa'.

[8] For general questions see A Gambaro and R Sacco *Sistemi giuridici comparati* (Torino 1996) for the analysis of specific sectors (source, contracting parties, contracts, civil responsability, access to justice) see the research coordinated by G Alpa *Corso di sistemi giuridici comparati* (Turin 1996); in its treatment of contracts, the work of B Markesinis is worthy of note: *The Law of Contracts and Restitutio, A Comparative Introduction* (Oxford 1997) and K Zweigert and H Koetz *Introduzione al diritto comparato,* translated by A Di Majo and A Gambaro (Milan 1992); M Vranken *Fundamentals of European Civil Law* (London 1997), also offers some useful indications.

[9] The continental jurist will find the contribution of HB Schaefer and C Ott on the subject of contracts particularly informative: *Lehrbuch der oekonomischen Analyse des Zivilrechts* (Berlin 1995) 321 ff.

ant factor, but seen rather as a sum of traditions and cultures to be decodified according to conventional analytical keys which are necessarily uniform. Thus the interests of salaried workers, professionals, consumers, and investors, as well as the dynamics of the market (domestic, community, and international) become guidelines in analysing normative models and for the establishment of uniform models.

However, we are not speaking exclusively of the circulation of juridic–formal models: there is also the question of the circulation of commercial and contractual practices as well as that of decisional models.

The circulation of practices invites us to consider the legal effects of commercial and economic exchanges. The circulation of decisions—in the comparative study of those cases which serve as the basis for normative texts or principles—induces us to expand our horizons, to verify what happens in other countries and to balance the effects of the application of laws and principles.

3.1.3. Systematic construction

To understand the processes at work in the harmonization of contract law it is advisable to begin by making a textual comparison congenial to the mentality of the continental lawyer who is accustomed to the analysis of written rules included in codes and statutes. This is a useful exercise, although it does not begin to exhaust the wealth of experiences available for study. In such a comparison, although didactic intentions predominate, the results may nevertheless be considered as indicative (even if not totally representative) of choices made and results achieved. The lawyer concerned with the formation of a *koiné* will be unable to shed his formative experience until the *koiné* is universally accepted; it is therefore advisable that he proceed in this direction by making a comparison of the various legal *corpora*. An Italian reader, for example, will be able to carry out a comparison with national laws in order to see how closely these converge with or how widely they diverge from other models.

The process of harmonization of contract law which is currently taking place is evidenced in three separate normative *corpora*:

(1) The construction of a European common core of contract;[10] the following directives will be considered here: 5/577/CEE on contracts negotiated outside commercial premises (incorporated in the Italian d.lgs 15 January 1992, n 50); 90/314/CEE on travel and holiday contracts and 'all-inclusive' packages (formalized as the Italian d.lgs. 17 March 1995,

10 This is the work of a team of researchers coordinated by N Lipari; the results are published in *Diritto privato europeo* (Padua 1997).

n 111); 93/13/CEE on unfair clauses in consumer contracts (incorporated in the Italian Civil Code as Article1469 bis-sexies); 94/45/CE on contracts relating to time-sharing, and 97/7/CE on long-distance contracts, not yet codified in Italy. Problems concerning the reception of these directives will not be considered in either their terminological or conceptual aspects, nor from the point of view of legislative options;
(2) The project of a European code of principles concerning contracts;[11] and
(3) The drafting of uniform principles of contract law in international trade.[12]

It bears mentioning that these three *corpora* differ among themselves in many ways.

(a) As regards the authority of the source. In the EC case we are dealing with legal rules, a type of regulation or directive providing principles and legal models for reception concerning special binds of contracts or special aspects of contractual relationships; these rules emanate from the regulatory powers awarded to the organs of the EU. In the second case (European principles) we are dealing with a theoretical elaboration, carried out privately by a commission of academics (headed by the Danish jurist professor Ole Lando) in the form proposals. This is currently nearing completion and it is to be hoped that it will subsequently be adopted by the EU. In the third case, we are dealing with an elaboration of principles serving to codify and renew the principles governing contracts in the area of international trade. This is also being undertaken privately by the Institute for the Unification of Laws (Unidroit);

[11] The text and comments are to be found in AS Hartkamp *Toward a European Civil Code* (Nijmegen 1994) (the text was later revised). See also O Lando '*European Contract Law*' in *Il Diritto privato europeo: Problemi e prospettive,* edited by L Moccia (Milan 1993) 119 ff. The construction of a European code of contracts has attracted the interest of Italian jurists; the question has been studied by esteemed scholars in a collection of P Stein (Milan 1996); in particular see G Gandolfi 'Per la redazione di un codice europeo dei contratti' in *Riv trim dir proc civ* (1995), 1073 ff; id, 'Sul progetto di un codice europeo dei contratti', in *Rass dir civ* (1996) 105 ff and Zeno Zencovich 'Il codice civile europeo, le tradizioni giuridiche nazionali e il neopositivismo', in *Studi in onore del Prof. P. Rescigno.*

[12] Text and comments in Bonell *An International Restatement of Contract Law* (Irvington, NY 1994); id, 'The Unidroit principles in practice: the experience of the first two years', in *Uniform L Rev* (1997),1,30; *Principi per i contratti commerciali internazionali e il sistema giuridico latino-americano,* edited by MJ Bonell and S Schipani (Padua 1996); single aspects of the 'principles' are the object of papers gathered in *Contratti* (1995) 5 ff; A Di Majo, 'I principles dei contratti commerciali internazionali tra civil law e common law', in *Riv dir civ* (1995) I, 609 ff. GB Ferri, 'Il ruolo dell'autonomia delle parti e la rilevanza degli usi nei principi dell'Unidroit' in *Contr e impr Europa* (1996) 825 ff; I myself participated in this debate: 'Prime note di raffronto tra i principi dell'Unidroit e il sistema contrattuale italiano' in *Contr e impr Europa* (1996) 316 ff.

(b) As regards their geographical application, the principles regulating international trade are tendentially of universal application, unlike those set forth in the first two *corpora*, which are more narrowly confined to Europe, or inside the European Common Market or inside Europe in a geographical sense; and

(c) In their scope, the European principles aim to systematize a 'general part' of the discipline of contracts, while the Unidroit principles are instead concerned with solving practical questions arising from the conclusion and enforcement of international trade contracts. EC law is based on the approval of Community Directives issued by the EU and on the manner in which single Member States have applied these Directives. Also, interpretations of the European Court of Justice (ECJ) have contributed to the formation of a sort of European contract law. Community directives, in any case, are aimed at implementing EC objectives in the realm of the free circulation of people, goods, services, and capital.

A comparison between the two 'codes'—the proposal of a text by the Lando Commission and the Unidroit text—can easily be made. The comparison with EC Directives is, instead, more complicated since these are neither designed nor approved with any systematic intention, but are presented as specific measures, field by field and subject by subject. In carrying out a comparison one must consider the origins of the single texts as well as their objectives and normative value.

The comparative examples require some further comments of a preliminary nature regarding EC Directives in the field of contracts. These comments concern either all the directives *tout court* or only those which regulate contracts, or some part of this latter group.

As was stated above, EC Directives are not emanated in any ordered fashion according to specific criteria or any identifiable logic. In other words, the 'Community legislator' (that is, those EC organs which have legislative power) has not set out to regulate contracts in general, nor any single aspect of contracts in a systematic way, either temporally or progressively. Since the planning, discussion, drafting, and approval of a directive is, so to speak, 'erratic'; there are directives which, even though they concern specific subjects, pave the way for directives of a more general nature. Being approved in different periods of time, they are not coordinated in terms of their contents or their validity; they thus come into existence with no coordination at their source. Consequently, it is up to domestic legislators to coordinate them at such time as they enter into effect (a complicated operation that is generally avoided). The directives originate with terminological and conceptual ambiguities since they are written during their drafting in French and English and afterwards translated into the other Member States languages. They have varying scopes: some concern specific operations (eg travel agreements or contracts relating to time-sharing). Others concern the procedures for contract formation (eg contracts concluded in the place of residence or long distance). Still others regard the contents, and the mention of specific clauses (eg the directive concerning unfair clauses in consumer contracts). Still others are not aimed at the construction of a common core of contracts, but explain certain effects resulting from the regulation of contracts (eg the directive on financial investments).

The construction of a common core of contracts under EC law is understandably difficult (and not always reliable) since each directive is implemented differently in the different member countries, depending on the legal sources and the options allowed to national legislators. Uniform implementation is further impeded by the terminology and the concepts employed as the directives are translated (or transposed) to national legal systems. Additional difficulties are represented by the lapse in time between the promulgation of directives and their implementation in member countries and by the way in which each country interprets both the directives and the rules concerning their application.

Despite this, and with all due precautions in view of the foregoing considerations, it is possible to identify correspondences and perhaps even a certain continuity in the various directives dealing with similar topics. In other words, an attempt can be made (and has been made quite successfully)[13] to construct a set of rules, assuming that each directive supplies the necessary guidelines, serving to regulate the negotiation, formation, and drafting of standard contractual models: this includes considerations of form, interpretation, integration, *ius variandi*, *ius poenitendi*, conformity to particular circumstances, protection of the weaker party, damages, remedies, arbitration clauses, etc. Same rules, or rules having the same content, are repeated in different directives, affecting aspects of the different kind of transaction. So it seems possible to say that the EC law, also if not devoted to create a general part of contract law, may be read all together as a common core of contract law.

3.1.4. Contractual freedom, good faith, fairness, and reasonableness

EC Directives in the area of contract law do not include general statements on the contractual freedom of the parties involved. Nevertheless, each of these directives presupposes such freedom both as regards the choice of the other party to the contract and the determination of the contents, as well as their formulation. What emerges, in terms of EC law, is not so much the

[13] I refer here to the research which was coordinated by N Lipari, op cit.

statement of this freedom (which is intrinsic to the system and co-natural with the very foundations of the Community market and its legal forms), but rather the limitations imposed on contractual freedom by directives.

These limitations have a dual purpose: that of annulling the legal effects of those agreements which impede circulation of goods, services or capital and of restricting the negotiating power of the stronger party who might 'take advantage of' this power to the detriment of the weaker party. The latter, in this perspective, is the consumer, in opposition to the 'professional', who is presumably better informed, better equipped, and stronger than the consumer. The category of the professional is postulated in abstract terms, because the particular circumstances which qualify the respective status of the contractual parties are left undefined.

The principle of contractual freedom is stated in both the draft of European principles (Article 1102) and the Unidroit principles (Article 1.1). Both formulas refer to the freedom of determination in stipulating a contract and the freedom of choice as to its contents.[14]

In legal phrasing, reference is often made to general clauses (*Generalklauseln* in German) and *standards* of behaviour. Aside from terminological remarks that may be the source difficulty in identifying a common ground ('*bonne foi*' is close in meaning to the Italian '*buona fede*', but is not precisely the same as the German expression '*Treu und Glaube*' or 'good faith'), the meaning of the general clause relating to good faith must be examined in relation to the context in which the concept is employed.[15] While it is possible to associate the 'good faith' in EC Directives (such as that on unfair clauses, where good faith is the parameter which controls the unlawfulness of a clause) with the 'good faith' referred to in the draft of European principles (Article 1102), it is difficult to see an identical notion in the Unidroit principles where 'good faith' or reasonableness refers to 'international commerce' (Article 1.7). In other words, the context awards relevance to the roles assigned to the parties: two 'merchants', that is two professional operators, have normal modes of behaviour which can not be identified with the behavioural codes of the 'contracting party' referred to

14 R Sacco in *I problemi dell'unificazione*, op cit., Part II, examined the common principle of contractual autonomy; as regards the Unidroit principles, see J Bonell *An International Restatement of Contract Law* (Irvington, NY 1994), 55 ff; more recently L Pontiroli 'La protezione del contraente debole nei Principles of International Commercial Contracts di Unidroit: much ado about nothing?' in *Giur comm* (1997) I, 566 ff. For a historical outline see the recent research carried out by P Di Lucia *L'universale della promessa* (Milan 1997) and the more dogmatic treatment by D'Angelo *Promessa e ragioni del vincolo*, I (Turin 1992).

15 There is a vast quantity of studies on this topic; by way of example see D Harris and D Tallon (eds) *Contract Law Today. Anglo-French Comparisons* (Oxford 1989); SJ Burton *Judging in Good Faith* (Cambridge 1992); A Fairnsworth *The Concept of Good Faith in American Law* (Rome 1993); P Schlechtriem, *Good Faith in German Law International Uniform Laws,* Rome, 1997; R Brownsword, 'Good faith in contracts revisited', in 49 Current Leg Probl (1996) 111.

in the draft of European principles, and even less with the behaviour of the consumer. The same may be said of 'fair dealing'. Different considerations pertain to the concept of 'reasonableness', which is a rare parameter in EC Directives and equally so in the draft of European principles, where reasonableness is placed alongside good faith (Article 1.102; 1.302); it is instead widely used in the Unidroit principles, appearing there more than 70 times.

3.1.5. Practices

It is understandable that usages are not considered favourably in EC Directives: usage calls to mind, first of all, legal particularism rooted in local traditions and is, therefore, ontologically in contrast with the creation of a common core of contract law. Also, usages in negotiation and in commerce tend to reflect the interests of the 'merchants' (now professionals) and thereby to impose on the consumer rules which are not aimed at redressing the imbalance between their positions in the sphere of contracts.

It is equally comprehensible that usages are exalted in the Unidroit principles, which are presented, ontologically, as general rules serving to codify (as well as renew, where such is the goal) the *lex mercatoria*. It is not surprising, therefore, that in the *corpus* of the principles a general rule is provided concerning 'usages' and 'practices', which is binding for both parties, the only limitation being unreasonableness (Article 1.8).

The draft of European principles makes a provision for usage as it is commonly understood, similar to that found in the Unidroit principles; in addition, it introduces a subjective notion of usage in considering as binding any usage that the parties have agreed upon or have established between themselves (Article 1. 105).

3.1.6. Protection of the weaker parties

Most of the regulation of contracts in EC Directives is aimed at protecting the interests of the weaker party which, as stated above, is understood to be the 'consumer'. In the draft of European principles there is no definition of the weaker party, but there are some provisions which indirectly consider the weaker position of one of the parties: eg as regards clauses which are not individually negotiated (Article 2.104), or unfair clauses which are not individually negotiated (Article 4.110) or in the case of interpretation *contra proferentem* (Article 5.103). In the Unidroit principles, even though these were conceived as a means of regulating relations between subjects who are more or less in a position of parity, there are rules concerning surprising clauses (Article 2.20), others regarding *contra proferentem* interpretation (Article 4.6), and still others concerning 'gross disparity' (Article 3.10).[16]

[16] *Contra* L Pontiroli op cit.

The general position in this area is substantially uniform in the three phenomena. The freedom of the contracting parties is established from the moment contacts are established, preliminary to the conclusion of the contract; the freedom to conclude a contract is also intended as a negative freedom, ie the freedom *not* to enter into a contract (Article 2.301 of the draft of European principles and Article 2.15 of the Unidroit principles). The failure to reach an agreement bears no responsibility whatsoever; both of these collections of principles, however, bind the freedom of negotiation to the concept of acting in good faith, since any behaviour in contrast with the principle of good faith implies responsibility. Responsibility is enforced in the case of unjustified withdrawal.

The behaviour of the parties in the course of negotiations, or in the phase prior to the conclusion of the contract, is carefully regulated in the EC Directives. Negotiations are seen in a dual perspective: as the phase during which the parties effectively express their freedom to negotiate, a phase of mutual discussion and reciprocal influence; and as the phase in which they exchange information. In the first case, the initiation of negotiations implies the exclusion of any control over the abuse of contractual power by one party to the detriment of the other (the most striking example is that in Article 3.2 of the directive on unfair clauses). In the second case, if the other party has been fully informed, this excludes the surprise effect and, above all, acts as a guarantee of an informed consensus (there are various examples in this sense: see Article 5.2 and 5.3 of the directive regarding contracts concluded outside commercial premises; Article 4 of the directive on long-distance contracts; Articles 4, 8, and 9 of the directive on travel contracts; and Article 3 of the directive relating to time-sharing contracts).

3.1.7. Formation, content, and form

Regulation of the formation of contracts seems to be fairly homologous in all the texts considered. These are probably the sections regulated in greatest detail in the draft of European principles and the Unidroit principles. Regulations on the formation of contracts are contained in the EC Directives regarding long-distance contracts and contracts concluded outside commercial premises, although their detailed examination is beyond the scope of the present chapter.

It is worth noting, however, that standard contracts are considered both in the draft of European principles (Article 4.110, relative to unfair clauses) and in the Unidroit principles.

Though it may seem curious that the Unidroit principles be concerned with safeguarding someone asked to sign a contract when the contents have been predetermined by another party, this practice is nonetheless considered in a moderately acceptable light. Though it respects the principle of contractual freedom, it ultimately places one of the parties at a disadvantage at the closing of the contract since the fine points hidden between the lines may be unknown. As a consequence, the weaker (ie uninformed) party must exercise all his persuasive and negotiatory strength in order to modify the text. This explains the numerous references to standard contracts in the principles (Articles 2.19–2.22).

In EC Directives the use of standard models is considered to be one of the means by which a professional attempts to impose unfair clauses on the consumer and it is thus carefully regulated by a directive specifically aimed at this purpose (n 13/1993).

EC Directives punctiliously regulate the *ius poenitendi* of the consumer, allowing him to revoke the offer or to withdraw from the contract ('cooling off period'). Such possibilities are not contemplated in either the draft of European principles or the Unidroit Principles. This is perfectly understandable since neither the normal contracting party nor the economic operator can withdraw unless this merely potestative condition is agreed to by both parties. In any case, it would be an unusual eventuality because, once the contract has been concluded, the obligation must be respected and cannot be annulled *ad libitum* by only one party. In EC Directives, the *ius poenitendi* is the best expedient by which to save the consumer from an operation whose meaning and eventual advantages are not totally clear to him. As for the meaning, when he or she receives the supporting documents for the contract, the consumer may re-examine them and eventually insert his or her own technical information. As concerns the advantageousness, by studying the legal and economic conditions, possibly with the advice of a third party, he or she may decide to abandon the business deal or decide to conclude a contract with another professional. It is for this reason that the *ius poenitendi* ('cooling off period') is inserted in the directives regarding travel contracts (Article 13), distance selling (Articles 5 and 6), time-sharing contracts (Article 5), and contracts concluded outside commercial premises (Articles 4–8). Considered as a safeguard for the consumer, the *ius poenitendi* must be included among the contractual clauses where required. If required only as a defence of the consumer, it does not create an imbalance in the legal positions of the two parties; if required only in favour of the professional, it is considered a negative condition and the clause in which it is contained is considered unfair.

Since the individual legal systems differ on what constitutes the essential terms of a contract, the draft of European principles does not list these requisites. This silence is more eloquent than any explicit statement to the contrary. The absence of any mention whatsoever of the 'cause' of the contract is particularly significant. Nor do the Unidroit principles, which consider a contract as a 'business deal', bother to enumerate these requisites; it is assumed to be natural that the contracting parties will not ignore the essential requisites, even if these are not specified.

Not even the EC Directives are concerned with these requisites. They do, however, concern themselves with what the continental jurist considers as the minimal essential contents of the object. This concern, yet once again, is inspired by the desire to protect the weaker party. This is, therefore, an 'interventionist' attitude because the directives prescribe certain essential terms in the absence of which the consumer would be deprived of the possibility of expressing his informed agreement and would thus be exposed to the risk of underwriting a voidable contract (with respect to those aspects considered as essential). The professional could consequently take advantage of this. It is for this reason that the minimal contents are specified in the case of travel contracts (eg Article 7) and those relating to time-sharing (Article 5).

EC Directives are also concerned that the contents of a contract be formulated in clear and intelligible terms so that the consumer may express his informed consent.

The rules of interpretation are largely similar in the different texts (eg in the draft of European principles, see Articles 5:101 and 5:107; in the Unidroit principles see Articles 4.1 and 4.7). But it is interesting to note that both the draft of European principles and the principles are inclined to accept the institution of the integration of the contract, perhaps in respect of the rules on 'implied obligations' which derive from English common law (see Articles 6:102 and 4.8 respectively).

EC Directives pay particular attention to the *ius variandi*: this introduction of mandatory law is a significant limitation to contractual freedom dictated by the need to protect the weaker party who might otherwise be subject to unfair treatment by the professional in terms of limitations imposed or the suppression of certain conditions or unexpressed obligations, disadvantages, costs, etc. Many of the provisions in the directive on unfair clauses are concerned with *ius variandi*, as is the directive on travel contracts (Article 12). In the Unidroit Principles as well there are rules indirectly aimed at limiting the power to modify contracts (Articles 1.3, 6.2.3b, 3.10), while this problem is ignored by the draft of European principles.

Control of the contents of contracts is the main scope of the directive on unfair clauses. But the Unidroit Principles are also concerned with the control of contents, both in relation to time limits and modality of compliance (chapter 6) and with regard to clauses concerning exemption from liability (Article 7.1.6).

Within the principle of contractual freedom, the freedom of form is also contemplated. This is to be expected in international trade, where the question of form could constitute an obstacle to the conclusion of business deals (see Articles 1.2, 2.18 of the Unidroit principles). It is likewise natural that in a variety of systems in which form is regulated in the most heterogeneous ways, it be considered an irrelevant feature of the contract (at present, this aspect is not specifically regulated by the draft of European principles).

On the other hand, even in this area, the directives take on an interventionist character. Form is intended in a dual sense: both as the means by which the weaker party, about to conclude a contract, is familiarized with the contents of the contract and as a means for drawing attention to the single clauses of the contract. The directive on travel contracts (Article 6) is eloquent in this respect as are the directives on long-distance contracts (Article 5), on time-sharing (Article 4) and those regulating contracts concluded outside commercial premises (Article 1.9).

3.1.8. Preservation of contracts

The rules concerning the termination and invalidity of contracts require a more detailed, in-depth analysis. Nevertheless, any comparison of the texts would be incomplete because EC Directives do not treat the question of termination or voidability in general, except in particular cases such as the voidability of single clauses. What must be emphasized is the tendency of the Unidroit principles to preserve the contract; in this text, in fact, the judge is given considerable power to modify the contents and so the draft of European principles.

EC Directives explicitly allow the judge to exercise strong control over the clauses, while they barely consider the preservation of the contract. When the consumer's interest is violated, it appears preferable to dissolve the contract or reduce its impact rather than uphold the agreement at all costs, unless its preservation is to the advantage of the consumer.

3.1.9. Closing remarks

In comparing EC Directives, the draft of European principles and the Unidroit Principles it is possible to draw several brief conclusions. Obviously, these conclusions are, in a sense, arbitrary, but they are indicative of trends, of the direction in which contract law is evolving and of the prospects that are opening up in this area. The 'contract'—whatever name is given to it and however it is conceived—is the legal guise of an economic operation and the terminology in which these texts are couched is sufficiently uniform in the English language (or perhaps 'jargon' is the more appropriate term). Concepts are simplified, since they respond to the practical, rather than theoretical, goals pursued by jurists.

The object or the contents of the contract prevail over the 'cause'; control of legitimacy is entrusted to national judges; a contract already concluded has precedence over the serious intention to enter into a contract and over fulfilment of the effects; a contract is considered as a source of obligations rather than as an instrument for transferral of property; it is seen as a general plan for the distribution of risks, advantages and disadvantages. It is common practice to assign a fixed duration to a contract as well as certain effects distributed along a curve, according to the specific scope which it aims to achieve; the form tends to be free so as not to create obstacles to the conclusion of economic operations. When envisaged, the form is intended as a means to protect the contracting parties so that they understand the binding nature of the operation and the terms of the obligations assumed. The weaker party is protected with respect to the stronger and is well informed and better equipped regarding the nature of the contract. An economic imbalance between services provided gives way to a legal imbalance, and it is the judge's concern to introduce corrective measures. The negotiating behaviour of the parties in the various stages of the operation is kept in check by the criteria of good faith and reasonableness. The economic operation is safeguarded insofar as possible by seeking solutions which serve to balance and adapt the relationship between the parties rather than dissolve the agreement. Interpretation and integration operate in an objective manner, in the sense that they are not conditioned by the subjective wishes of the parties; these parties are not considered as neutral operators but their *status* is given due importance. The base model is still that of sale (though this may be undeclared, it is nevertheless transparent), or in any case, that of a contract of exchange (goods, services).

Though an economic–commercial tone pervades the various disciplines, the traditional austere concept of a 'neutral' contract seems to have definitively vanished.

3.2. TRADING ON-LINE AND THE PROTECTION OF THE CONSUMER

3.2.1. The legal framework

In the trading of financial services on-line, two models of analysis tend to conflict—more visibly than in other sectors—and these models of analysis also correspond to two different models of legal policy. The first concentrates attention on the fairness of behaviour of the operators but enhances freedom of action and the freedom of contract of the professionals, basing itself on competition and customer satisfaction. The other sets out to ensure the protection of the economically and contractually weaker party, the customer–consumer, who is guaranteed by means of a set of non-negotiable rights, through the introduction of rules which cannot be waived by the parties, and control mechanisms regulated by public authorities, the legal capacity to sue of consumer associations.

It is merely worth noting that *customer satisfaction* and *consumer protection* do not extend over coinciding areas but only partially overlap.

The former, on the one hand, is wider than the latter because it addresses all contracting parties, regardless of their *status*, but on the other hand it is narrower, because it implies measures selected spontaneously by a company, or measures which the company has committed to assume, on the basis of corporate agreements or by virtue of codes of conduct or agreements negotiated with customers' associations (be the latter professionals or simply consumers).

The latter includes measures that a firm must compulsorily satisfy, because they are imposed by an authority. In the case of investment contracts there are a number of authorities, albeit coordinated according to criteria of hierarchy and cognisance, such as, in fact, EC agencies, parliaments and governments, and independent public authorities.

The first relies on self-regulating bodies, and in any case aims at marginal intervention by the state, limited to fixing the general principles which intermediaries and customers must abide by. The second assumes intervention by the state, both as a regulator and as controller.

Community directives on the subject matter tend towards a mix of the two models, facilitating the realization of forms of self-control and self-restraint, but at the same time introducing certain provisions which are not subject to variation by agreement between the parties.[17] This solution is suggested by the fact that the imbalance of information between the parties can be corrected only partially and that the market is unable, through the mere techniques of self-discipline, to strike a fair balance between the different interests at stake.

Furthermore, in the financial market the interests of the consumers have only recently emerged; health and safety issues tended to dominate and only subsequently did attention focus on the protection of the economic interests of consumers, even though economic interests were already considered one of the main features of the EC Resolution of 1975 on consumers' rights. EC policy on this matter has mainly concerned the sectors of consumer credit and excessive indebtedness of consumers and only recently has the figure of the consumer become identified with that of the saver.[18]

[17] See Craig and de Bùrca (eds) 'The evolution of EC law' (Oxford 1999), *passim, et ibi* More, *The Principle of Equal Treatment: From Market Unifier To Fundamental Right?* 517 ff; Weatherill *Consumer Policy* 693 ff; Armstrong *Governance and the Single European Market* 745 ff; Micklitz and Weatherill (eds) *European Economic Law* (Dartmouth 1997), *et ibid* Hommelhoff *Civil Law Under the Influence of European Legal Harmonization* 362 ff; Weiler *Methods of Protection: Towards a Second and Third Generation of Protection* 526 ff; de Bùrca, 'The language of rights and European integration', in *New Legal Dynamics of European Union* (Oxford 1995) 29 ff.

[18] See the 'Green Book' of the EC Commission on *Financial Services* (COM96/209) and the following: Communication on *Consumers Expectations* (COM 97/309), in Alpa (ed) *Codice del consumo e del risparmio* (Milan, 1999) 605 ff, and comments by Gaggero *I servizi di investimento* 657 ff; National Consumer Council, *Consumer Concerns 1999. Consumers' Views of Advice and Information on Financial Services* (London Nov 1999), Alpa 'Commento sub art 21 24 Feb 1998, n 58', in Alpa and Capriglione (ed) *Commentario al testo unico delle dispo-*

Today, the combined provisions of Articles 2, 3 c.1 item t) and 153 (formerly 129 A) of the EC Treaty in the version derived from the Treaty of Amsterdam show that the protection of the consumer has become one of the fundamental objectives of the EU and one of the essential tasks of EC policy inherent to the realization of the internal market. The harmonious, balanced, and sustainable development of economic activities is pursued even through the strengthening of the protection of consumers—ensured at a high level—regarding, *inter alia*, their economic interests. These objectives are pursued through ever closer legislative, regulatory and administrative provisions (Article 94, formerly 100) of the Member States and the harmonization of the forms of direct protection aimed at avoiding discriminations (Article 95, formerly 100 A).

The problems regarding the protection of the consumer are now joined by the problems regarding the protection of consumers who rely on electronic means for the purchase of goods and services. The aims to be pursued in this new dimension, which belongs to the so-called 'information society', have been underlined in a report devoted to the construction of 'networks for the citizens and their communities',[19] where the need is highlighted to guarantee individuals access to the nets, transparency of transactions, adequacy of information, fairness in the conduct of professionals.

From this perspective, which merges the trend that aims to protect the consumers in their dealings with professionals with that which aims to protect the users of information technology in their dealings with the services providers and with the professional users of the same services, the issue of the distribution of financial services on-line is centred.

Electronic commerce, digital signatures, payments, and obviously, the conclusion of a contract on-line, unfair terms in consumer contracts, the protection of personal data, the remedies available and the out-of-court settlement of disputes are, *inter alia*, some of the problems—certainly the most significant—which emerge in this new dimension.

The layout of the legal framework, at EC law level and at the level of domestic law is, therefore, necessarily complex.

To these rules we must add the general rules on the protection of personal data, which regard not only natural persons but also legal entities

sizioni in materia di intermediazione finanziaria (Padua 1998), I, 212 ff; Banakas 'Liability for incorrect financial information: theory and practice in a general clause system and in a protected interests system', in (1999) 7 Eu Rev Priv L, 261 ff; James, '*The application of the EC recommendations on the principles applicable to out-of court procedures to the new arrangements for the settlement of consumer complaints in the UK financial services sector*' in 7 Cons L J (1999) 443 ff; Domont-Naert, '*The right to basic financial services: "Opening the Discussion"* ', in 8 Cons L J (2000) 63 ff.

[19] Forum Information Society *Annual Report* (1996) Andersen *Electronic Commerce: A Challenge to Private Law?* (Rome 1998); Report of the European Consumer Law Group on E-Commerce, n 194/2000.

and both the data relating to aspects of personality and data with an economic content (Directive EEC 24 October 1995, n 46 and law 31 December 1996, n 675, and relative provisions of the authority for the protection of personal data).

In the subject matter, the framework is tendered by two directives which have a general bearing: Directive n 93/22/EEC of 10.5.1993 on brokerage in the financial market and Directive n 2000/31/EC of 8 June 2000 on electronic commerce. Both have been definitively implemented in Italy in the uniform text on financial markets (Legislative decree n 58 of 1998), and through a legslative decree n 70 of 2003.

On the first Directive—which does not have the direct protection of the consumer as its principal aim—there is not much to be said. It is sufficient to highlight that it proposes to establish rules of conduct for the intermediaries, in order to ensure that their conduct is 'fair' in their dealings with investors and in avoiding conflicts of interest. In addition, the Uniform text envisages general criteria of conduct (diligence, fairness, transparency) in the interest of the customers and for the integrity of the markets, it is provided that the intermediaries must 'reduce to the minimum risks of conflict of interest and, where conflicts of interest arise, act in a manner as to ensure in any case to their customers transparency and fair dealing'; rules are envisaged on distance marketing and on the right of withdrawal by the customer within seven days from the moment in which the contract for the placement of financial instruments or the management of individual portfolios is underwritten; referral is made to the rules of the surveillance Authority (Consob) for the regulation of promotion and distance placement of investment services and of financial products.[20]

The other Directive, on e-commerce, is far more articulate.

3.2.2. The Directive on electronic commerce

Directive 2000/31/EC, within the principle of subsidiarity, introduces rules which ensure legal certainty and consumer confidence (Recital 7), the free movement of services, and a high level of protection of objectives of general interest, such as consumer protection (Recital 10). The Directive is coordinated with those Directives, separately recalled, which regard unfair terms in consumer contracts, misleading and comparative advertising, consumer credit, prices of products offered to consumers, distance marketing of goods and services, and the future Directive of the European Parliament and of the Council concerning the distance marketing of consumer financial services.

The protection of investors is also the main concern of Recital 27, which sets forth the reasons for the rules of conduct imposed on professionals

[20] Regarding the Italian experience see Alpa *Commento op cit.*

providing on-line financial services. These are rules of both a legislative and regulatory nature, but also rules deriving from the codes of conduct which are considered the best means 'of determining the rules on professional ethics applicable to commercial communication' (Recital 32). The Directive is concerned with giving legitimacy to contracts concluded by electronic means (Recital 38), with reiterating the duty of services providers to act with fairness and diligence, and their duty of compensation in the event of liability (Recitals 40, 48), with identifying actions inhibiting unlawful conduct (Recital 45), together with appropriate court actions also through alternative disputes resolution (Recital 52).

In particular, the Directive on electronic commerce establishes rules, which are so detailed as to be considered directly applicable in domestic legal systems, as regards the general information to be provided to consumers (Article 5), information regarding commercial communications (Article 6 et seq), information regarding contracts concluded by electronic means (Article 10 et seq).

3.2.3. The distance marketing of consumer financial services

This framework of EC action, always concerned with ensuring a 'balance between the different interests at stake' (Recital 41 of the Directive on electronic commerce) is to be completed with the approval of the two Directives which are still missing: the Directive on the marketing of financial services on-line and the Directive on the liability of services providers. The first seems closer to the draft text of 2000 (working document CONSOM/00/14) provides a systematic version, being the only alternative to the previous, and sufficiently consolidated, certainly more significant than the previous draft prepared (n 12932/99 of 19 November 1999).

The harmonization of Member States' legislation is not however—nor could it be in this particular phase—complete: n 2 of the text under review points out that a same financial service may receive different legal qualifications in the different legal systems and that the rules of the Directive proposal regard only the initial agreement, and not the successive operations. It is left to other Directives, possibly to a European civil code, to unify the discipline on services and therefore on financial services, distributed by whatever means.

The proposal complies with the Directive on the marketing of goods and services other than financial services and with the Directive on electronic commerce in the objective of providing information to consumers. It is interesting to note that the proposed rules by themselves establish obligations on the intermediary and that the products under consideration refer not only to services of a banking, credit, personal pension, investment and payment nature, but also insurance services, whose inclusion among financial services is not (indeed was not) taken for granted in all legal systems (Article 2, item b).

The provision of information to the consumer—a right which entails an equal number of obligations on his professional counter-party—has always been, since the general Resolution of 1975, one of the primary objectives of the Community. This, for several reasons: to ensure transparency and fairness in the performance of economic activities, to facilitate competition among professionals, to ensure certainty in legal relations, to eliminate—or at least to curtail—the imbalance of information between the parties. An adequately informed consumer has not only a greater capacity to understand the importance of the actions he is about to undertake, but is also capable (or we assume it should be so) to make more convenient choices in the investment of his savings.

The identity of the supplier and of the other intermediaries with whom the consumer comes into contact, the economic consistency of the product, the currency, the additional costs, the right of withdrawal, the risks associated with the financial service, the existence of redress mechanisms, the applicable law, the court having jurisdiction are the subject of information of a general nature (Article 3, c.1).

Information must be provided in a clear and comprehensible manner, in accordance with the principles of good faith, and the principle of protection of those who are unable to give their consent, such as minors (Article 3 c.2).

The relevance of this information (ex Article 3) is such that—together with the right of withdrawal (Article 4) and sanctions (Article 10 a)—where the rules pertaining to the same were not harmonized, the Directive proposal sets forth that they are to be subject to the discipline of the country of residence of the consumer (with the exception of Directives n 92/49/EC and 92/96/EC) (Article 16 a).

Among the many areas governed by the Directive proposal we note, in particular, the communication of contractual terms and conditions and of the prior information (Article 3 a) and the right of withdrawal (Article 4).

The provision according to which 'the choice of means of communication is agreed between the parties' (Article 3 a, c. 3) is ambiguous: it is obviously a referral to the freedom of the contracting parties, but in insurance contracts, in which the policies are normally prepared by the company, the choice is already made by the company and therefore is the result of a predetermined clause, which may result unfair, as it is imposed on the consumer and implies a contractual imbalance; the alternative is that the consumer should be the one to choose among the alternatives offered by the company; but this still leaves the problem unresolved as to whether this solution may imply that the clause is negotiated and therefore removed from the test of unfairness.

The right of withdrawal is the subject of a complex discipline: it is upon the Member States to establish the extent of duration for the exercise of such right (from 14 to 30 days).

The fraudulent use of a payment card implies a risk which is placed on the company (Article 8 a); the text does not specify whether this risk includes fraudulent acts by persons which are external to the company (eg the intermediary), but requirements of consistency dictate a positive solution of the issue; it shall be up to the company to claim against the intermediary or third parties for damages.

Unsolicited services and communications (Articles 9 and 10) imply instead that it is the consumer who has to take the initiative to obtain services and communications, and that there be his consent for the supply of the same.

As regards specific clauses, the proposal points out that the burden of proof in respect of the supplier's obligations to inform the consumer and the consumer's consent to the conclusion and performance of the contract is placed on the supplier, and that any contractual term or condition placing the burden of proof on the consumer is to be considered unfair (and therefore void) (Article 13).

The choice of law applicable to the contract and the choice of court having jurisdiction are for the parties to decide, always provided that they have been the subject of prior information; but the proposal itself takes care to advise that the Brussels Convention must be abided by; the problem, therefore, arises as to the compatibility of these provisions with those of Directive n 13 of 1993 on unfair terms and conditions, and whether there is a waiver of the regulations provided therein, in favour of the consumer.

As for the further requirements envisaged by the proposal, on the one hand the need is noted for the preparation of codes of conduct on the part of the operators and, on the other hand, for the establishment of organizations for conciliation and arbitration for the out-of-court settlement of disputes.

The Community proposal does not purport to establish either the time or the place of conclusion of the contract.

Not even Directive n 97/7/EC and the rules for implementation provided by Legislative decree 22 May 1999 n 185 address the issue, which will therefore have to be resolved in accordance with the provisions of the domestic law applicable to the contract and by the Rome convention on the discipline applicable to obligations of 19 June 1980, ratified by Law 18 December 1984, n 975 (which came into force on 1 April 1991) in the event of contracts concluded between subjects of different states.

It is worth noting that as regards the time and place of conclusion of the insurance contract the same are established by Italian law, where this is applicable, ie the implementation of EC Directives on 'life' and 'non-life' insurance.

Also as regards remedies, the proposal refers to the applicable law chosen by the parties.

3.2.4. *The distance marketing of consumer financial services in Italy*

Some ten million Italians today are Internet users. The marketing of products and services other than financial services is taking off. The use of the Internet for business-to-business operations is becoming more widespread, already reaching 25 per cent of the entire market. For transactions between business and consumers this has reached 15 per cent. The marketing of financial services on-line is only at the beginning, even though many banks and investment companies are fully equipped, and some insurance companies rely on the Internet for their institutional advertising and description of their products, as the majority of contracts are still concluded through the agencies. The forecasts, however, are favourable to the development of this means of distribution, and the phenomenon seems at the same time unstoppable and irreversible. Furthermore the rules of competition are forcing Italian professionals to utilize this system, in order to keep up with foreign rivals.

Since 1992 (with law n 50 on distance marketing) our system has been dealing with contracts concluded by electronic means. The provisions, however, regard only the right of withdrawal.

As regards distance marketing of consumer financial services, for the time being we note only a rule of referral, contained in Article 32 of the uniform text on financial brokerage services (legislative decree 24 February 1998, n 58). Furthermore, Article 100 of the said uniform text excludes 'insurance products issued by insurance companies' from the discipline of the chapter regarding solicitation of investment.[21]

The discipline is not uniform, but fragmented. In addition to the rules of self-discipline of the operators, and to the regulations introduced by the independent authorities (who have already made adequate provisions as regards our own country), we must take into account the general rules concerning the conduct of intermediaries of financial services contained in the Uniform text previously mentioned and, as regards banks, also in the uniform text on banking, legislative decree 1 September 1993, n 385, and likewise, as regards insurance companies, in the discipline of insurance activities set forth in legislative decrees of 17 March 1995, n 174 and 175.

[21] See Gentili, *Commento sub art 32 d.lgs 24 Feb 1998*, n 58, supra at n 2; Antonucci, *Profili giuridici del commercio elettronico di prodotti finanziari*, in *Mondo bancario* [2000] 49 ff.; Lener, *L'uso di Internet per la distribuzione di servizi finanziari*, paper (Milano, 2000); Parrella, *La disciplina speciale dell'offerta a distanza di 'prodotti finanziari' e di 'servizi di investimento'*, in *Dir.banca e del merc.fin.* (2000) 38 ff.; Delfini, *Commercio elettronico e servizi di investimento*, in *I contratti* (2000) 716 ff.; Carriero, *Vendite a distanza, informazione precontrattuale, disciplina comunitaria: la tutela del consumatore di servizi finanziari*, Paper (Rome, 2000).

It is worth noticing that, until the issue of a uniform text, containing provisions relating to the entire insurance sector, (one which has by now widely penetrated the financial market), the rules devoted to banks and financial intermediaries are considerably more far-reaching and systemized than those currently applicable to insurance companies, giving the latter's clients, whether they be 'professionals' or 'consumers' a far more desultory and erratic protection than is reserved for the clients of banks and financial intermediaries.

Of the three authorities that have jurisdiction to elaborate rules on the matter, the Bank of Italy is developing a specific set of rules as regards financial services on-line, Consob has approved certain deliberations in this respect, and the Italian insurance watchdog, Isvap, has approved circular n 393/D dated 17 January 2000.

As regards the deliberations of Consob, it is worth mentioning:

(a) communication n DI/99052838 dated 7 July 1999 which defines the Internet as a means of distance communication; in this elaborate communication, Consob sets forth the fundamental rules for the activity under review;
(b) communication n DI/99065403 dated 3 September 1999, which brings the promotion and placement of shares of unit trust funds through a website under the discipline envisaged for prospectuses, which must be communicated together with the forms for subscription (as can be seen from Consob regulations n 11971/1999 and n 11522/1998); in this communication, Consob remarks that there is full compatibility of the Internet means with the timely information of the investor and that the possibility of printing the documents to be communicated to the investor is not an impediment for the delivery of the prospectus and of the document on the general risks pertaining to investments in financial instruments; and
(c) communication DI/99091709 dated 15 December 1999 with which Consob specifies the rules applicable to the activity under review, in particular as regards the procedures for which one has to rely on a financial promoter.

As regards Isvap, circular n 393/D dated 17 January 2000 specified that:

(a) foreign companies with head offices in a Member State of the EU which intend to place insurance products through the Internet in the territory of the Italian republic, if they are not already admitted to operate under a regime of establishment, or of freedom to provide services, must abide by the conditions of access envisaged in Articles 70 et seq of legislative decree 174/95 and Articles 81 et seq of legislative decree 175/95; for companies of non-Member States the authorization of Isvap is required, to operate as an establishment; Italian companies intending to operate through the Internet in other States must comply with the revisions set forth in Chapter IV, title II of the legislative decree n 174 and of Chapter V, title II of legislative decree n 175 already mentioned;

(b) companies must assume prior 'full responsibility' for the activity performed by the individuals actually entrusted with the management of the web-site and/or the interaction via e-mail; this is the application, in this specific sector, of the provisions of Article 1228 of the Italian Civil Code, regarding contractual liability of associates, and of Article 2049 of the Civil code regarding unlawful acts committed by employees and assistants;

(c) companies must carry out periodic and systematic checks on the completeness and regularity of communications;

(d) they must also ensure that the marketing initiatives for the products envisage payment procedures that guarantee certainty, security, and confidentiality of payments effected by the contracting parties; and

(e) offers of insurance services must include the identification of the company and its entitlement to perform the said activity, the prior information, the authenticity and delivery of the conditions of policy, the certainty of the time of conclusion of the contract and the start of the insurance period, the conduct to be complied with after the conclusion of a contract, the right of withdrawal (which regards the phase after the conclusion of the contract) the law applicable to the contract and the court having jurisdiction, the written form as regards the policy, any representations by the insured, in accordance with Articles 1892 et seq of the Civil Code, the consent of the third party on whose life the insurance is stipulated, a statement by the insured that he has acquired, on paper or other durable means, the prescribed prior information.

The Isvap circular also draws the companies' attention to the need to exclude unfair terms and conditions in accordance with Article 1469 *bis* et seq of the Civil Code; and sets forth rules on the conduct of agents and brokers operating through the Internet.

With the exception of the warning regarding unfair terms and conditions, the rules introduced by the circular concern all insurance contracts concluded through the Internet and e-mail, without any distinction between the status of a 'professional' and that of 'consumer'.

The role of Isvap in this matter has therefore been essential, because it has made it possible to advance, on the basis of the law currently in force, a series of requirements which the Directive and the implementation discipline will articulate and specify in greater thoroughness. However, it should be noted that—as has been highlighted by observers—the market for on-line insurance services has failed to develop in Italy with the same speed and intensity that the use of the Internet could have allowed and which has occurred in other countries. A simple consideration emerges from a surf on the Internet, as regards the different conduct of companies: there are companies that merely make a presentation of their web-site, their activities and their 'credentials'; others which illustrate the type of products available on-line, and refer to the list of agents operating in the various areas for the conclusion of the relative contracts; others actually operate on-line negotiations.

In this latter case, the information offered tends to be a simple description of the products. However, the company is able at the same time to acquire two essential data: the first regarding the type of risk that the potential customer wishes to insure and secondly, his propensity to risk (in the event of policies with contents and aims of a financial nature). It seems, however, that in most cases the customer is able to acquire knowledge of the policy conditions, as reported in the text of the contract, only *after* he has confirmed his interest in subscribing the offered policy and *after* he has transmitted his data to the offeror. The expression 'offer' and that of 'offeror' relate to the product on offer and to the supplier, but in the contractual practice of insurance companies (as with the other financial intermediaries and with banks), the role of the parties is overturned: it is the client who requests a service and therefore assumes the role of the 'offeror' in a purely technical sense.

3.2.5. Some critical observations: the legislative approach

Faced with this phenomenon, and until the legal framework is completed with the definitive approval of the EC text on-line financial services and of the text on the liability of services providers, we may ask how we could improve the system of consumer protection, bearing in mind the requirements of striking a balance between the different interests at stake which the EU aims to ensure.

First of all, we may consider the legislative approach.

The harmonization of legal rules is indispensable to realize an efficient single European market. In this respect, we are faced with a dilemma. In order to facilitate information and the criteria for comparison of products and services by consumers, it appears advisable to seek harmonization at maximum level. However, such harmonization inevitably does not progress beyond a modest level as a result of the fact that operators are subject to constraints and limitations.

In order to allow companies freedom to offer differential and improved conditions, it appears advisable to have minimal harmonization with optional areas entrusted to the individual Member States. But excessive diversification pre-supposes a consumer so highly aware—from a linguistic and technical point of view—as to be able to fully appreciate the differences and profit from the advantages.

A balanced solution could be articulated in two objectives:

(a) to attain maximum harmonization in the legal dimension, as regards terminology, concepts, legal devices (the latter objective is being pursued by the current initiatives for the drafting of a 'European Code of Private law', comprehensive also of the discipline of the provision of services, including financial services); and[22]

(b) to maintain a differential treatment for the forms of enhanced protection, compared to the minimum required threshold, as regards remedies and guarantees and a differential treatment, dictated by the requirements of the market, in respect of the economic contents regarding price, risks, advantages, etc.

From this perspective, it is pointless to refer to the rules of the conflict of laws, to the Brussels Convention and to the Rome Convention for the application of procedural and substantive rules. The competition among national statutes creates more obstacles than benefits.

By the same token, it is pointless to refer the discipline relating to the conclusion of a contract, or the rules of dispute resolution or of other contractual remedies, to the national statutes or the 'conventional' rules of the parties.

The presence of unfair terms and conditions in contracts implies the bringing of action by the consumers and their associations before the courts having jurisdiction, with a consequent work-load, for the judicial process (which appears to be overloaded in almost all Member States) and with a waste of money, time, and energy, which on the whole are damaging to the market, and to the individual investors. In the sector of financial markets it is more practical to prevent conflicts rather than trying to somehow remedy the same. By their inherent features, financial services and products are quite different from any other service or product, which can be replaced or repaired more easily; in any case, they imply a far higher economic incidence than the latter.

The remedies offered by alternative dispute resolution (ADR) are not comparable in all countries: in some countries, like the UK or Spain, these systems are advanced and fully operational, while in others, like Italy they are still in the fledgling phase. ADR constitutes a secure and useful device for the resolution of disputes, but it cannot resolve entirely the issues of the certainty of legal relations and speed.

[22] Hartkamp et al (eds) *Civil Code* (London 1998) 2nd rev and exp edn.

Nor do the codes of conduct, which the recent EC Directives render compulsory in all countries, appear to provide a complete solution. Every country has its own history and the English model, though it has been successfully exported, is not devoid of criticism. Codes of professional ethics are usually written by the operators themselves, and the control bodies normally do not envisage the inclusion of representatives of the users of the services.

Agreements between professionals' associations and those of consumers pursue important aims, but turn into a boomerang when a court has to examine conducts or terms which have been negotiated, and have therefore been approved by consumers' associations, and the court must take into account the evaluations that the interested parties, on both sides, have already performed.

3.2.6. The marketing of financial services on-line

Before providing the information to the consumer on the features of the service, many operators require the consumer who has accessed their site to illustrate his propensity for risk-taking, so as to guide him on the choice of products on offer. But in addition to this, usually before communicating the contractual terms and conditions, the consumer is requested to reveal his identity and his personal data with reference to the forms of payment. This is a risk which is imposed on the consumer, which is not required for the acquisition of statistical data, but for the appropriation of data which may be used in other ways.

Moreover, for unsolicited communications, the option between *opt-in* or *opt-out* systems, which is entrusted to the national legislatures is detrimental, because in a single market consumers must anyway be protected against aggressive practices.

The features of the information to be provided mandatorily by professionals—in a clear and comprehensible manner—which often are mentioned in the EC Directives are vague and imprecise: clarity can be replaced by technicalities, which have little to offer to the consumer; comprehensibility is not ensured by the use of terminology and expressions that vary from country to country.

The burden of proof in respect of compliance with the rules on mandatory information cannot be an optional subject entrusted to national legislatures, because the use of such a sophisticated and highly volatile technical means, such as the electronic system, implies uncertainties and difficulties which are coped with far more easily by the professional than by the consumer.

These are only borderline remarks, which may be more thoroughly analysed only after the approval of the definitive text of the Directive.

Taking previous experience into account, it is desirable that the Directive, once it is approved, can be updated and amended from time to time, bearing in mind what can be ascertained in the various countries, in respect of the ways in which it is applied and complied with.

4. LAW AND MORAL VALUES

4.1. THE MEANING OF 'NATURAL PERSON'

4.1.1. Will European constitutional law have an impact on the 'European Civil Code'?

To speak of a 'person' in the legal world is to invite the problems inherent in some very diverse concepts and meanings. Today we are accustomed to regard the person as dignified by his entitlement to fundamental rights, but we should not forget that the idea of a person, understood as a human being who is inherently the owner of rights and obligations, as the outcome of a long and eventful journey. A journey that has, so to speak, been the reverse of what one would rationally have expected. It would be reasonable for the fundamental rights (such as those of life, health, and liberty) to come first, and to be followed by political, then economic and then civil rights.

But if we follow the course of history, the idea of inherent rights, belonging to the person as such, comes into being in the 17th century; but in codes and statutes the rights that are the first to be asserted are economic, then civil, then political; and finally human or fundamental rights. And even here there are differences between the various concepts of the categories of rights of the person underlying the meta-legal (philosophical, sociological, and religious) views of the person, not to mention the differences in the concept of a right, or claim, and so on.

Since we have the concept 'legal subject' (*soggetto di diritto*) denoting those capable of holding rights, is it necessary also to have the concept of 'person' (*persona*) to organize legal relations? Why did the concept of 'person' begin to make its timid appearance in the 19th century and why is it only now that it has erupted into continental legal culture, to the extent of being regarded as essential to a model legal system that is democratic and inspired by the basic values of any civil society?

Terminology, as always, has a great deal to tell us about history and about the concepts that are reflected in the creation of legal rules and in the theoretical elaboration of legal categories. But the legal system of a country also offers useful pointers to an understanding of the spirit of its legal history.

In European private law, one of the most difficult tasks is to unify the concept of the person, that is, to discover convergence between those legal systems that explicitly focus on it—such as the French, German, and Italian legal systems—and those legal systems that presuppose it, but do not explicitly locate it as their foundation, as is the case with the common law. A brief summary of these concepts may be a useful means of explaining the stratification of these theories, their political tendencies, and their transpositions into legal terms in the course of legal history and of highlighting the way in which the concept of the person has become second nature to every civil code: not only the codes of the 18th and 19th centuries but also to a future European civil code.

Whatever meaning one prefers to assign to the expression 'European private law': whether it is a *convergence* of the national legal systems, according to the meaning proposed by Sir Basil Markesinis; whether it is a *common core* of the legal systems of the Member States, according to the meaning pursued by the 'School of Trento'; whether it consists of the results flowing from the *acquis communautaire*, as the researches of various study groups would have it; or whether it is the subject matter that Ole Lando and Hugh Beale, Christian von Bar, and their respective groups are attempting to *codify*:[1] inevitably the legal concept of 'person' must figure in any of these models. However, it is not an easy matter to identify a single definition that will satisfy all the learned legal writers involved in these research programmes. Moreover, in order to arrive at a worthwhile definition, it seems essential to consider private law and public law jointly in the European dimension. Since *convergence* is a matter of fact and the *common core* is a basic exercise to comparative law, it will be worth examining the question in more depth in the light of the other models of study.

The *acquis communautaire* does not treat the person as a single concept but fragments that concept according to the legal positions the person assumes in the context of legal relations between individuals. In other words, it treats the person as a citizen, a worker, a consumer, a saver, a user of the environment, and as the owner of personal data.[2] These are admittedly facets which, when reconstituted as if they were the tesserae of a mosaic, restore the image of the person. But, as has been pointed out in legal commentary, in the first phase of its formation the trend of the *acquis* was the achievement of the single market. It obeyed a functional logic, which was corrupted by the prevalence of economic interests over every other different kind of interest. Thus, the person was treated as *homo oeconomicus*, the manufacturer or recipient of goods, services, and capital. Taken in this reductive sense, the *acquis communautaire* has nevertheless been useful for the development of European Community law as also for

[1] For a survey of the meanings of 'European private law' see G Alpa 'European Private Law: Results, Projects, Hopes' in [2003] Eur Bus L Rev 379–403.

[2] In the now vast literature I would like to point out certain Italian contributions which have the merit of being systematic: Rossi (LS) 'I cittadini, gli stranieri', in Tizzano (ed), *Il diritto privato dell' Unione europea* (Torino 2000), I, 97–147; Livi et al '*I soggetti*', in Lipari (ed) *Trattato di diritto privato europeo* (Padova 2003) I, cap II, 293–603.

the development of some national laws, such as the Italian, in which the culture of consumer protection had not been particularly significant. One should add, however, that the *acquis communautaire* is now acquiring new goals, which are a long way from the functional logic either of the law or of economics, since the new European Union texts reflect the growing awareness in the national cultures of the meta-legal values relating to the person.

The plans for a European code or codes do not appear to contain any statement of the legal status of the person. They are dedicated to the drawing up of rules to harmonize and unify the laws of contract, of civil liability, of the other sources of obligations, and of single contracts relating to sales, services, personal guarantees, the transfer of property and insurance. Thus they remain in the domain of property and economics and are not concerned with the legal implications of the Constitution for Europe. They do not even lay down rules for the interpretation of the law that would form an explicit link between the text of the Constitution and the text of the Code. In other words, to the eyes of the continental legal commentator they show a major legislative deficiency. But how is one to remedy it?

Since in the continental legal culture the rules of the Constitutions prevail over all others, one is entitled to suppose that the same must hold good for the rules of the Constitution for Europe compared with all the other rules, principles, *frames, restatements,* or actual codes.

And one is also entitled to suppose that the same techniques should be used for linking and interpreting the rules of the Constitution for Europe and the other legal rules of lesser rank. This is the phenomenon known (even in Italy) as *Drittwirkung.*

The principle that the rules of Constitutions are directly applicable to legal relations between individuals has now gained acceptance and cannot be given up. Similar phenomena have shown themselves even in those countries, such as the United Kingdom, which do not have a written Constitution but have introduced a law on Human Rights.[3] Will the application of the Constitution(s) be vertical or horizontal? Will uniform methods or a variety of methods be used?

The question directly affects the legal boundaries of the person, who has a legal face in the (draft) Constitution for Europe and ought to have a face also in the European civil codes.

But we should not overlook the fact that the constitutional dimension of the person involves also another phenomenon: it requires interpretation certainly, but an interpretation that is 'axiological', or based on value judgments.

[3] The Human Rights Act 1998.

In Continental Europe, the Constitutions not only fulfil the function of dictating the political, administrative, and legal organization of a country, they not only enshrine a list of rights of the person, but they fulfil another important function: they constitute for the interpreter of the law a list of values from which he must take his inspiration in the interpretation and application of the law. A judge, who is an interpreter of the law, must take account of these values at all times; and when he considers that the law to be applied is in conflict with them, he has a twofold choice: either he must bend the meaning of the law to achieve an 'adjusted' interpretation, adjusted, that is, to the rules of the Constitution, or he must refer the question of the legitimacy of the legal provision to his (own) constitutional court. The list of Constitutional values acts as a guide to the interpretation of the law.

In this way, Constitutions have also a didactic function: the construction of the science of law, of legal reasoning, of the elaboration of the fundamental principles on which a legal system is based, finds in the Constitution an immediate, certain and necessary reference. And if the Constitution for Europe (like almost all the Continental Constitutions) enumerates the values of the dignity of the person, equality and solidarity, likewise these values permeate legal relations between individuals through the application of the law.

The Constitutional aspect of legal relations between individuals thus affects the way in which the drafts of a European civil code should be drawn up. This effect can be seen at various levels: (i)in the text, with its laying-down of rules about the person; (ii) in the content, with its provision of rules to ensure that proper attention is paid to the values of the person; and (iii) in the interpretation, in which the rules of the Codes are adapted to the values enshrined in the Constitution.

This means that the rules of the Codes should not become entrenched behind the individual aspect of the person but must also deal with his social aspect. This prospect concerns all the areas of private life and in particular the area of contract law.

But the rules of contract law also cannot escape a value based interpretation, nor can they express only choices of a technical nature, asserted to be 'neutral', nor can they express only an individualistic (and thus egotistical) conception of relations between individuals. This conception, dictated as it was by the rules of the market, characterized the statutory codes of the 19th century, but was called into question in the 20th and no longer seems appropriate to the 'codes' of the new millennium.

In the final decades of the 20th century, constitutional law—especially Italian and German—showed evidence of the necessity of considering the values pertaining to the person in the contractual relation, when the person is placed in a position of inequality with the other contracting party.

Memorable judgments on the dignity of the person have ratified limitations to that freedom of contract that would be the means of violating this fundamental value.[4] And even in the case law of the lower courts' decisions on the merits and on legitimacy there are judicial pronouncements which, applying the principles of good faith, mutuality or balance between performances, public order, just cause and abuse of the law, tend to guarantee the values relating to the person, which are assured by a real 'contractual justice' which takes its inspiration from the principle that goes with dignity, namely the principle of solidarity.[5]

Now it is precisely the drawing-up European civil codes that would make it possible to make use of provisions that would be the same for all and that would explicitly be able to link the values of the person to the control of the financial transaction achieved by means of the contract.

But this is a new chapter in the process of the integration of the European Union and its configuration and destiny are still to be explored. It is sufficient to have summarized the long history and development of the concept of the person, to see how the European dimension—starting with the process of the constitutionalization of private law which has been seen in some national experiences—is a determining factor in the modernizing elements being added to the European Civil Codes. The process encounters many problems, among which are the origin of the person and the now received concept of 'life'. It is a prospect in which legal definitions overlap with ethical, social, and political.

4.1.2. *The individual in the Civil Codes of (Member) States: the 'legal subject'* (soggetto di diritto)

The civil codes of the 19th and 20th centuries generally start with provisions relating to the natural person, which are followed, in many cases, by provisions concerning the legal person. Even a 'model code' intended to be used in the European context should therefore proceed in that way, both for the sake of good order and because a code governing relations between individuals cannot exclude a description of the legal position of the *person*. Portalis (1746–1807), in his introduction to the rules contained in the Napoleonic Code, stressed the fact that the Code was centred on the individual and dedicated to him. His admonition is still valid today. To deal with the person in legal terms means establishing when a being is a 'person', when his life begins and when it ends, when the person can take valid legal actions, and so on. It is clear, moreover, that the conception of the person

[4] Markesinis et al *The German Law of Obligations, Vol 1, The Law of Contracts and Restitution,* (Oxford 1997) ch 1.

[5] Alpa and Bessone (eds) *Il Contratto in generale, vol 1, Il Contratto e i fenomeni negoziali* (Turin 1991) ch 1.

varies according to the epoch and the cultural and political climate sustaining the law.

Even the legal concept of the person must therefore be placed in its historical context. For Portalis, apart from statements of a general nature, the person was a '*citoyen*', he was the owner, the contracting party, the individual responsible for the unlawful act, the merchant.

It is with Pufendorf that we discover the essence of the person in his *human dignity*, that characteristic feature that must be recognized in every individual, whatever his social role. However, in contrast with Holmes and Grozio, Pufendorf does not justify, but condemns slavery. His ideas haunt and pervade French legal culture, which becomes a real trigger for the re-establishment of civil law.

In the same period in which Pufendorf wrote his seminal work on the law of nature and of peoples (published in 1672) Domat wrote his *Loix civiles*, which was not published until 1689.

Domat can be taken as a prototype of the model of legal reasoning as to the conception of the person (Lib Prel, tit II, section II). He divides the state of the person—that is, the complex of *qualities* of a human being—into the natural and the civil. The *natural* state pertains to the sex, birth, and age of the person; the *civil* state on the other hand is determined by the 'arbitrary laws' of men; it springs either from the concepts of status created by the Roman legal tradition (of liberty, citizenship, and family) or from local laws. In France he considers the division of persons into noble and low-born, ecclesiastical, citizens and plebeians, free or in servitude, the latter however not being a condition of a person but linked to his home or the nature of his assets.

While admitting that there are no slaves in France, Domat describes their condition according to Roman law. Even as late as 1796, in an Italian language edition of his *Loix civiles* published in Naples in that year, there is a commentary on the pages where he states that in the Kingdom of the Two Sicilies there are not known to be any slaves except the Turks who have been 'taken in the act of piracy'; they can be sold but their free circulation is legally permitted only within the borders of the Kingdom; they can be freed; but even when freed they cannot cross the borders without royal authority, on pain of being again enslaved.[6] Although it is remarkable, Domat's conception—to the eyes of legal commentators of today—is not without defects.

Several flaws are noticeable in his conception of natural law: the first is the confusion of the laws of nature with civil laws or legislation; the second is the separation of natural from civil law; the third is the idea that the

6 *Le leggi civili nel loro ordine naturale di Giovanni Domat, avvocato del Re in Clermont*, translated into Italian from the French (3rd edn Naples 1796) 188.

social status cannot be modified. More precisely: birth out of wedlock—with the attendant acquisition of the status of 'bastard' limiting the rights of succession—should not be considered as a condition deriving from nature. It is obvious that the natural fact of birth does not confer any distinction as to the inherent rights of the person, except that of equality. In Domat's assessment, the legal construction of the person seems to be a distillation of categories, prejudices, and social conditioning, which codify *objective* inequalities. It thus consists in an interpretation of the external data in accordance with preconstituted models. It does not distinguish that which is called natural from that which is superimposed on nature; or rather, it attributes to that which is called 'natural' a selective function, apparently carried out according to the canons of preconceived social convictions.

One cannot understand therefore how the distinction between the laws of nature and civil laws can be drawn. Domat describes first what he calls natural laws and juxtaposes them with civil laws, which are indeed 'arbitrary'; but he does not say that the former are better than the latter, that they constitute the ideal model of the latter or be its corrective.

Finally, the notion of status, which is drawn from Roman law—where Domat laments the absence of a definition—is not clarified as to its origins and its causes. Status is not regarded by him as a legal instrument, a social selector, a mainstay of society; but rather as a fact of nature, impressed on the natural order and therefore coming from the Creator who imposed this order on the world.

To sum up, the cornerstones of the construction of the concept of the *person* in the past (Roman law, medieval law, natural law, and pre-Napoleonic civil law) are the results of hypostases or anti-historical operations: anachronisms to which the legal commentator harks back in order to justify primacies, immunities, and privileges. Tradition is used to justify the present and to argue for the need for its continuity with the past; in other words, to engage in operations whose ideological orientation is not made plain.

The fact that in some national legal traditions the concept of the person is codified does not therefore mean that individuals' rights are protected; nor does it postulate the superiority of those national traditions that contain rules and treatises on the person over those that have none. It is the results of the application of such rules and treatises that count.

Nor should one overemphasize the conceptions of the person that emerge from the Codes. As stated above, in the Napoleonic Code the person is treated in his capacity as owner, and in the *Code de Commerce* in the role of *marchand.*

The Austrian Civil Code of 1811, whose first chapter is dedicated to the law of the person, specifically to the rights relating to social status and interpersonal relations, includes certain rules which represent the cornerstones of 17th-century 'natural law'. Paragraph 15 relates to the rights of the person in connection with his social status, to inter-personal relations and to the status of the family; paragraph 16 refers to the 'personality', acknowledges that every human being has 'innate rights' and abolishes slavery or ownership in a human being; paragraph 17 presumes rights to extend except where there is evidence that they have been restricted; and paragraph 18 acknowledges that everyone has—subject to the conditions laid down by the law—the capacity to acquire rights. The Code does not say what the natural rights are 'or that they are to be apprehended by the light of reason alone' but at least it gives one to understand that a human being—because he is a person—cannot be the subject of rights and thus preserves his quintessential freedom. This Code, however, is to be regarded not so much as a forerunner of the modern theories of the person but rather as the mirror of an antique society, poorly adapted to the economic needs of a modern industrial society.

A century later, the Swiss Civil Code seems to be an updated version of the Austrian Code. It does not mention natural rights but, in contrast to the Napoleonic Code and the German Civil Code, which allude to the person only in the title but do not make it the subject of pronouncements, it opens with a proclamation of the universality of civil rights.

It should not escape us, however, that apart from the rhetoric of the Civil Codes of the past, the person is encapsulated in apparently neutral formulae and in formal categories. The Civil Codes reflect the needs of a bourgeois society which only considers those persons subject to the law (*soggetti*) who are economically prosperous, legally free, who undertake reciprocal obligations on a level playing field, according to the rules of an individual ethics, and whose legal relations are symbolized and to a large extent also actually realized in accordance with the model of the individual contract. The legal order, like the economic order, has the task of guaranteeing the *person* the *maximum freedom* consistent with the freedom of every other person *sui iuris*. But the person as such has validity in the world of law only insofar as he fulfils a social role.

4.1.3. Remarks on the English common law

The common law does not offer a systematic picture of the discipline of the person, treated as such, but irregular facets of it. In the legal literature one does not find manuals or treatises or even sections of works dedicated to the 'law of persons', except in texts dealing with Roman law. One speaks about the person (*natural person*) in the manuals dealing with individual areas or aspects of private law, but these are only incidental descriptions. On the subject of contract law, there are the rules as to natural capacity and the contracts of minors; in family law, legal relations between parents and children or between spouses; in the law relating to legal medicine and bioethics, the rules relating to birth and death, the embryo and the foetus; in the law of torts, the protection of certain rights that in continental jurisdictions form part of the discipline of the person since they relate to his attributes, that is, the 'rights of the personality' such as honour and reputation (expressed in the common law by way of libel, slander, defamation), confidentiality (expressed as privacy), and the integrity of the person or his right to remain whole (expressed in the common law system as personal injury). In other words what comes to the fore is the assessment of damage to rights and the remedies offered to their owner in satisfaction.

This sphere of rights borrows its rules both from civil and from constitutional law. And it is interesting to note that these rights have received a new impetus in England from the debate on citizenship and on the rights of minorities, which debate has been extended since the Human Rights Act was passed in 1998 and came into force in the year 2000.

The English 'law of the person', therefore, does not have its roots in private but in public law. This can be seen in John Austin's philosophical work entitled *The Province of Jurisprudence Determined* of 1832,[7] where he deals with the natural (single or individual) person only as a member of a group or body, so that the person is perceived as an individual who, together with other members of the group to which he belongs or of which he is a member, contributes to the formation of the will of the group, whether this is a company or Parliament itself.[8]

The approach of Buckland and McNair[9] is more realistic. They confirm the impression of the civilian, starting their chapter on the subject—and it is no accident that the subject is explained from the viewpoint of legal territoriality and personality—with the unequivocal statement: 'the rubric "persons" is of comparatively small importance in our law, since the law is territorial and every subject of the State is a citizen of it.'

Other authors, on the other hand, following the methodology of the current institutional manuals of Roman law, adopt the civil law categories. This is shown in the studies of the Roman roots of modern law:[10] they start with the origin of life and its end, consider the *imbeccillitas sexus*, the role of the minor and the legal position of the unborn child.

[7] Cambridge (1995) 126 ff.

[8] According to Stein it is possible to identify common characteristics in the common law and civil law in the law relating to persons, which are due to the promulgation of canon law in England; but apart from these faint echoes, it is the last two centuries that have drawn the European systems closer together, with the coming of the modern law modelled on the requirements of the industrial economy (op cit, pp 135–136).

[9] *Roman law and Common law* (Cambridge 1936) 20 ff.

[10] Watson, *Roman foundations of modern Law* (Oxford 1957) 1053 ff.

The Institutions of Justinian[11] are the starting point of the argument. Here, in addition to the classical arguments, it was an open question, whether a slave was a 'thing' (chattel) or a 'person'. The answer was 'both', because the slave was considered to be the *object* of rights (other people had rights over him) but to the extent that he was (also) a *person*, in late Byzantine law, influenced as it was by theology, he was 'a being with capacity for rights and duties'.[12]

There are therefore a wide gaps in understanding, between the concept and discipline of the person to be found in the models of the Civil Codes, the idea of the person in the common law, and the new needs of a modern society.

4.1.4. *From 'individual' to 'person': the charters of supra-national rights*

Legal identity is perceived by the common man, the bystander, the 'average person', as a complex of permissions and prohibitions laid down by the 'law'. In other words, the person as such is identified according to certain parameters, which correspond to the fundamental characteristics of a State, nation or social group. If one asks a passer-by what is the most striking legal aspect of national identity, the reply that immediately comes to his mind will be that component of the legal system that is sought to be defined in terms of *public law*. In order to simplify the translation of these considerations into archetypes, it is enough to think of the discrepancies between States based on socialism or free-trade, dictatorship or the rule of law, extended or limited representation (the latter may be in terms of census, literacy, caste, sex, etc), between States that are federal or unitary, monarchist or republican, religious or lay, that recognize collective or individual ownership, with matrimonial, monogamous or polygamous regimes.

It does not follow that the legal component that denotes the model of identification will also correspond to the opinions expressed by all those belonging to the community concerned; it may be shared only by a minority or only by a minority that has imposed itself on the majority.

After the Second World War two significant processes evolved in parallel: the emergence of fundamental rights acknowledged as belonging to the individual in the supra-national Charters and Conventions on Human Rights and the emergence of human rights acknowledged in some continental Constitutions. In both cases the problem arose, whether the rules concerning human rights were applicable to relations between individuals.

[11] V Lee *The Elements of Roman Law* (London 1956) 46 ff; the first edition is that of 1944.
[12] Nicholas *An Introduction to Roman Law* (Oxford 1991) 13 ff.

(a) The Universal Declaration of Human Rights

The basic text of which to enquire whether human rights can be linked with legal relations between individuals is the Universal Declaration of Human Rights, adopted and proclaimed by the General Assembly of the United Nations in 1948. Here one does not find, in the catalogue of human rights, a provision referring to contracts, or to the principle, which better expresses the power to undertake obligations (or not to undertake them), of *freedom of contract*. Looking at the letter of the law, therefore, the answer to the enquiry must be in the negative, since Article 2 of the Declaration provides that 'Everyone is entitled to all the rights and freedoms set forth in this Declaration'. Since freedom of contract is not specifically proclaimed, one must conclude that it does not constitute a fundamental right (or right of man, or human right, or inviolable right).

However, the interpreter of the law can fill these gaps (in a scientific sense, not in a political or evaluative sense) by bearing certain considerations in mind. Only some of these are listed below.

There is mention in the list, of freedom and equality (Article 1). Thus, one considers that these expressions relate to the public law position inherent in the relationship between the individual and authority, and not to private legal relations between individuals.

Then, there is a reference (in Article 2, paragraph 1) to the prohibition against discriminating against individual human beings on the grounds of sex or other criteria; in counterpoint to this prohibition is the entitlement to equal protection of the law, against discrimination (Article 7). The matter of discrimination directly affects the right to work and thus the contract of employment, since it relates to the equality of treatment of persons of the opposite sex or of different sexual orientations from those practiced by the majority, of persons belonging to ethnic or religious groups or professing political opinions or speaking languages different from those of the majority.

The right to life, liberty and security of person, and the prohibition against slavery and servitude (Articles 3 and 4), can also affect the contractual relationship: servitude and slavery relate to it and to marriage, at least when marriage is regarded as a contractual bond; life and security can come into consideration for those contracts in which life and security can be compromised or where the health, life or security of oneself or others is at risk. The right (in Article 6) to recognition as a person before the law can affect a contract wherever there are distinguishing criteria available, such as the name, even the ideal image, personal data collected by computer, etc.

The right to matrimonial freedom affects contracts where marriage is considered to be a contract (Article 16) and the same is true of freedom of association, which affects the contractual tie inherent in membership of an association (Article 20). Then the economic and social rights (Article 22) must be considered.

On this view, questions as to the identity of the fundamental human rights, the legal status of the person, and the applicability of the values enshrined in the Constitutions, to legal relations between individuals, overlap and give rise to a diversity of solutions,[13] as a consequence of our diverse cultures and legal systems. However, the direct applicability to legal relations between private individuals, of the provisions contained in the Universal Declaration of Human Rights, remains in doubt. The provisions seem rather to be meant to be used as reference models to evaluate the totality of the definition of the person, perceived as the owner of fundamental human rights.

(b) The European Convention on Human Rights (Convention for the Protection of Human Rights and Fundamental Freedoms (Rome, 4.IX.50 as amended by Protocol 11)).

A no less problematic fate has been reserved for the European Convention on Human Rights. The question of the direct applicability of the rules of the Convention, which acknowledge and enshrine human rights, is still under discussion and this problem is linked to the recognition of the fundamental human rights in the European Community context.

In that context, discussion has centred on the interpretation of the new rules introduced by the 1999 Treaty of Amsterdam, which (in Article 1 paragraph 8) amended what is now Article 6 (formerly Article F) of the Treaty on European Union, to state that 'The Union is founded on the principles of liberty, democracy, respect for human rights and fundamental freedoms, and the rule of law, principles which are common to the Member States', thus stating these rights as principles of Community law and consequently making them directly applicable to relationships between individuals.

The case law of certain courts of the States that are signatories to the European Convention on Human Rights and of the Court of Justice of the European Communities, and the rules set out in the Treaty on European Union as amended by the Treaty of Amsterdam, seem to confirm the possibility of directly applying the Convention to legal relations between individuals, with particular reference to the safeguarding of private life, the right to abortion, and the right to freedom of expression.

The authors who have written about the problem refer to the question

[13] An interesting discussion of this view was offered by a conference organized by Alfredo Mordechai Rabello and Peter Sarcevic in Jerusalem in Sept 1994. See the proceedings now published by the Hebrew University (Jerusalem 1998).

of *Drittwirkung*, specifically in the German legal experience[14] and to the question whether the EC Directives are applicable only vertically or also horizontally. The idea has, however, been put forward that the German concept of indirect applicability is not the same as the applicability of its rights acknowledged by the European Convention on Human Rights.[15] In the former, reference is made primarily to determination of the content of the general clauses of good faith and public policy, whereas, in the context of the European Convention on Human Rights, this notion would refer rather to the theory of the positive obligations imposed on the public authorities, which is resolved in the liability of the State for breaches of the fundamental rights of individuals.

But it is not out of the question that one may speak of *direct* applicability of the European Convention on Human Rights to relations between individuals.[16] Many arguments have been adopted to this effect.

One of these is that it follows from the intention expressed by the States that signed and ratified the European Convention on Human Rights, that 'it is possible to impute obligations deriving from international law, to the States that have signed the Convention and ratified it for the individual';[17] another argument refers to the case law of the International Court of Justice at the Hague, according to which 'the fundamental rights of the person create obligations *erga omnes*';[18] reference is made to the intention expressed in the text of the Convention;[19] and in particular in the declarations in the Preamble.[20] It is also thought that the provisions of the Convention are an expression of public policy and therefore binding individuals;[21] and it is argued that—like the Universal Declaration of Human Rights—the provisions of the Convention are applicable both against the public authorities and against individuals.[22]

A literal interpretation of Article 1 of the Convention cannot be unequivocal, since the English expression, that the High Contracting Parties *shall secure* to everyone within their jurisdiction the rights and freedoms defined in the Convention appears stronger than the French expression *reconnaissent*

[14] D Spielhagen *L'effet potentiel de la Convention européenne des droit de l'homme entre personnes privées* (Brussel 1995) 26.

[15] MM Hahne *Die Drittwirkung in der Europeeischen konvention zum Schutz de menschenrechte und Grundfreiheiten* (Heidelberg 1973) 26.

[16] Spielmann, *L'effet* cit, 30.

[17] Ibid 31.

[18] M Forde 'Non-Governmental Interferences with Human Rights' *BYIL* (1985) 265.

[19] Ibid.

[20] MA Issn *La Convention et des devoirs de l'individu, La protection internationale des droits de l'homme dans le cadre européen* (Paris 1961) 190 ff.

[21] Spielmann. L'effet cit, 45, a commento della decisione dell'App. Bruxelles, 25 Feb 1988 (1989) JLMB 1132.

[22] WJ Ganshof van der Meersch *La Convention Européenne des Droits de l'Homme a-t-elle dans le cadre du droit interne une valeur d'ordre public?* (Bruxelles and Manchester 1968). See also D Fairgrieve, M Andenas, J Bell *Tort Liability of Public Authorities* (London 2003),

(shall acknowledge that they exist). Thus, different meanings can be given (and thus opposite solutions to the question of direct applicability) according as one ascribes more importance to the wider meaning of the English or the more restrictive meaning of the French.

Not all the provisions contained in the Convention are applicable to legal relations between individuals. Those which are certainly applicable, according to the proponents of direct applicability, are those concerning forced labour (Article 4), freedom to marry (Article 12), and the provisions as to fundamental freedoms. There is some dispute as to whether the provision on respect for private life is also directly applicable (Article 8); though in Italy the question is resolved by its application in the case law on the right to privacy.[23] It is generally thought that Article 1 of Protocol no 1 on the right to ownership and Article 14 of the Convention which provides the principle against discrimination are directly applicable.

In the case law of the countries that have ratified the Convention, learned legal writers point out a number of significant cases; though for obvious reasons these are quite rare.

Among the Belgian cases, reference is made to the decision of the Judge of Peace of Tubize who refused to execute a judgment ordering a mother with children in her care to vacate a dwelling house, because she was in difficult financial circumstances and could not have found adequate shelter in the winter;[24] to the judgment of the Court of Appeal of Brussels, which refused to suspend the power supply to a debtor on the grounds that it was a measure contrary to human dignity;[25] and to the judgment of the Civil Court of First Instance of Brussels, that a term in a contract providing that the losing party should pay all the costs of the other party, was contrary to public policy.[26] Other Belgian cases relate to the right to dismiss an employee for behaving in a manner contrary to the values upheld by his employer's organization. This question is well known in our own legal system as the safeguarding of the so-called orientation organization, whose right to dismiss employees for opinions, behaviour or religious beliefs incompatible with its own aims is under question.[27]

Among the Dutch cases, the significant ones are those concerning direct applicability to relationships of obligation. These are cases in which condi-

[23] See G Alpa and B Markesinis '*Il diritto alla privacy nell'esperienza di common law e nell'esperienza italiana*', Riv trim dir proc civ (1997) 417.

[24] Juge de paix de Tubize 27 Oct 1981, JJP (1982) 171, commented on by Spielmann *L'effet* cit. 45.

[25] App. Bruxelles, 25 Feb 1988 cit.

[26] Trib, Bruxelles, 23 Nov 1967 JT (1967) 741.

[27] In favour of the organization see, eg, Pret Roma 23 May 1994, Riv it dir lav (1995) 11, 624; Triti Roma 29 July 1987, Dir lav (1987) II, 501. In favour of the employee see, eg, Pret Milano 24 July 1987, Dir lav (1987) III, 498; Pret Milano 8 Jan 1980, Riv giur lav (1981) II, 205.

tions in letting contracts for buildings were held to be void because they discriminated against the lessee on the basis of ethnic origins, religious beliefs or nationality.[28]

The case law of the European Court of Human Rights in Strasbourg offers examples of direct application in the sector of the rights of the personality, while, with regard to relationships of obligation, the judgments are almost exclusively concerned with contracts of employment.[29]

The conclusion drawn by learned legal writers from the whole picture of these references, is not so much that the European Convention on Human Rights is directly applicable, as that it is *indirectly* applicable, and that this translates into the liability of the State to the individual who suffers the breach of a fundamental right in the context of a private legal relationship, or the obligation of the national judges to apply the law of the Convention to the legal relationships between individuals: this obligation becomes a *secondary positive obligation.*[30]

4.1.5. The concept of the person in the written Constitutions and in the EC legislation

With the Constitutions that followed the Second World War—in particular the Italian Constitution of 1948 and the German Basic Law of 1949—we see the transition from the notion of the individual perceived as the abstract subject whose rights are recognized to the notion of the 'person' per se, as such. The terminology used and the formulae which are the means to understanding this great innovation signal a major turning-point in continental legal culture. Article 2 of the Italian Constitution acknowledges and guarantees the inviolable rights of man, both as an individual and in the social formations in which his personality is exercised.

The Italian Constitutional Court has made extensive use of Article 2, often in conjunction with Article 3, which states the principle of equality. This is with regard to the fundamental freedoms, the right of freedom of association, freedom of thought, the rights of members of a family, and the right to health. The person has thus come to be understood not in the abstract, but as a real person with biological and social needs.

Similar and perhaps more significant, is the case law of the German Constitutional Court.

In the EC context there has been lengthy discussion as to whether the principles acknowledged in the national Constitutions already form a kind of European constitutional law. But there has also been discussion as to

[28] App Arnhem, 25 Oct 1943, NJ (1949) 331, 612, cit, Spielmann *L'effet* cit, 57.

[29] See the survey of cases cited for the various European countries by Spielmann, *L'effet* cit, 79.

[30] Così Spielmann *L'effet* cit, 88.

whether the fundamental human rights could be amalgamated into EC law and whether the EC should be a signatory to the European Convention on Human Rights so as to make them its own in a formal manner.

The question was resolved by the Opinion of 28 March 1996 given by the European Court of Justice in answer to the question whether signature by the EC of the European Convention on Human Rights was compatible with the EC Treaty.[31] The opinion made it clear that given the text of the EC Treaty then in force, the EC did not have competence to sign the Convention. Only an amendment to the text would make it possible, even though the judges considered that respect for human rights constituted a prerequisite for the legitimacy of the acts of the EC. [32] The opinion has been criticized but it has been remarked on the one hand that the classic fundamental human rights do not relate to EC law and on the other hand that the opinion would not prevent the drawing up of a *bill of rights* at EC level.[33]

It is important for our purposes to draw attention to the replacement first paragraph of Article 6 (formerly F) of the Treaty on European Union: 'The Union is founded on the principles of liberty, democracy, respect for human rights and fundamental freedoms, and the rule of law, principles which are common to the Member States.' (The first paragraph of Article F formerly read: 'The Union shall respect the national identities of its Member States, whose systems of government are founded on the principles of democracy.')

The new text seems not so much ambiguous as restrictive, despite the appearance that the new formulation reinforces respect for human rights in the EC context.

It has been pointed out that the new text has a noticeably political meaning, inasmuch as in Article 49 (formerly Article I 59) it makes the accession of new countries to the Union dependant on their respect for human rights as set out in Article 6. But it has been observed that the amendments that have been introduced 'fall short (. . .) of the expectations that had been growing on the subject'.[34]

Admittedly a procedure has been introduced (by Article 7) for the disciplinary sanction of States that persistently breach the principles that protect human rights in Article 6(1). But the procedure is exclusively within the competence of the Council of Ministers rather than the European Court of Justice. The Court of Justice may apply the principles of EC law which acknowledge the fundamental human rights implicitly; but it may not

[31] Opinion 2/94 of 28 Mar 1996, ECR (1996) I, 1759. The opinion was given on the basis of the Text of the 1992 Treaty of Maastricht.

[32] Thus para 34, of the Opinion cit.

[33] By L Betten and N Grief *EU Law and Human Rights* (London 1998) 120.

[34] A Tizzano *Il trattato di Amsterdam* (Padova 1998) 38.

appeal to an EC catalogue of such rights, nor do individuals have specific recourse directly to the Court for breach of their rights.[35]

On the other hand, certain rights of the personality are reinforced, such as the rights relating to personal data, certain rights in relation to access to the acts of the EC and the rights of consumers and savers.

4.1.6. The Charter of Fundamental Rights of the European Union ('the Charter') and the Constitution for Europe

When it first appeared, the Charter of Fundamental Rights of the European Union, approved at Nice in December 2000 ('the Charter') was considered, at least in the statements made by its proponents, as a text whose value and contents were purely *political*. In reality (in legal reality, that is: in the imaginary world of terms, concepts, instruments, and especially legal *symbols*) the process of institutional innovation has taken a different course. In the first months of examination and interpretation of the Charter, both the judges of the European Court of Justice and some national judges treated it as a document having legal effect. To use the words of an illustrious writer on constitutional law, Costantino Mortati, here too, a phenomenon of 'actual constitution' materialized at Community level. Already, therefore, the Charter acts as a list of values, a picture of general principles or programme of action for the EU *as if* it actually had legal effect. This function will be reinforced when the Constitution for Europe comes into effect.

This kind of reasoning, which uses formal arguments but contains implied political value judgments, is second nature to the Italian or German learned legal writer. In modern constitutional experience, however, there is no shortage of situations very different from this model. In France, the venerable Declaration of the Rights of Man originating in the Revolution is considered by most people to be a political document and the French Constitution as a legally relevant document which is intended only to delineate the institutional structure of the State. In the United Kingdom, a written text with the function of 'Bill of Rights' has been introduced with the Human Rights Act of 1998, in which the European Convention on Human Rights signed at Strasbourg in 1950 is reproduced with some mutilation; and the constitutional structure rests on the democratic tradition of the country, but has an habitual nature, not being entrusted to a written text. In the experience of almost all other countries, including the Italian, the (written) Constitutions consist of both the commandments of fundamental rights and provisions delineating the structure of the State.

[35] Tizzano *Il trattato* cit 41.

The Constitution for Europe is closer to the Italian and German models.

The draft presented by Giscard d'Estaing and the proposal signed in Rome in 2004 provide (in Article 2) a list of the European Union's values, including respect for human dignity, equality, and solidarity—the fundamental rights. These are the cornerstones of democracy, of the rule of law, and of tolerance.

In reality, Article 2 as formulated, might be sufficient to guarantee to all citizens the respect for the fundamental rights, but the incorporation of the Charter into the Constitution (in Part II) has the merit of listing all the rights of personality now acknowledged as belonging to individuals, distinguishing, where necessary, the rights acknowledged to belong to all from the rights only acknowledged to belong to European (EC) citizens.

The Constitution for Europe presented on 28 October 2003 thus gives a sufficiently clear response to the questions put in the Declaration of Laeken. Are we to consider that the response is full and complete?

Does the Charter and now the Constitution for Europe, enhance only the individual dimension of the person, treating him as a single entity who claims rights from the authorities, as was the case in the bourgeois codes of the 19th century, or does it also emphasize his social dimension, as many of the 20th century Constitutions do?

The Constitution for Europe maintains its focus on the social dimension of the rights of the person and of his social groupings. The mention of the principle of solidarity, already present in the Charter, enhances the social role of the person, and safeguards the collective interest and not only the egotistical, individualistic positions to which today's fashionable free market philosophy would otherwise inexorably lead.

In any case, the text could not be understood as a list of merely individual values closed to any social yearnings: human dignity is necessarily a value of *relating*, as also are *tolerance* and the *fundamental rights* (which include the right of freedom of association) and, it goes without saying, *democracy*, which cannot have, if understood in a modern sense, a merely monist dimension. But to be more precise even a *value* must be of a *relational* and *community* nature: a value has its citizenship in the awareness and life of a people only if it is shared and complied with, not because it is printed on paper.

Arguing from the idea that a 'right' is the product of the interrelation of sources of law, sources of case law and sources of learned legal commentary, the construct or syntagma *fundamental rights and relations between individuals* can be unpacked by bearing in mind: (i) the notion of 'fundamental rights', (ii) the notion of the social contract, (iii) the statements of judges who have posed the question and answered it in the affirmative (the problem exists and has a solution) or in the negative (the problem does not exist, or it does exist but has no solution), (iv) the trends in learned legal commentary, among which distinct tendencies can be discerned, to emphasize natural law (whether religious or non-religious), positive law (whether state-based or pluralist) or realistic law.

The expression *fundamental rights*, or *fundamental human rights* in this article is intended in the widest and most generic sense, to indicate the claims or freedoms acknowledged in international texts, in the texts of the national Constitutions, in judicial practice, in supranational practice, and so on. Similarly the term *legal relationship between individuals* is used generically, as of an obligation or promise freely expressed or as a contract giving rise to civil liability. Now, considering only the written texts most frequently used in the comparison, such as the Constitutions of the western countries and their civil codes, in addition to individual special laws and international conventions and treaties, one does not find an explicit legislative formula that specifically links 'fundamental rights' and 'legal relations between individuals'. However, the interpreter of the law can enquire as to whether it is possible to make this link on an interpretative level, whether the link has been made, and what the results have been.

The Charter, to some extent amplifies and updates the rights of the person. For example, it provides for a right to respect for private life (Article 7), which Italian case law had been construing on the basis of Article 2 of the Italian Constitution. This right—understood as the right to privacy—is not set out in the written Italian Constitution, but is the fruit of an interpretative process (of case law and learned commentary) which started in the 1960s. But the Charter adds to this right another right, pertaining to the protection of personal data (Article 8). This right was dawning in Italy and was ratified by the Law no 75 of 1996 on the protection of personal data, now the Consolidated Law on Personal Data (Legislative Decree 2003, no 196). To elevate this right to the level of the rights guaranteed by the Constitution is a further step towards a modern statute of the rights of the person.

In the same way the Charter, acknowledging the right to found a family (Article 9), goes beyond the dictate of the Italian Constitution, which treats the family as a natural group founded on marriage and acknowledges the importance of an actual family only by implication, as one of the social groupings in which the personality of the individual develops (Article 2 of the Italian Constitution). The Charter not only includes among the fundamental rights of the person the right to form a family not founded on matrimony, but is open to the acknowledgement of families formed of persons of the same sex, which is not yet the case under Italian law.

Likewise in terms of the principles of equality and non-discrimination (Articles 20–6) the Charter extends the rights of the person as acknowledged and guaranteed by the Italian Constitution, since it inserts in the list of rights a prohibition against discrimination based on colour, genetic features, birth, disability or sexual orientation.

In addition the Charter makes some rights explicit which only an imaginative interpretation could find in the Italian Constitution, such as the rights of the child (Article 24), of the elderly (Article 25), and of persons with disabilities (Article 26). Then in addition there are the provisions relating to protection of the environment (Article 37) and consumers (Article 38).

For protection of the environment the Italian Constitution already has a provision (Article 9, which mentions the countryside or landscape, which by means of an wide interpretation has been applied so as to restrict the rights of the landowner and compensate the loss and damage suffered by the individual person and by the community as a result of pollution. But the word 'consumer' is not known to the Italian Constitution, and is a recent acquisition to the vocabulary of Italian lawyers, except in the judgments of the courts at every level, as a result of EC interventions on the matter.

This process, which is moving away from the neutral concept of the individual person as legal subject (*soggetto di diritto*) towards a conception of the individual as a person deserving protection per se, is not complete.

The problems relating to the beginning of human life and its quality have still not been resolved in a uniform manner. Can the embryo be regarded as a 'person'? And does the embryo, or the foetus, have the right to be born healthy?

Only a few scraps of legislation expressed in the EC texts can be called upon to provide an answer to these disturbing questions. The Charter does give some guidance on the matter: Article 2 refers to the right to life, but this right is reserved to the individual or 'everyone' (not the embryo); the Charter prohibits 'eugenic practices' and 'human reproductive cloning' (Article 3); and Article 35 guarantees a high level of protection for human health. But how are we to use these provisions to answer the two questions posed above?

These questions can only properly be answered in greater depth and in another chapter, which cannot be provided here. But in any case, a modern civil code cannot neglect these aspects relating to human life.

4.1.7. Conclusion

The foregoing pages pose questions rather than making assertions; but it is hoped that they serve to demonstrate that the concept of the person in the European civil codes cannot be ignored and that this concept must not be confined to private law because it is so closely linked with the values deriving directly from constitutional law. Thus, the making of European private law for the future cannot but go hand in hand with the making of European public law.

4.2. THE USE OF EMBRYOS IN ARTIFICIAL PROCREATION

4.2.1. Is the embryo a person?

To provide a complete definition of the person it is necessary to identify the moment at which, from a legal point of view, the person comes into existence.

The year 2004 is an important one for Italian legal writers. It is the 20th anniversary of the publication of the Warnock Report,[36] which started the debate in Italy about artificial procreation (or assisted conception)[37] and posed the problem of the need to define the legal status of the embryo and to legislate to protect it.[38] It is also the year in which the Law on Medically Assisted Procreation (*Norme in materia di procreazione medicalmente assistita)* (Law no 40 of 2004), was passed after troubled debates by Parliament, constituting a complete departure from the intentions of the draft consolidated Law presented to the previous legislature and indeed from actual practice. The new Law contains important rules on the uses of the embryo[39] which, in a sense, provide a kind of constitution or statute of its rights for this 'entity' which is so difficult to define.

[36] The Warnock Report, drafted by the Commission on Human Fertility and Embryo Research, 1984, provided a framework of 'recommendations' reported in *Procreazione artificiale e interventi nella genetica umana,* Atti del Convegno di Verona 2–4 October 1986 (Padua 1997) 357; its story is recounted by its Chairperson, Mary Warnock in her Introduction to *A Question of Life* (London 1985). Mary Warnock, now Baroness Warnock, has continued her involvement in the problems of bioethics and the legislation dealing with the techniques of artificial procreation. She has published explanatory books and in some ways has altered her original opinions: see *Making Babies: Is there a Right to Have Children?* (London 2002).

[37] This debate came to a head at a conference in Genoa, of which the proceedings were collected by G Ferrando in *La procreazione artificiale tra etica e diritto,* (Padua 1987); see also Ferrando's earlier *Procreazione artificiale: verso una regolamentazione per legge,* in *Pol dir* (1986) 501 ff. The contributions of Stefano Rodotà defined the boundaries of the debate, made intellectuals think, and stimulated legal writers to form opinions: *Per un nuovo statuto del corpo umano,* in *Bioetica,* edited by Di Meo and Mancina (Roma-Bari 1989), 41 ff; *Questioni di bioetica* (Roma-Bari 1993); *Tecnologia e diritti,* (Bologna 1995). During the same years see A Trabucchi '*Procreazione artificiale e genetica umana nella prospettiva del giurista*', in Riv dir civ (1986) I 495 ff; Patti *Verità e stato giuridico della persona,* ibid (1988) I 231 ff; Ascone e Rossi Carneo *La procreazione artificiale: prospettive di una regolamentazione legislativa nel nostro paese* (Naples 1986). A comprehensive reconstruction of the situation is offered by Lenti *La procreazione artificiale. Menoma della persona e attribuzione della paternità* (Padua 1993). On the subject of biotechnological research the essays collected and introduced by CM Mazzoni *Etica della ricerca biologica* (Florence 2000).

[38] See especially the proceedings of the conferences organized by Politeia *La bioetica. Questioni morali e politiche per il futuro dell'uomo,* edited by M Mori (Milan 1991); *Quale statuto per l'embrione umano. Problemi e prospettive* ed M Mori (Milan 1992); and the essays collected in *Bioetica. Rivista interdisciplinare* (1993) 1.

[39] On the debate in the Italian parliament and the questions that preceded the text of the Law as definitively approved, there is an abundant literature, mostly circumstantial, published in the press and on the Internet; but see the essays collected in *Testimonianza. I diritti dell'embrione* (2000) no 412.

Consulting the calendar and making the conceptual link between the two events is not merely a feat of memory. Between the two dates is the whole history of the biomedical, ethical, and legal debate in Italy, which got under way with a lively, open and fascinating discussion—full of hope—in expectation of a legal enactment that would be satisfactory to all. It then dragged on through doubts and second thoughts, as well as through many attempts at regulation, with more and less support; but few people would have imagined that the outcome (at least as it appears to be today) would be Law no 40 of 2004. The new Law, of which an analytical description follows below, prohibits the provision of assisted procreation to single women and reserves the procedure to heterosexual married or unmarried couples; it prohibits the use of the semen or egg-cells of donors, the creation of multiple embryos, and the use of embryos or gametes in order to achieve aims not connected with procreation, eg to cure illnesses, as well as their use for commercial purposes or cloning.

4.2.2. Legislation and solutions throughout Europe

Only seven years ago, surveys of assisted procreation in Europe listed Italy among those countries in which techniques were practiced to reach the goal of giving a child to people who could not have one naturally. Many countries, Italy not among them, had, according to these surveys, introduced legislation to govern the means of reaching this goal. The United Kingdom, the Netherlands, and Spain had enacted legislation to permit a woman of an age at which women are usually capable of procreation to subject herself to treatment for assisted conception. Our own situation was one of fact, not law, in which the donation of the gametes and egg-cell, and 'micromanipulation' of the gametes were allowed. Italy did not, according to the surveys, practice the selective reduction of fertilized embryos for the purpose of preventing multiple births. Nor did Italy permit research on embryos as an end in itself, but it permitted both the preservation of embryos by freezing them and the destruction of supernumerary embryos.

The present situation in Europe generally is varied.

The German model (governed by the *Gentechnikgesetz* of 1990) is apparently restrictive: the formation of embryos is only permitted for procreative purposes. The principle of human dignity prevails and applies from the moment of fusion of the nuclei of the cells of the fertilized ovocyte; the embryo is defined as the 'human ovarian cell which from the moment of the fusion of the nuclei is capable of development'.

The English model by contrast is apparently permissive: in the Human Fertilisation and Embryology Act 1990[40] the embryo is regarded as an

[40] On which see Douglas, in *Family Law* (1991) 110 ff.

object (rather than a subject) and the logic of ownership is applied to it, so that donation of gametes is permitted subject to the consent of both donors. This contrasts with United States case law, in which there are judgments (such as *Davis* v *Davis*)[41] in which the embryo is regarded as an 'unborn child'. In any event, less rigid restrictions are imposed under the English legislation: the embryo can be formed for purposes other than procreation, under a licence for research (as set out in Schedule 3 of the Act), in order to promote advances in the treatment of infertility, to increase knowledge about the causes of congenital diseases, or about the causes of miscarriage, to develop more effective techniques of contraception, to develop methods for detecting the presence of gene or chromosome abnormalities in embryos before implantation, and for such other purposes as may be permitted by future secondary legislation.

The French model on the other hand appears to be a compromise; human dignity is protected from the beginning of life (Article 16 of the Civil Code); forming embryos for purposes other than procreation is forbidden; all forms of commercialization of and experimentation on embryos are prohibited (Law 94-654 of 1994); the conception of embryos by means of *in vitro* fertilization is forbidden; the keeping of them must not exceed five years; subject to consent, the embryo may be used for the artificial insemination of other couples; the couple need not be legally married; the mixing of seminal liquids is forbidden; and medical operations on the embryo are subject to authorization.[42]

The fundamental principles common to all these models are that:

(i) the embryo must not be treated as a *thing*,
(ii) the embryo's identity as an individual precludes any operation upon it that would be unthinkable for a human being.

4.2.3. *Principles and guidelines laid down by the European institutions*

A further step towards the convergence of these models has been taken by the intervention of the European institutions. They have been engaging in discussions between themselves and with the various national legislatures and have been attentive to the organizations that have been formed and mobilized in each national civil society. Essentially, they have been trying to act together in this field. The Council of Europe and the European Parliament have concerned themselves particularly with the embryo.

In its Recommendation no 1046 of 1986, the Council of Europe set itself the problem of restricting the use of embryos, permitting their diagnostic,

41 *Davis v Davis*: Case no E-14496, Circuit Court for Blount, Tennessee, 10 Aug 1989.
42 On this point see Carusi '*Le nuove leggi francesi sulle biotecnologie*' in Riv dir Civ (1996) II 537 ff.

therapeutic and scientific uses, and excluding industrial or commercial uses, as being contrary to human dignity. This principle was repeated in its Recommendation no 1100 of 1989.

The European Parliament expressed the same view, when dealing with the techniques of genetic engineering and *in vivo* and *in vitro* artificial insemination in its Resolution of 16 March 1989; in another Resolution of 28 October 1993 it expressed an opinion against the cloning of human embryos; and by three further Resolutions it expressed itself, again restrictively, on human cloning (on 15 January 1998, 30 March 2000, and 7 September 2000). Resolutions are merely persuasive, but Member States are invited to follow their prescriptions. In any case, a clear principle emerges from these Resolutions: in addition to all the restrictions concerning the protection of human dignity, the use of embryos is to be permitted only if it is made for the purposes of procreation or for *diagnostic*, *therapeutic* or *scientific* purposes.

Subsequently the Council of Europe drew up a Convention 'for the protection of Human Rights and the dignity of the human being with regard to the application of biology and medicine: Human Rights and Biomedicine'. It was adopted in Strasbourg on 19 November 1996 and opened for signature at Oviedo on 4 April 1997.

This text is particularly important and worth examining in detail.

The Convention consists of a Preamble in which the precursors of the new legislation are mentioned: namely The United Nations' Universal Declaration of Human Rights of 1948, The Convention for the Protection of Human Rights and Fundamental Freedoms of 4 November 1950, The European Social Charter of 18 October 1961, the International Covenant on Civil and Political Rights and the International Covenant on Economic, Social and Cultural Rights of 16 December 1966, the Convention for the Protection of Individuals with regard to Automatic Processing of Personal Data of 28 January 1981, the Convention on the Rights of the Child of 20 November 1989 and Recommendation 1160 on the preparation of a Convention on Bioethics of 1991. The Preamble stresses the need for international cooperation in biology and medicine and the urgent necessity to guard against the dangers to human dignity arising from the misuse of biology and medicine.

In the text of the Convention, certain general principles are laid down, including that the interests and the welfare of the human being must prevail over the sole interest of society or science (Article 2); a code of conduct must be established for medical treatment (Articles 3–9) including provisions as to the consent of the person to be treated; the right to respect for one's private life in relation to information about one's health is asserted (Article 10); and in the context of the human genome there is a prohibition against discrimination based on genetic characteristics; there are measures to safeguard persons volunteering, and those unable to volunteer, to be used in scientific research; and there are rules on the extraction of organs for the purposes of transplants and a prohibition against making a profit from the use of any part of the human body.

These and other provisions are manifestly aimed at the protection of human dignity and rights.

Among these, Article 18 makes two provisions about the embryo. One is that where the law permits *in vitro* research on embryos, the law must ensure adequate protection for the embryo. The other prohibits the creation of embryos for the purposes of research.

The Convention thus provides a general framework within which the signatory States are to make their enactments;[43] and to some extent it takes account of the various legislative provisions that have been gradually enacted in the principal European States.

Among the latter it is worth noting the French intervention, which is set out in two measures: Law no 94-653 of 29 July 1994, renewing Articles 16.16-1 to 6-12 of the French Civil Code) and Law no 94-654, enacted on the same date, on the use of the human body. The former Law confirms the dignity of the person and the respect due to any human being from the beginning of life; it affirms the right of each person to his own body; and restricts operations on the person and the human species. The second is concerned with transplants and assisted conception. A lively debate has started among French legal writers about these innovations.[44]

On 6 July 1998, the European Parliament and the Council of Ministers approved Directive 98/44/EC on the legal protection of biotechnological inventions—which also relates to the human embryo. In the recitals it specifies that 'patent law must be applied so as to respect the fundamental principles of safeguarding the dignity and integrity of the person' (recital 16) and that in the then state of patent law 'the human body, at any stage of its formation or development including germ cells, or the simple discovery of one of its elements . . . cannot be patented'. In recital 17 it acknowledges the need to encourage research and medicinal production by means of the patenting system. In Article 5 it proceeds to provide that 'an element isolated from the human body or otherwise produced by a technical process, including the sequence or partial sequence of a gene, may constitute a patentable invention'; but in Article 6 (since patenting implies commercial exploitation) that such inventions 'shall be considered

[43] It is interesting to note that as of Sept 2004, the UK and Germany have not signed the Convention; and France and Italy have signed it but not ratified or brought it into force.

[44] For the debate among French legal writers see, eg, B Mathieu '*La dignité de la personne humaine: quel droit? quel titulaire?*' in Dalloz (1996) chron, 281; C Philippe '*La viabilité de l'enfant nouvaeau-né*' ibid, *chron*, 29; J Hauser '*Un nouveaù-né: l'enfant conventionnelle?*' ibid, chron, 181; Ch Byk, *La recherche sur l'embryon humain*, in *Sem. jur* (1996) 3949.

unpatentable where their commercial exploitation would be contrary to *ordre public* or morality'; and that certain processes, including processes for cloning human beings, or the uses of human embryos for industrial or commercial purposes, shall be considered unpatentable.

By another Resolution of 7 September 2000 on Human Cloning, the European Parliament specified that human dignity and the value of each person is and should be the constant aim of the legislative activity of the Member States; and that medical research resulting from advances in knowledge of human genetics is necessary but must be carried on within rigorous ethical and social limits. It refers to a proposal by the UK Government to permit therapeutic cloning, which involves the creation of human embryos solely for research purposes. It calls upon all Member States to reaffirm the ban on patenting or cloning human beings; it urges the use of stem cells taken from adult subjects; and it calls for the adoption of techniques of human artificial insemination that do not produce an excess number of embryos.

Finally, the Charter of Fundamental Rights of the European Union, approved at Nice in December 2000, now the European Constitution (Article II-3) includes in its provisions as to the 'right to integrity of the person' a prohibition against 'making the human body and its parts as such a source of financial gain' and a prohibition against 'the reproductive cloning of human beings'.

Thus there are clear and precise restrictions upon the production, use and patenting of embryos.

But it is equally clear that the production of embryos—albeit not in excessive numbers—is permitted by the EC authorities for diagnostic, therapeutic, and scientific research purposes.

However, the new Italian legislation on the status of the embryo does not follow this process of convergence. The Italian model is not informed by the principles of freedom and responsibility. It is informed by restrictions and prohibitions.

4.2.4. *The new Italian Law*

The Italian Law of 19 February 2004 (no 40) contains 'Rules governing medically assisted procreation' and is not actually intended to regulate the legal status of the embryo. Its purpose is rather to 'enable the solution of reproductive problems deriving from human sterility or infertility'. The embryo is one of the means of solving these problems, which could also be solved in other ways. But the Law is all about a particular method, because in order to reach the goal that the Law aims to achieve, it is necessary first of all to create an embryo, then to process it, establish the manner of its processing, as well as to establish who must take the decisions inherent in the processing, and finally to decide the fate of any embryos that have not been used.

The Law gives some answers to these questions but does not resolve all of them.

The whole of Chapter VI is devoted to the embryo; but it consists mainly of prohibitions, so that the protection of the embryo appears indirectly. There is a prohibition against experimentation on embryos (Article 13 paragraph 1); a prohibition against research not intended for the protection of the health and for the development of the particular embryo that is the subject of the processing for the purposes of fertility (Article 13 paragraph 2); a prohibition against producing embryos for the purposes of research and experimentation or any purposes not specifically permitted by the Law (Article 13 paragraph 3 letter a)); a prohibition against any form of selection of embryos for eugenic purposes (Article 13 paragraph 3 letter b)); a prohibition against cloning by transfer of the nucleus, and against premature fission etc of an embryo even for the purposes of procreation (Article 13 paragraph 3 letter c)); a prohibition (Article 14 paragraph 1) against the preservation of embryos by freezing (except temporarily, for reasons of a sudden crisis in the health of the prospective mother, pursuant to Article 14 paragraph 3) and against the destruction of an embryo (Article 14 paragraph 1); and a prohibition against the production of supernumerary embryos (beyond the number three) (Article 14 paragraph 2).

Although the embryo is mentioned many times in this Law, 'embryo' is nowhere defined: one has therefore to refer to its technical, scientific definition to be able to assign a meaning to the term.

From the mere enumeration of the above prohibitions, it is apparent that this is not a well-organized piece of legislation: not only is the embryo not defined as an entity, or even treated as equivalent to a person (except perhaps in passing, in Article 1 paragraph 1, where the rights of the '*concepito*', the 'subject' or 'person' conceived, are referred to), but the rights that the title of Chapter VI would lead one to expect—'Measures to protect the Embryo'—are not defined in it.

The irrationality of this Italian Law on assisted procreation emerged only weeks after it had been passed, in a case brought before the Court of First Instance of Catania.[45] Two spouses had for a long time been trying to have children, using a permitted technique of assisted conception. Several times the wife had been subjected to the painful and distressing procedure but, because of the husband's low fertility and also due to physical complications in the wife's reproductive organs, these attempts had failed. The spouses had then discovered that they were both afflicted by thalassemia, an hereditary disease. During the course of their latest

[45] Ord (judgment of) 3 May 2004.

attempt, the Law on assisted procreation came into force and as indicated above, it is very restrictive. Since the assisted conception procedure had been started and consent for its continuance had also been signed, together with a declaration that they had been properly informed, the spouses applied to the judge for an emergency order that the doctor at the medical centre to which they had gone to have the operation, do not implant diseased but healthy embryos in the wife's uterus. However, the Italian legislation does not permit selection, even for the purposes of predetermining the genetic characteristics of the embryo, nor does it permit the preservation of the egg-cells by freezing (except temporarily), or their destruction: all the egg-cells produced in the course of the operation must be implanted in the uterus of the would-be mother. Thus, it is not possible to sort out the healthy embryos from the diseased ones and the doctor is obliged to implant any diseased ones in the uterus also. Nor is it possible for spouses who have given their informed consent, to revoke that consent. Consequently, the judge refused to make the order applied for, leaving the mother with a difficult choice: either to continue the pregnancy, thus running the risk of bringing a child with thalassemia into the world, or to have an abortion, always supposing that the requirements for obtaining it were satisfied. Abortion, in the Italian legal system, can be freely effected if within three months of conception, but after this time limit a pregnancy can only be terminated for serious reasons of the health of the mother, not that of the foetus (Law no 194/1978).

The judge, in his reasoned judgment, examines the rights that are in conflict, and refers to the Italian Constitution[46] (but not to the Charter of Fundamental Rights signed in Nice and not to the provisions of the international conventions). The conflicting rights in the case, as described by the judge, are: the right of the embryo to life; the right of the mother and father to procreation; and the right to collective health for the good of society. So, in this conflict of rights, the judge, treating the embryo as equivalent to a person (even though the Law does not explicitly so provide), found that the embryo's right to be born prevailed, and that neither the mother nor the father had the right to choose between the embryos produced from their bodies, or to permit only the healthy ones to complete their development.

Thus, if a child is consequently born, he will not be able to claim damages against his parents or against the doctor, because all of them have acted in accordance and compliance with the Law. Even if it were possible to overcome the problem of the existence of a right to be born healthy, and the problem of the causal connection between the event of his birth and the disease (the child would not have been able to be born except in those

[46] Specifically to Art 2, which recognizes and guarantees the inviolable rights of man (ie of the person), individually and in a social context, and reminds the person of his (social etc) responsibilities.

conditions, otherwise he would not have existed), the child would still have no right to damages because the conduct of the parents and the doctor would have been lawful. Possibly, the legislature could be sued in damages for not having allowed diseased embryos to be cured.

The question is complicated by other questions concerning human life, such as, specifically, the birth of genetically diseased children. We are in a difficult area of the law, in which judicial findings sometimes conflict with each other and sometimes differ from ethical assessments. The '*affaire Perruche*', decided by the French judges, is a typical example.

4.2.5. Does a person have the right to be born healthy?

The *affaire Perruche*, decided by the French *Cour de Cassation*, sitting in plenary session on 17 November 2000, is one of the 'problem cases' on which learned legal writers have tested their most sophisticated techniques of imaginative interpretation. It is indeed a case that lends itself to an enquiry into how the resources of the law answer the requirements of justice, in a society which in one way is multiplying the demands of the person and in another is preoccupied with mediating between rights and interests that are in conflict with each other. But the case also lends itself to a discussion as to whether all the problems of the person can (or should) be made the subject of legislation and if so, which models (Italian or foreign) are to be considered satisfactory. There are models that claim an absolute respect for the techniques of formalism without any reference to 'values' and others that are ready to incorporate into legal rules, fundamentally assumed ethical and moral values. In its peculiarity, and because of the dramatic twists it presents, the case also lends itself to an enquiry into how to practice the 'art of judging' and to a comparison of the reactions of the judiciaries of different countries when faced with similar facts.

The procedural developments of the case may be reconstructed by reading the account of Conseillen Pierre Sargos,[47] the pleadings of the Advocate General to the *Cour de Cassation* Jerry Sainte-Rose[48] and the numerous commentaries by learned legal writers.[49]

Greater problems are posed by the extreme brevity of the reasoning in the judgment of the *Cour de Cassation* sitting in plenary session, whose main function is to check the legal correctness of the judicial reasoning of the courts below.

Here therefore are the main events in the proceedings.

[47] In *Sem jur*, 10438 (13 Dec 2000) no 50, 2293 ff.

[48] Ibid 2302 ff.

[49] eg Chabas ibid 2309.

(i) By its judgment of 13 January 1992, the *Tribunal de Grande Instance d'Evry* found that a doctor and a pathology laboratory were liable in damages to a pregnant woman, who had applied to them find out whether she had the antibodies of German Measles. The court found that both were in breach of contract for having given her incorrect information, which convinced her that it was possible to carry the pregnancy to term without damage to the not-yet-born child; it found further that damages should be paid both to the child, for damage to his physical integrity, and to the parents.

(ii) By its judgment of 17 December 1993, the Court of Appeal of Paris, to whom the doctor had appealed, on the grounds that the error was to be attributed, in his submission, only to the laboratory, held that the doctor also was in breach of contract (for breach of an obligation to provide all the means at his disposal) and that he was jointly and severally liable with the laboratory and with both their insurers, to the mother and to the father, since the mother, in reliance on the erroneous result, had decided not to terminate the pregnancy, whereas she would have decided to terminate it in the event of danger to not-yet-born child, which intention was well known to the doctor.

(iii) The pronouncement in the judgment at first instance that the defendants were jointly and severally liable to the parents became unappealable, since it amounted to *res judicata*.

(iv) The Court of Appeal did, however, reverse the pronouncement in the judgment at first instance, concerning liability to the child: according to the appeal judges, there was no chain of causation between the damage suffered by the child and the wrongs (torts) found to have been committed. It held that the effects of the German Measles did not derive from the error of the doctors but rather from the fact that the mother had contracted the illness at the beginning of her pregnancy and because the mother's decision to carry the pregnancy to term could not, of itself, amount to an actionable wrong against the child, recoverable in damages, since the effects of the German Measles were constitutionally inherent in the person and absolutely irreversible.

(v) On being seized of the question, the first section of the *Cour de Cassation*, in its judgment of 26 March 1996, reversed the judgment given on appeal, only on this question of causation. It held that the wrong diagnosis had led the parents to believe that the mother was immune to German Measles and that the child had consequently no *chance* of suffering the devastating consequences of the disease. The case was therefore sent back, on the single point of the causal connection, to the Court of Appeal of Orléans, which, however, by its judgment of 5 February 1999, refused to follow the principle of law declared by the *Cour de Cassation* and decided that there was no causal connection between the tort of the doctor (and the laboratory) and the damage suffered by the child.

(vi) On a fresh appeal to the *Cour de Cassation*, the *Cour*, now sitting in plenary session, held:
  (a) that the wrongs (torts) which the doctor and the laboratory were held to have committed in their performance of the contracts entered into with the pregnant mother had led her to rely on the exactness of the information and on her own immunity and thus had prevented her from exercising her own right to terminate the pregnancy in order to avoid giving birth to a handicapped child; and
  (b) that the child was entitled to obtain compensation for the damage resulting from his handicap and caused by the torts found to have been committed.

(vii) The parties were referred to another appeal judge to establish the quantum of damages.

The extreme brevity of the text of this final judgment of the *Cour de Cassation*, which consists of a few lines of reasoning, does not satisfy the learned legal writer, though he is aware that French judgments are concise. But the legal logic with which the Court arrived at the result is one thing; its effect is quite another.

In order to examine this final judgment it is necessary to dismiss certain matters, even though they are worth considering: the placing of the judgment in its context of learned legal writing and case law and also in the cultural context of the time. Then, there are doubts about the legislation referred to in it (Article 1165 of the French Civil Code, on the effect of a contract on third parties and Article 1382 on unlawful wrongs (torts)); and then again about the failure to reconstruct the causal connection, though it was evidently held to have existed; moreover the appeal judges (deciding on points of law) say nothing about the nature of the damage for which they say compensation should be paid.[50]

It is essential to limit the scope of the enquiry. Considering the circumstances in which the case arose, it is scarcely necessary to point out that the damage was neither inflicted directly by the doctors on the physical integrity of the pregnant woman, who had contracted German Measles before submitting herself to the tests, nor was it inflicted directly on the foetus, to whom the German Measles was transmitted by the mother, nor was it damage suffered by the parents for non-termination of a pregnancy

[50] From a comparative point of view see B Markesinis, '*Réflexions sur l'affaire Perruche et la nécessité d'un recours accru au droit étranger par les juridictions nationales*', Revue trimestrielle de droit civil (2001) 77 ff; A Verbeke *Contract and Torts in a Comparative Perspective* <http://www.jurawelt.com>.

resulting from errors in sterilization of the husband or the wife. Of all of these, our case law by now has copious examples.

4.2.6. *Italian case law on medical malpractice and assessment of damages*

The circumstances of the *affaire Perruche* are well known to the Italian observer, since our national experience by now has registered numerous cases dealing with similar facts. In its judgment of 16 February 2001 (no 2335) the Italian Court of Cassation found in favour of compensation for the physical and psychological damage suffered by a new-born baby on the occasion of a caesarean section, for asphyxia and subsequent episodes of apnoea with a consequent loss of working capacity and loss of the amenities of life, and also for the loss and damage suffered by the parents in terms of expenses and moral suffering; the liability of the doctor was founded on negligence (*colpa lieve*) pursuant to Article 1176 of the Italian Civil Code.

In its judgment of 9 August 1985, the Court of First Instance of Padua found that compensation was payable for (extra-contractual) loss and damage suffered by a mother because a doctor had failed to inform her that an operation to terminate her pregnancy had been unsuccessful; and similar decisions were given by the Court of Appeal of Bologna in its judgment of 19 December 1991 and by the Court of Cassation in its judgment of 8 July 1994 (no 6464).

Other decisions have found that parents could sue in damages, for medical malpractice, consisting in a wrong diagnosis and consequent failure to inform a mother about the malformations of her unborn baby, which led to the fundamental impossibility of her procuring an abortion; judges have highlighted the fact that in such a case it is the mother whose interests are infringed by the damage: namely her right freely to choose to terminate the pregnancy, but it is thought that an action brought by the father would also be admissible, since he would have been involved, if not in the mother's decision, at least in its shared consequences. Some judgments have found a doctor liable for not having informed the parents of the fact that their foetus had malformations and would be born with Down's Syndrome.

However, in similar cases the Court of Cassation has found that for the purpose of proving a causal link between the conduct of the medical professionals and the damages complained of by the mother (or both parents) it is necessary to prove that the conditions laid down by law for termination of the pregnancy are fulfilled. The right found to be infringed is the right of the mother to terminate the pregnancy. In the Court of Cassation's judgment no 12195 of 1998 compensation for the loss and damage suffered by the father is described as 'indirect damages'.

In its judgment of 23 February 1995, the Court of First Instance of Cagliari awarded (contractual) damages to a mother for having given birth to a healthy but unwanted child following an unsuccessful operation to terminate the pregnancy.

Further, in its judgment of 20 October 1997, the Court of First Instance of Milan awarded (extra-contractual) damages to both parents on the grounds that, following an incorrect operation to sterilize the husband, their right to conscientious and responsible procreation had been infringed. It should be stressed, however, that the Court considered the damaging event to have been not so much the birth of the child—since life is an immeasurable good, and bearer of joy to the parents, and such as to compensate for the drawback of having to maintain a child—but rather the infringement of a right of personal freedom belonging to the parents. The joys of paternity and maternity likewise provide compensation in themselves, of which the judge must take account when evaluating the *compensatio lucri cum damno* (set-off of gain against loss and damage). As to the nature of the loss and damage, case law is divided; but this is another question that is beyond the scope of this chapter. In any case, these problems are not germane to the purpose of understanding the innovation in the judgment of the plenary session of the Court of Cassation in the *affaire Perruche*.

4.2.7. *New challenges concerning the* affaire Perruche

This innovation consists in the *locus standi* acknowledged by the final judgment to exist in the child. Of course, the innovation is relative, given that the first judgment on the merits in the same proceedings had already found in favour of damages payable to the child, as had the first section of the *Cour de Cassation*.

The case can be stripped down to its essentials and, taking it as an hypothesis for teaching purposes, and overstepping the boundaries of its facts, the challenges can be summarised in a few questions. The parents' right to damages, agreed to by the Italian judges subject to the remarks and limitations described above, can be taken as read, but one wonders:

(a) whether from a methodological point of view, the problem can be exhausted in the discussion of the existence of the causal connection, or whether there can or must be other factors in the evaluation;
(b) whether, under the rules of law, the child is entitled to claim damages;
(c) for what loss and damage; and
(d) against whom.

At this point further questions arise:

(a) whether the child can claim in damages against the doctor and the laboratory on the grounds that he came into the world handicapped, even though that condition was not caused directly by the defendants but only by a combination of two factors: one being the error in the information that would otherwise have determined the decision to terminate the pregnancy and the other, the mother's continuance of the pregnancy in ignorance of that error;

(b) whether a child is entitled to sue his mother for having knowingly decided to carry the pregnancy to term; and

(c) whether he is entitled to claim damages from the father as well as the mother.

Probably the only case recorded in Italy whose *ratio decidendi* is really relevant to that of the *Perruche* case is the much-discussed one concerning a baby girl with hereditary syphilis, long ago decided by the Court of First Instance of Piacenza on 31 July 1950.[51] This is because in all the judgments so far mentioned and in others that could be mentioned, damages are always claimed by one or both parents but not by the child.

The Court of First Instance of Piacenza awarded damages to the child, and overcame the problem of the causal connection with these words:

> life is a great gift, an immense gift. Now, transmitting by the act of generation (. . .) a diseased condition which transforms this great gift into an immense unhappiness is unlawful, contrary to the law, and is not the proper conduct of a person on whom the legal system imposes a duty to recognise and elevate this gift.

The strength of the criticism of most commentators, which (with the exception of a few favourable opinions) has greeted this judgment, has been sufficient ever since to dissuade children born handicapped from starting actions in damages in Italy against their parents. It should however be pointed out on the facts, that the infection of syphilis had been transmitted from the father to the mother and that she was possibly not aware of it and in any case (at the time) did not have the right to an abortion. We have to remember that abortion has only been legal in Italy since 1978.

The similarities of the French case and the Italian case decided by the Court of Piacenza, mentioned above, are not completely coincident.

The *Perruche* case also was an action in damages, but the action was not against the parents, but against the doctors and the laboratory, so that it is not possible on the basis of that case, to pose the question whether parents are immune from being sued by their children for having caused them to be born in a disadvantaged condition, or the question whether damages should not be awarded because to do so would infringe the right of the parents to procreation or the right of the mother freely to choose to terminate a pregnancy. However, even if the old Italian case was somewhat different from the *affaire Perruche,* the question of the causal link remains open. The alter-

[51] In *Foro it* (1951) I, 987.

natives, simple but obvious, are 'being' and 'non-being': living with the affliction of an incurable handicap or not being afflicted by it and consequently not being born. The choice between these alternatives, where there is medical liability, does not arise in either the old Italian or the new French case, because in both the child has been born and is condemned to live in disadvantaged conditions. The words of the judges of the Court of First Instance of Piacenza, at the distance of half a century, still seem (extraordinarily) up-to-date, even though, strictly speaking, they do not offer an adequate reasoning in the strict sense.

Today those judges, pilloried by some, respected but criticized by almost everyone,[52] would enjoy quite another sort of consideration.

To resolve the matter, are we to follow a line of strict legal reasoning or a line which accommodates the principles underlying that reasoning?

It is possible to reach opposite conclusions using the formal method or using reasoning grounded on values, or underlying principles.

On strict, formal legal reasoning, it appears clear that 'the concept of life as of incomparable value' is a non-legal concept 'superimposed on a purely formal concept'. If we distinguish between the moment of the damaging act and the moment it shows its consequences, it is possible to overcome the difficulty of the causal connection even in rigorously formal terms.[53] But these considerations apply in the context of extra-contractual liability. If the question is put in the contractual context, either we must consider that the mother entered into a contract with the pathology laboratory for diagnostic services and a contract with the doctor for medical services and that both contracts can be construed as including an obligation to protect the third party (the foetus); or we must consider that the legal effect of these contracts is specifically that services are to be provided in favour of the foetus, whose condition in the uterus is to be ascertained. In either case, it is impossible to deny that the interests of the foetus-to-be-born have a bearing on the matter, just as it is impossible to deny that the absence or inexactitude of information affect the foetus at least indirectly. On this construction, the problem that there can be no right not to be born does not arise, nor does the question whether there is a right to be born healthy: the problem that arises is that of the difficult condition in which the baby finds itself when born, by reason of the absence or inexactitude of information:

[52] See the careful reconstructions of the history of this in Patti *Famiglia e responsabilità civile* (Milano 1984) 112 ff, where there are references to the German and American legal experiences; Z Zencovich '*La responsabilità da procreazione*', in Giur it, (1986); IV, 113, with further comparative references; and for other instances compare von Bar *The Common European Law of Torts, I* (Oxford 1998) 581 ff; and A D'Angelo (ed) *Un bambino non voluto è un danno risarcibile?* (Milano 1999); where there are essays and opinions by Lupoi, Canale, Busnelli, Lipari, Ruffolo, Cendon, Passio, Brunetta d'Usseaux, A D'Angelo, Bregante, Ferrando, De Matteis, Spallarossa and Monateri.

[53] According to Rescigno '*Il danno da procreazione*', in Riv dir civ (1956) I, 634.

the baby has been born in the only condition in which it could have lived, that is, afflicted with a handicap. The doctors' error is mirrored in the tragic condition of the child that has been born.

To be sure, if one makes a distinction between factual and legal causality, it is apparent that the error of the doctors was a contributing cause (*concausa*), but not the only cause (the mother could have decided not to have an abortion). If the doctors had not erred, the admitted fact of the child's tragic condition would not have given him grounds to sue his mother, because there would have been no fault (*colpa*) attaching to her; she would only have freely made the choice to procreate, which choice is not open to criticism and should not be governed by the possibility of a claim from the child in damages.

If, on the other hand, we take the line of reasoning that accommodates the values or principles underlying it, we might agree with those jurists who have remarked that the idea that a birth is always a 'precious gift' (a recurring theme in judgments in decided cases), 'highlights the value of human life and its right to be protected in such a way as to obscure the need to evaluate the connection between the event of the birth and the person of the parent: which connection can make one see the birth as an event whose significance is not unequivocal—but as the bearer on the one hand of 'gifts' and on the other of difficulties'; so that 'to connect birth and motherhood in a single fate and a single estimation really adds to the sort of confused priorities that acknowledge the value of human life only if it is 'wanted'.[54]

The parents can thus be acknowledged to have suffered loss of a capital nature as well as biological and natural damage in the strict sense; since damage cannot be duplicated, the child can only be acknowledged to have suffered moral damage.

Is this a just and equitable decision? Or is it one that holds doctors, hospital managers, and insurers, all subject to the law, liable for a loss that should 'lie where it falls' or at least be absorbed by the insurance system? How far should we follow the logical and formal line of argument? And if we do not follow it, are we not stepping *tout court* into the quicksands of 'free law'?

Pietro Rescigno, commenting on the old Italian judgment, concluded his essay on the question of loss and damage caused by procreation with the penetrating observation that '. . . the theme of the not-yet-born child, in the peculiarity of this case, reveals the law's incoherence. It is this contradiction that explains the painful uncertainty of the judge and the bitter anxiety of the reader'.

But it is precisely with that painful consciousness and from that point of departure that we must start the reasoning again today.

[54] Rescigno op cit.

5. LONG-TERM PERSPECTIVES

5.1. EUROPEAN COMMUNITY RESOLUTIONS AND THE CODIFICATION OF 'PRIVATE LAW'

By resolution of 6 May 1994,[1] the European Parliament reconfirmed the resolution made on 26 May 1989 concerning harmonization of certain sectors of private law in Member States.[2] The justification for this initiative is illustrated in the preamble in which it is stated on the one hand that the communities have already proceeded with harmonization of certain sectors of private law, and on the other that progressive harmonization is essential for realization of the European common market. The desired result is the development of a 'European common code of private law', to be developed in various phases of progressive rapprochement of the prevailing rules in the systems of Member States, which would lead first to partial harmonization in the short term and then to a longer-term more complete harmonization. Within the scope of the resolution reference is made to organizations which already concern themselves with harmonization of laws such as Unidroit, Uncitral, and the Council of Europe, as well as to the works of the Commission on European Contract Law, known as the Lando Commission, from the name of the Danish professor Ole Lando who chairs it.[3] The resolution was sent to the Council of Ministers, to the Commission

[1] In OGC 205 of 25 July 1994, 518. In Germany the precursor of European codification was Konrad Zweigert, '*Il diritto comparato a servizio dell'unificazione giuridica europea*', in Nuova riv dir comm, dir dell'economia, dir sociale (1951) I, 183 et seq; in Italy the precursor was Rodolfo Sacco '*I problemi dell'unificazione del diritto in Europa*', (1953) II, 49 et seq (republished in *I Contratti* (1995) 73 et seq). On the history of scientific and institutional initiatives for harmonization, uniformization, unification and codification, see Bonell '*Comparazione giuridica e unificazione del diritto*' in Alpa et al *Diritto privato comparato. Istituti e problemi* (Rome and Bari 1999) 4 et seq. On the problems of legal communication in Europe, on the role of comparison in European private law, on the perspectives for unification, and on the training of the European lawyer, L Moccia (ed) *Il diritto privato europeo: problemi e prospettive* (Reports of the Macerata international conference, 8–10 June 1989) (Milan 1993); among the contributions see the introduction by Moccia vii et seq; Sacco *Il sistema del diritto privato europeo: premesse per un codice europeo* at 87 et seq and Grande Stevens *L'avvocato europeo*, 173 et seq. On the reconstruction of Italian law in the light of EEC law, v Lipari (ed) *Diritto privato europeo* (Padua 1997) and on the private law aspects of EEC law, Tizzano (ed) *Diritto privato comunitario* (Turin 1999).

[2] In OGC 158 of 28 June 1989, 400.

[3] Since 1982 Professor Ole Lando has been gradually constructing the culture of European codification, dedicating himself particularly to the rules of contract. Numerous contributions include: *European Contract Law*, in 31 (1983) Am J Comp L 653 et seq; '*Principles of European Contract Law*', in *Liber Memorialis François Laurent* (Brussels 1989) 555 et seq; '*Principles of European Contract Law/An Alternative or a Precursor of European Legislation?*' in RablesZ (1992) 261 et seq; '*European Contract Law*' in *Il diritto privato*

and to the governments of Member States of the EU. For its part, the Lando Commission has worked prolifically and drafted a text of rules for contract law.[4]

The work did not stop at this point because, through carrying out wide research, it is reaching the other sources of obligations (ie torts, restitution, unjust enrichment), which is the responsibility of a committee coordinated by the German professor Christian von Bar.[5] In connection with this work research is being conducted also on securities, insurance contracts, and sales.

The tasks of the jurists who are involved with this harmonization are very ambitious and also very difficult.

The expression 'private law' is not further defined in the resolutions of the European Parliament, so that some problems of interpretation arise in translation.

1. As there is no definition of private law available in the texts creating the European Communities, it is necessary to interpret the expression taking account of the meaning or meanings that have been given to this expression in the *koiné* (the common language) of the legal culture of Member States. In continental Europe private law may be considered as a sufficiently uniform notion, in that in Italian law (no differently, for example from French law, Spanish or Portuguese law, German or Austrian law) private law signifies the law governing relations which are instituted on an abstract basis between private persons or between the state, public and private entities. Thus one is referring to rules of ordinary law, or to formulae or techniques governed by civil codes and traditionally ascribed to this subject. It is more difficult to identify a notion of private law in the jurisprudence or case law of common law, where the division between private law and public law is not easy and in any case does not correspond to the division on the Continent.

europeo, cit 117 et seq; *The Harmonization of European Contract Law through a Restatement of Principles* (Oxford 1997) (conference held at the Institute of European and Comparative Law organized by Professor Basil Markesinis).

[4] *Towards a European Civil Code*, edited by Hartkamp et al (London 1994) (in this volume we can find in a general overview the introduction by Hondius, 1 et seq; the discussion of various drafting techniques for rules by Mueller-Graff, 19 et seq; a description of the contents of the rules collected in the first edition of the contracts code by Hartkamp, 37 et seq; the foundation on the tradition of the *ius commune* by Zimmermann, at 65 and by Bollen and de Groot, at 97; there follow essays on specific themes in the law of contracts and guarantees.); Lando and Beale *Principles of European Contract Law* (London 1995) in which there is a commentary on the rules of the 'code' drafted by Beale, Drobnig, Goode, Lando, Tallon.

[5] von Bar, translated in English as *The Common European Law of Torts* (Oxford 1998). The original *Gemeineuropaeisches Deliktsrecht* is being translated into Italian; von Bar has also edited *Deliktsrecht in Europa* (Cologne 1993).

2. We must also note that in all the continental countries mentioned above, the traditional distinction between private law and public law is in a state of crisis. For some time in these systems there has been a trend towards 'constitutionalization' of private law that is the direct or indirect application of rules contained in the respective constitutions to relationships between private persons. In France this process is rather slower, but has also started.
3. Beyond these definitions, the expression private law has an academic content (with reference to university teaching) and a formal content, which includes two branches of law, civil law and commercial law.
4. From the point of view of the sources of law, private law consists then of rules contained in the constitutions, rules contained in the codes and rules contained in particular statutes. Each system of the Member States uses sources which are different from each other, which also include regulations, administrative orders of independent authorities, and so on.

If one should try to simplify the argument—and thus the tasks of the lawyers who involve themselves in harmonization of the rules in a European context—one should make reference to the rules contained in the civil codes and codes of commerce of European nations. At this point, two further problems emerge.

1. The reference models of the codes in force in continental European Countries are essentially two. These are the French Civil Code, introduced by Napoleon in 1804, and the German Civil Code, approved in 1896 and brought into force in 1900. To these one can add the models of commercial codes, which followed each other throughout the 19th century and in our own time were incorporated in Italy in the Civil Code of 1942 and in Holland in the Civil Code whose publication in several volumes started in 1980.
2. In the English common law and Irish common law there are no codes in the continental law sense, but statutes as well as the case law. In various States however one meets situations which are still more complex, as in the Scandinavian countries. Taking account of this classification, the approach of the Commission for the project of a European code has been cautious. The division between the rules of civil law and rules of commercial law has not been followed. Using a flexible and generic understanding of 'private law' it is intended that the rules developed by means of harmonization may apply to either civil law or commercial law.

No restrictions have been imposed on the method of drafting. The harmonized rules may be considered a sort of 'restatement' of the rules applied in Member States, or otherwise to constitute the fruit of unification of already existing laws with adaptations and simplifications required for a genuine codification.

One must add that for certain sectors of private law there already exist unitary models of reference. Even if developed for difference purposes, the principles of contract in international commerce developed by the International Institute for the Unification of Law (Unidroit) constitutes a 'restatement' of contract laws consisting of general and balanced rules.[6] The Lando Commission on European contract law has referred to the Unidroit text in order to develop its own contract law proposal. There are also in progress other initiatives, such as the identification of a 'common core' in contracts, undertaken by academics of the University of Trent, Italy, and the drafting of common principles in the French and German law of obligations on the initiative of the Sorbonne and University of Louvain-la-Neuve. There is also a further proposal for the drafting of a European code for provisions of consumer law.

The history of the initiatives attempted and achieved for unification, uniformity, and harmonization of the law has run for over a century and taken many diverse forms.[7] In any event, the numerous directives which the European Community has approved on subjects relating to the interests of consumers concerning unfair clauses, door-to-door sales, distance selling, time-sharing, etc, already constitute a form of codification of private European law in the relevant sectors.[8]

What should be illustrated here is on the one hand the purposes of harmonization (or unification) and on the other the doubts which have arisen in the discussion of this initiative.

[6] See generally Bonell *An International Restatement of Contract Law* (New York 1994) '*The Unidroit Principles in Practice: The Experience of the First Two Years*', in [1997] Uniform L Rev 2, 34 et seq; *The Unidroit Principles: What Next?* in [1998] Uniform Law Rev 3, 275 et seq.

On the discussion of the 'Unidroit principles' in Italy, see the reports of the conference organised at the Unidroit premises in Rome by J Bonell and F Bonelli in 1995; among the various contributions, see the essays by Di Majo, Ferrari, and Alpa in *Contratto e impresa/Europa* (1996) I, 287 et seq.

For the construction of lines of development of contract law *for* an understanding of the evolution of the principles elaborated by Unidroit, the effect of European Directives and the principles of the Lando Commission, see Alpa *Nuove frontiere del diritto contrattuale* (Rome 1998) (summarized in the volume *Diritto privato comparato,* cit); Koetz and Flessner *European Contract Law*, I (Oxford 1997) (English translation by Weir); Vranken *Fundamentals of European Civil Law* (London 1997); for a comparison of models of judgment, see Markesinis, Lorenz, Dannemann *The Law of Contracts and Restitution: A Comparative Introduction* (Oxford 1997).

Italian scholars have considered these initiatives with great attention: see eg Gandolfi '*Pour un code européen des contrats,*' in Rev trim dr civ (1992) 707 et seq. Rescigno, '*Per un "Restatement" europeo in materia di contratti*', in Il diritto europeo, cit, 135 et seq; Mengoni *L'Europa dei codici o un codice per l'Europa?* (Rome 1993) (lecture given at the Center for Study and Research in Comparative and Foreign Law directed by J Bonell).

[7] On this point, see Bonell op cit 4 et seq; Monaco 'I risultati dell "Unidroit" nella codificazione del diritto uniforme in Il diritto privato europeo', cit. 35 et seq.

[8] The directives and the relative rules for their implementation are gathered in Alpa (ed) *Codice del consumo e del risparmio* (Milan 1999).

5.1.1. *The purposes and advantages of a European Civil Code*

Next to the 'economic space' and the European jurisdiction,[9] one is now seeking to create a unitary legal space. The EC's sovereignty is limited by subject matter. The European Civil Code therefore cannot extend to subjects outside the powers of its Charter. Areas such as family law, succession, and real property law are off-limits. However, the law of obligations is included within the jurisdiction of the Community, including contracts and tort, commercial dealings, restitution and remedies. Obviously, also matters arising from commerce, corporations, construction contracts, etc, are included.

Article 100 and later Article 100A of the EC Treaty attribute to the Council of Ministers the power to establish directives intended to bring together the 'legislative, regulatory and administrative provisions of Member States which have direct consequences on the implementation and operation of the Common Market.' Reference may be made to these provisions for the justification of the European Civil Code initiative, and to make them compatible with the so-called 'principle of subsidiarity', which means any effort to avoid regulation. The ECC may choose between the instrument of regulation or the use of directives, or a mere recommendation in order to work toward a European Common Code.[10] But why breach the barriers of the national systems on these subjects? The subordination of national barriers is a necessary part in achieving the single market. In other words, the diverse treatment of legal relations in private law in different countries is a considerable economic cost, an obstacle, a complication, which obstructs the implementation of the single market. A European Civil Code would enhance the free exchange of goods, services, capital, and labour within the single market, that is of the free circulation of goods, services, capital, and labour within the EU. There is a strict correlation between open and free economic activity and the method and structure of civil law. In this light the initiatives of a European Civil Code encourage the market without dictating that legal rules by their nature must 'mimic' economic rules. This follows the economic legal analysis as thought in America by professor Richard Posner.[11] In his sophisticated analysis concerning European law of contracts, Professor Juergen Basedow has underlined how rules in conflict between themselves in the various countries of the EU can develop as a real market hindrance, while uniform

[9] On which, see Carbone (SM) *Lo spazio giudiziario europeo* (Turin 1997).

[10] Basedow 'Un droit commun des contrats pour le Marché commun', in *Rev int dr comp* (1998) 26 et seq.

[11] For a survey of the views and objectives of professors Coase, Posner, Calabresi and other American scholars, see the anthology *Analisi economica del diritto privato*, ed Alpa (Milan 1998).

private law rules emerge as conditions precedent for the implementation of the single market. Thus a European Civil Code would indeed constitute a 'building block' of the single market.

An important objective of a European code is the simplification of the legal rules applicable to economic relations, too often dispersed among codes or national laws. Uniform rules would help to prevent or simplify disputes, to ensure harmonious application of the rules to disputes that have arisen, to eliminate conflict between national systems, the dominance of one over the other, or recourse to choice of the most convenient national law.

5.1.2. Criticism of the initiative

The initiative to develop a European Civil Code has raised much enthusiasm, but also many doubts. Examination, as objective as possible, of the many and strong expressions of doubts and criticisms must take account their origin, their reasoning, and their ambition.

First of all there is the 'fear of the unknown'.[12] Lawyers typically are affected by this fear, because of their desire to maintain familiar notions, well worn texts and their own method of reasoning. The abandonment of rules proven over time and easily predictable judicial resolutions of disputes remove an anchor point for jurists who perceive in the introduction of a new text a jump into the unknown. This attitude however can be easily overcome, if one understands that to know and confront a matter exorcises the phantom of the unknown. All those who dedicate their time to comparative law and those who are interested in understanding what happens in other countries far and near, share the idea that today it is more important to understand what unites us, rather than what divides us. There are many research studies organized for the purpose of constructing an ideal bridge ('bridging the continents' as Professor Sir Basil Markesinis defined it)[13] between different legal experiences in order to identify the convergence's between systems and in order to compare common law and civil law in a constructive manner.

The dream of 'bridging the continents' is ripe for realization in Europe, owing to the making of a common European legal culture, whose existence

[12] Legrand, 'Sens et non-sens d'un code civil européen', in Rev int dr comp (1996) 779 et seq. A perceptive criticism of the theories of Legrand has been conducted by Zeno-Zencovich, 'Il "codice civile europeo", le tradizioni giuridiche nazionali e il neo-positivismo', in Foro it (1998), V, 60 et seq.

[13] Markesinis (ed) 'The gradual convergence. Foreign ideals, foreign influences and English law on the eve of the 21st century' (Oxford 1994); *Foreign Law and Comparative Methodology* (Oxford 1997).

is denied by some scholars[14] even in the wide meaning of the German *Rechtswissenschaft*.[15] Today, the books, essays, and encyclopaedias of European jurists transcend national frontiers and contain ever more often references to the law and decisions of other countries. This comparative approach is used attain a better understanding national law as well as to receive suggestions and models from other experiences. Without doubt, the circulation of models (codes, laws, and principles) which cross over political and cultural boundaries is a phenomenon increasing in an ever faster and wider way.

In the mean time, common legal values have consolidated in Western Europe.[16] This is true without considering the Roman law tradition or the mediaeval law (so called *ius commune*, common law) which are quite different from the '*European Ius Commune*' of today.[17] In all countries of the EU there exist fundamental rights of an identical nature. In fact, the constitutional law of the EU has materialized from the principles accepted in the written and unwritten constitutions of Member States. Moreover, the European Convention of Human Rights has further been ratified by all Member States.

Criticisms that codification is taking an excessively long time are less troubling,[18] as also the fact that codification of rules related only to economic relationships would leave in the shade human sentiments or would sacrifice the 'narrative function' of law.[19]

The authority under which the proposed European Code has been drafted is somewhat in doubt.[20] In this case one is dealing with authority understood in a moral sense, not in a legal or institutional sense, since in the scope of powers conferred on the Community the provisions of the treaty do not prevent, but rather favour, the creation of a unified legal space. A code of this kind appears also deprived of any systematic order, while each codification needs a systematic order. It is true that the code is being born section by section. But harmonization may well proceed by degrees. Functional and practical demands prevail over those of order and efficiency.

14 Schulze '*Le droit privé commun européen*', in Rev int dr comp (1995) 31 et seq (with extensive bibliography).

15 Legrand, op cit 785.

16 Stein and Shand *I valori comuni dell'Occidente* (Milan 1970) (on which, see Alpa *I principi generali* (Milan 1993)); Hinestrosa Des principes généraux du droit aux principes généraux des contrats, in [1998] Uniform L Rev, 3 501 et seq.

17 Among others, Schulze, op cit, 10 et seq.

18 Markesinis 'Why a code is not the best way to advance the cause of European legal unity', in 5 (1997) *Eur Rev of Private Law* 519 et seq.

19 Jayme, *Cours général de droit international privé* (London 1995); Zaccaria *Il diritto privato europeo nell'epoca del postmoderno* in Riv dir civ (1997) I, 367 et seq.

20 Legrand, op cit, 798, 803.

More worthy of consideration are criticisms of a different nature, though even these are in my view surmountable. They may be summarized in the following way:

(a) the structural difference in theory and practice between common law and civil law;
(b) the elimination of the original national characteristics and the value of legal pluralism; and
(c) the appropriateness of using techniques of harmonization other than the drafting of a unified civil code.

As for the first criticism—the structural differences between the common law and the civil law—the opinion of professor Alan Watson must certainly be taken into consideration. 'The legal tradition—he said—has a considerable impact on the shaping of the law, and the individual sources of law have different effects on the growth of the law'.[21] The formation of a legal system on the basis of legislative sources rather than on the basis of judicial sources is one thing. But one hardly needs to be reminded that now in English law and in Irish law not all creation of law relies upon case law. The province of statute law in those countries has become ever wider. The collections in English law edited by Blackwells are organized by subject matter, and the numerous legislative rules dedicated to the area of contract and commercial law are contained in various copious volumes. Also membership by the UK and Ireland in the EU requires application of all Community regulations and community directives, which obviously occur by means of written law. The attitude of many common law lawyers has also changed concerning codification as a technique of consolidation of legal rules. In his conclusion on future developments of commercial law in the UK, one of the most prestigious scholars of the subject, Professor Roy Goode, looks forward to the arrival of an internal codification of the rules in force today relating to economic transactions.[22]

At the same time, in the European countries with civil codes it would be näive to pretend that there has been no case law, which enlivens the written text, adds to it and corrects it. The role of ascertaining facts is relevant in all legal systems. Reasoning by induction (as in common law systems) or reasoning by deduction (as in civil law systems) is apparently diverse in its process, but similar in substance. The classification of rules is uncertain in one or the other system when case law can be found in both as also can statute law. The identification of protected interests in terms of subjective

[21] Watson, 'Roman Law and English Law: Two Patterns of Legal Development' in *Il diritto privato europeo*, cit, 10

[22] *Commercial Law in the Next Millennium* (London 1998), 100 et seq, and on the comparison between the technique of restatement and codification, '*International restatement of contract and English law*', in (1998) 3 Uniform L Rev, 231 et seq.

rights is now common to both systems. Contractual text are now ever more extensive, many of which are drawn from the experience of common law countries language and thus with regard to new type of contracts, methods of formation of contracts, techniques of notification, and transfers of money and title. This is so true that in a new treatise on Italian private law, edited by Professor Rodolfo Sacco, there appears together with a volume on written sources another volume on 'non-written' sources of law, such as custom, case law, interpretation, commercial practices, and so on.[23]

As for the second criticism—the erosion of natural differences and the value of diversity—the elimination is not so important. Certainly, the rules contained in individual codes will no longer be applied individually, but they will continue to survive in the historical culture of the individual countries. It is of course true that the legal system is one of the fundamental characteristics of a country, but it is also true that one can easily renounce this and that its existence and importance is obvious only to jurists. Realistically speaking it is not considered an identifying characteristic by the ordinary citizen.

The appeal to history and codification (or in any case to legal organizations passed down by tradition) must not be undervalued, but nor must it be overvalued. It is overvalued when a tradition emerges only to achieve finality or to prevent finality of a purely technical nature. Now, it is known how the Mediaeval *Ius Commune* developed in the context of a common legal culture in Europe[24] and that this formed the tree from which grew as so many branches, the national laws of continental countries and island areas (England, Scotland, and more recently Ireland). In the mediaeval period important changes took place, so important to be defined in terms of being revolutionary.[25]

Yet the legal history of European Western Countries is a fragmented one, which shows progress (such as codification) and regression (such as the development of 19th century dogma). Strange diversions have occurred, for example the greater affinity between Roman contractual law and common law rather than with the Napoleonic or Germanic models; incredible combinations, such as the translation into English of a code of Napoleonic origin which has become the Code of Quebec or the translation into English of the former Italian Civil Code, which has become the Civil Code of Malta and the Code of Quebec; unexpected influences, such as those of canon law on English equity. This very evolution of models is not monolithic and uniform as the critics of the Roman/French tradition would want to repre-

23 Sacco *Le fonti non scritte* (Turin 1999).

24 Santini L'Europa come spazio giuridico unitario: un armonia nel rispetto delle dissonanze, in Contratto e impresa/Europa (1996) I, 43 et seq; but then see Grossi, *L'ordine giuridico medievale* (Rome, Bari 1997).

25 Berman *Law and Revolution. The Formation of the Western Legal Tradition* (1983).

sent it. One only has to think of the differences of application of the Napoleonic Code in France and in Belgium where the force of the same written rules leads to notable divergence in interpretation in doctrine and case law. Differences are also observed in the common law family, not only between English and United States common law, but also between English common law and that in Ireland or in other common law countries politically connected with the UK. History provides a formidable reservoir of facts, experiences, techniques, and models which can be used to achieve convergence.

In the old Europe new codifications have taken place or are in the course of implementation, as in Holland, recodifications, as in Italy and Germany, without mentioning the great modifications occurring in all countries as a result of implementation of Community directives. One should also consider that EC law is showing an expansive force, since it tends to influence also the general common rules which are not affected by directives.[26]

In any event, it is only a question of the level at which one wants to place the codified rules. One is still always talking of rules of a general nature, which leave the Member States free to introduce rules of a particular type applicable to individual regions. The dichotomy between State law and regional law, or the law of individual nations may be saved for sectors which do not concern economic relations.

As for the third criticism that other techniques of harmonization techniques are more appropriate, obviously the argument is open. We could continue with the introduction of directives scattered over sectors, but already this system of EC law-making creates difficulties of coordination of the laws in terms of coherence, simplicity, and applicability. We could turn to conventions or treaties but this would not change much towards the desired solution. We could also think of a restatement or a collage of general principles,[27] but the rules of the Lando Commission, even if not very different from this proposal, are the result of a more creative process.[28]

These are alternatives have been fully considered by the Lando Commission and now are taken up by the von Bar Commission which is proceeding with the work in the remaining part of the law of obligations. In any case these options are not new: they had already been assessed immediately after the Second World War by Professor Rodolfo Sacco, who announced that the choice could not be left only to the solution of technical problems, but incorporated above all considerations of a political nature.[29]

[26] See the references in Alpa and Dassio 'Les contrats des consommateurs et les modifications du code civil italien', in [1997] Rev int dr comp 629 et seq.
[27] Zeno-Zencovich op cit 67.
[28] Lando '*European Contract Law*', in *Il diritto privato europeo*, cit 218.
[29] Sacco *I problemi*, *cit* 77 in the republished edition.

The other proposal seems less worthwile because instead of the drafting of a European Code one would substitute the drafting of common rules of uniform international laws. However, this would be an intermediate provisional solution and certainly not definitive. It would give rise to the application of common choice of rules to be applied.

5.1.3. Problems of codification

Before turning briefly to the advantages of European codification, we should reflect further on some additional problems concerning the initiative.

The first problem is language.[30] The European Code must be drafted in all the languages of the EU States. The rules already established for contracts in general have been written in English. As is known, English is now the *lingua franca* (language without borders) of commercial traffic. Together with French, English is one of the most practiced languages in the EC offices. English is destined to prevail. This is not so much by the merit of the power of the dominance of England, but above all by the expansion of the economic and political power of the United States and also by the practicality and the simplicity of its grammar. English is the language of this work in progress, but a translation into the language of Member States will be inevitable.

It is then fundamental to choose written rules rather then those derived from case law. The choice of codification is no rejection of the common law system. Many common law jurists and writers are now convinced that codification presents considerable advantages, such as simplification, certainty, and predictability of the rules. We must remember that 'the citizen of a European State has not the same easy access to the laws of his sister states'. Very often he or she 'cannot read them in the original' and may not fully understand.[31]

And then there is the structure. A code of this type and for certain purposes cannot be conceived like the old codes of the 20th century. It will be constituted by rules intended for individual sectors provided by an internal coherence. It will not be complete, but concern only economic relationships to them. It will contain rules of wide extent, rather than rules applying only to narrow circumstances. A European Code will contain rules situated in a dynamic reality, not a static reality. They will thus be proved by their application and modified where gaps are found.

[30] Among the numerous contributions, see Palmisciano and Christoffersen, 'Aspects linguistiques de la communication juridique en Europe: pratique et problèmes des "juristes-reviseurs" de la Commission des Communautées europénnes', in *Il diritto privato europeo*, cit 69 et seq.

[31] Lando op ult cit 118.

A comparative approach is necessary for this purpose, to be carried out with sophisticated instruments, and in the right perspective. 'The task of science is (. . .) to exorcise the absurd and contradictory positions.'[32]

There will remain questions which are not simple to resolve. For example, the identification of mandatory rules with respect to the individual systems from which the common rules derive, the constitutionalization of private law rules, the meaning of blanket rules (in German, *Generalklauseln*) such as 'good faith', 'public policy', 'reasonable man', and so on.[33]

We could think about the unification of remedies since the law may not just be considered from the point of view of substance but also from the point of view of procedure. We could even consider the unification of systems of administration of justice.

5.1.4. Conclusion

Beyond the many advantages already shown, it is worth saying that unitary codification re-enforces economic unity and promotes political unity. But if it is true that the legal component—that is the entire organization of law in a community—constitutes an essential characteristic of that community, the drafting of a unitary code at a European dimension will become one of the aggregate factors in cementing that same European Community, and a factor in defining the collective European identity.

The European lawyer will no longer have to negotiate his way through dusty research sources, commentaries, and case law of other jurisdictions, encountering linguistic, conceptual, and practical problems. There are advantages for the judge, who in the administration of civil justice, will not have to have recourse to deciphering the formulae of foreign law.

None of this will bring about the levelling of values nor the standardization of our work. The panorama will be varied. Differences will be maintained, and uniformity consolidated. The motto of Europe '*E pluribus plures*' for the Civil Code could be converted into the American '*E pluribus unum*'.

The countries, regions, cities, and villages will keep their splendid and marvelous traditions, an irrepressible aspect, their individual and diverse beauty. The unity of private law will not make Rome more similar to Paris or to London, the Italian language more like Swedish or German, Italian art like the Flemish. But to paraphrase a famous saying of Voltaire: while travelling, we shall no longer be constrained to change law every time we change horses [now aircraft]. Each of us will keep our own distinctive char-

[32] Sacco, op ult cit 98.
[33] Rescigno, 'Per un "Restatement" ' cit 142.

acteristics, will not have to renounce our own historic inheritance, which constitutes the fundamental heritage of Europe, as Hans Gadamer reminds us.[34] Though, each one of us by studying, interpreting and applying the unified Civil Code will be and feel more European.

5.2. THE PROJECT FOR A UNIFIED CODE AND THE PRINCIPLES OF EUROPEAN CONTRACT LAW

Soon after the publication of the latest version of the 'Principles of European Contract Law' (hereinafter 'The Principles') which is a work reflecting the intelligence, culture, and experience of the 'Lando Commission'[35] public discussions of this text have taken place in the academic and professional legal world in the various Member States.[36] This seems to be a further logical step toward the cultural and technical unfolding of the drafting of a 'European Civil Code',[37] a subject about which many contributors have now turned their attention. This section aims to understand—from a very simple and synthetic perspective—which the convergences and the differences between the Principles and the Italian Civil Code (Article 1321 et seq).

5.2.1. General Provisions

The Principles do not contain a definition of *contract*. The definitions

[34] *L'eredità dell'Europa* (Turin 1991) ix.

[35] At Utrecht, on 16 Dec 1999. A commentary of this text is provided by Ole Lando and Hugh Beale (eds) *Principles of European Contract Law. Part I and II, prepared by The Commission on European Contract Law* (The Hague 2000). About the aims and the content of the work undertaken by the Commission, the other groups, and the Steering Committee coordinated by Christian v Bar, see *Towards a European Civil Code. Second Revised and Expanded Edition* (Nijmegen 1998).

[36] Mainly in Rome and Coimbra, during spring and summer 2000. In Rome the meeting had been organized by the (Italian) National Council of Lawyers and the Institute of Private Law (University of Rome 'La Sapienza'). Ole Lando sent a text on *The Spirit of the Principles of European Contract Law*; Christian v Bar made a report on the working process (*The Study Group on a European Civil Code*); the Italian reporters (Guido Alpa, Adolfo di Majo, Luigi Rovelli, Vincenzo Roppo) discussed the style and content of the Italian translation of the 'Principles' provided by the Department of Justice (in *Rivista critica di diritto privato* n 3, 2000).

[37] Among the last contributions see Hondius 'European Private Law –Survey 1998–2000' in 2 (2000) Eur Rev Priv L 8, 385 ff; Grundmann, 'General principles of private law and *ius commune modernum* as applicable law?', in Baums, Hopt, Horn (eds), *Corporations, Capital Markets and Business in the Law* (London 2000) 213 ff; Basedow 'Codification of private law in the European Union: the making of a hybrid' (inaugural address delivered at the Erasmus University, Rotterdam, 9 May 2000); Whittaker 'Unfair contract terms, public services and the construction of a European conception of contract', in 116 (2000) *L Q Rev* 95 ff; Campana, 'Vers un langage juridique commun en Europe?' in 1 (2000) Eur Rev Priv L 33 ff.

which are included deal with other terms, in particular that of '*act*', but only inasmuch as this terms includes 'omission' (Article 1.301). A definition is given of '*promise*', but only in the sense that 'A promise which is intended to be legally binding without acceptance is binding' (Article 2.107).

The definition of 'contract' is therefore left to interpretation.

The '*commentary*'[38] specifies that the notion of contract utilized in the Principles includes agreements through which two or more parties undertake an obligation to perform (a certain task), agreements in which the offeree accepts the offer by performing the act or tolerating the act which the offeror desires to be performed, agreements in which only one party assumes obligations and his promise requires acceptance on the part of the offeree, promises in which the party legally bound does not require acceptance of the other party (ex Article 2.107).

The omission of the definition contained in Article 1321 of the Italian Civil Code does not create particular problems, in so far as Article 2.101 does not exclude the possibility that the contract may be intended not only to create obligations, but also to transfer property. It will be necessary to verify the text which will be prepared by the Commission currently working on the project of drafting a 'European Civil Code', chaired by Christian von Bar, on the transfer of property and on the regulation of sales and of the other contracts which transfer property rights, to ascertain the actual extent of the notion of contract. In any case, the fact that a contract may be intended to modify or terminate legal relations is envisaged—in more restricted terms, because reference is made to an already existing contract—in Article 1.107, which sets forth that the Principles are applicable, in so far as they are compatible, to agreements intended to amend or terminate a contract.

The requisites for a contract to be 'deemed to have been concluded' (in accordance with Italian legal categories, we would rather say that the contract was '*valid*' or '*validly concluded*') do not correspond precisely to the requisites envisaged in Article 1321 of the Italian Civil Code; in fact the following are given as conditions: (a) the *intention to be legally bound* and (b) that the parties have reached a *sufficient agreement*. Requirement (a) may be compared to the 'agreement' as per Article 1321, n 1, of the *codice civile* and the requirement (b) may be compared to the 'object' or the 'content' as per n 3; in any case, however, '*causa*' and 'prescribed form' are omitted.

The *commentary* to requirement (a), says that it is not to be read in the subjective or psychological sense of the word, but in the objective sense,

[38] *Principles of European Contract Law* [hereinafter, Principles] above n 1, at 157; about the concept of *contract* see Sacco '*Contract*', in 7, 2 (1999) Eur Rev Priv L 237; Alpa and Delfino, 'Towards a New European Common Law of Contracts', in Gambaro, Rabello (eds) *Towards a New European Ius Commune* (Jerusalem) 5759–1999.

that is in the reliance created in the co-contracting party. The meaning is inferred from the specification set forth in Article 2.102, which refers—among the criteria to ascertain the intention to be legally bound—to the statements of the party whose intention is to be ascertained, and that party's conduct, as both were reasonably understood by the other party.[39] A promise which creates reliance is binding also in the Italian legal system, therefore there is no incompatibility with the Principles.

Requirement (b) is spelled out in Article 2.103, to the effect that the content must be sufficiently defined between the parties for the contract to be enforceable, or must be capable of being determined under the Principles. Two problems are therefore solved in one requirement whereas these two problems are distinct in our own experience: the so-called 'completeness' (or sufficiency) of agreement, and the determination or determinability of the object of the contract. The formula utilized is not in contrast with the solutions adopted by Italian courts and legal scholars: to take some examples, we come across the same problem when contract is agreed through a long proceeding of negotiations, when a draft of the text already keeps the essential elements and so can be considered 'binding', when the parties leave aside and postpone the solution of marginal questions, considering the agreement already complete and binding with regard to the progressive formation of contract, the contract draft and the definition of the essential elements of agreement. What appears useful is paragraph 2 of Article 2.103, which sets forth that if one of the parties refuses to conclude a contract unless agreement is reached with the other party on a specific matter, there is no contract, unless it is ascertained that agreement had actually been reached on that specific matter. The impact of such a refusal, however, is tempered by the evaluation of the conclusion of '*in idem*' agreement; and in any case, it must be unequivocally clear which was the item deemed to be essential by one party, a sort of 'element', so vital as to exclude that party's intention to create legal relations, and to exclude the possibility that the other party could rely on agreement having been reached.

The Principles lay down no requirement of form, but rather adhere to the principle of freedom of form. The omission of any requirement as to form is justified by paragraph 2 of Article 2.101, but this principle contrasts with the legal form required for conventions contracts, by the Italian Civil Code or by special laws. We may wonder, furthermore, whether the conventional form of the Italian Civil Code, that is, the form not requested by the civil code, but chosen and agreed by parties is compliance with Article 2.101. Nevertheless, given that Article 2.101 does not claim to be 'mandatory' and given that in the '*commentary*' to Article 1.103, Article 2.101 is not quoted

[39] *Principles* 143.

among the 'mandatory' principles, we may assume that the conventional form is accepted by the Principles.

As to the legal form requested by law, the matter is different. The same Article 1.103 does not seem to give effect to rules of form which are imperative under national laws when the parties have decided to apply the Principles, unless the same norms are mandatory under the principles of international private law.

5.2.2. *Formation of a contract and representation*

We have been speaking about the essential elements of agreement. The rules governing the formation (or conclusion) of a contract (Article 2.201 et seq) are quite similar to those contained in the Italian Civil Code (Article 1327 et seq).

As regards proof of contract, we note some friction with the provisions of the Italian Civil Code (Article 2721), given that Article 2.101, paragraph 2, second part, also accepts proof by witnesses. This rule of our Civil Code is deemed to be mandatory when the contract must be in written form 'ad substantiam', in the event of riders and added clauses and when one party is opposed to the testimonial evidence requested by the other party. There are, however, exceptions regarding the events listed in Article 2724 and in particular statement of will, promises to pay, acknowledgments of debt, and the reasoning for the interpretation of a contract.

Another new concept envisaged by Principles, is found in Article 2.104, which refers to terms 'not individually negotiated'. These are binding only if the party invoking them reasonably brought them to the attention of the other party, either previously or during the conclusion of the contract.[40] These requirements are not fulfilled by a party making a mere reference to these terms in a contract document, even if the document is signed by the other party. The *commentary* refers to two instances: to the distinction between 'express' and 'implied terms', which are a feature of common law and to the terms prepared by one of the parties. The first distinction, it is unheard of in our own experience for the contents of an agreement to be distinguished and divided into 'express' and 'implied' term. Interpretation of the contract may go beyond the actual wording employed by the parties, and the judge may establish the circumstances common to the parties in order to understand their pre-supposition, etc. We shall return to this later on. As to the second instance, this is envisaged for terms prepared and printed by one party and submitted to the other party, but the Italian Civil Code is more liberal in this regard, because it deems such terms effective if they could be understandable in accordance with ordinary diligence. The

[40] *Principles* 149 ff.

party invoking them need not have taken particular steps to bring them to the attention of the other party. The two positions coincide when the signing of the terms by and of itself is deemed to be equal to knowledge of the same, provided that (as regards the Principles) the signing is separate and refers to a document and not the same contract text and (as regards the Italian Civil Code) the terms are not unfair, because in this case the terms must be underwritten, ie formally signed separately (Articles 1341 and 1342); also in this case, a separate underwriting is effective.

Two references are conspicuous in this provision of the Principles. Reference is made to the EC Directive on Unfair Terms in Consumer Contracts (EC dir N 93/13)—even if there is no mention here of the unfairness of the terms—and a reference is also made to contractual good faith, which forbids one party from taking advantage of the inattentiveness of the other. The *commentary* adds that either party can exclude an obligation to disclose information through the terms of the offer or by other means. The other party, however, before or during the conclusion of a contract, may renounce its right to such disclosure. However, usages are still binding and these may exclude an obligation of disclosure (Article 1.105).

The expression 'terms individually negotiated' carries with it the problems which arose in the application of Directive no 13 of 1993. 'Negotiation', according to the Directive, means either a proceeding toward an agreement, a choice among different opportunities offered by one party to the other, etc. But the meaning of this expression involves a sort of vagueness which has to be restricted. As regards the procedures of negotiation, the drafting of terms negotiated separately and subsequently to printed clauses, the printing of alternative terms, with a restricted choice offered to the consumer alone, etc.

Another new concept is introduced in the provisions on the so-called 'merger clause' (Article 2.105). These are regulated in analytical terms in the principles, while, in our own Code, an added clause is deemed to prevail on a printed clause only in respect of contracts concluded by means of forms or printed texts (Article 1342). We should, however, note that in practice, especially as regards contracts concluded between businessmen, it is customary to find a clause that binds the parties only to what has been expressly agreed by them in the contract text. The 'merger clause' is, however, attenuated by Article 2.106, which refers to the presumption that the contract cannot be amended or terminated except in writing and also refers to precluding the use of a merger clause when one party has reasonably relied upon certain statements or conduct by the other party.

As regards the rules relating to the conditions for the formation of a contract (Article 2.101 et seq) we may say that they are substantially similar to the provisions of the Italian Civil Code (Article 1326 et seq).

Also as regards the rules on dealings there are, with the exception of a few minor details, no great differences compared to the same provisions of the Italian Civil Code, as enhanced by various court rulings (Article 2.301 PECL, Article 1337 It Civ Code). We should note, however, that the principles contains a rule on breach of confidentiality that corresponds to clauses habitually inserted in commercial agreements (Article 2.302).

The same applies to the authority of agents (Article 3.101) and to contracts concluded on behalf of an unidentified principal (Article 3.203).

5.2.3. Validity

As to validity, the Principles do not deal—for the time being—with the problems relating to unlawfulness, immorality, and legal incapacity of the parties, which are left to further investigation to determine whether it is feasible to draft European principles on these subjects.

It is interesting to note that initial impossibility (Article 4.102) does not render a contract invalid, but the parties may avoid the contract if, after it was concluded, performance becomes impossible. According to Italian legal scholarship and jurisprudence, on the contrary, the impossibility of the object of a contract, which renders a contract invalid, arises when performance cannot be objectively carried out due to hindrance '*ab origine*' of a material or legal nature which totally impedes the result which said performance aims to achieve.[41] By the same token, an impossible condition, if it is a condition precedent, renders the contract void (Article 1354).

There is a difference in wording between the English and the French versions of the Principles as regards invalidity. On the subject of mistake, the English version utilizes a formula which is akin to avoidance, in as much as Article 4.103 (1) sets forth that: 'a party may avoid a contract for mistake . . ., while the French version uses an expression which is close to invalidity' ('*la nullité du contrat pour un erreur* . . .'). Bearing in mind the 'possibility' of voiding the contract, it appears more appropriate to the Italian view to refer to this category as one of voidability.

As regards the regulation of mistake, particular note is to be taken of Article 4.103 (2) which does not consider an 'inexcusable' mistake to be fundamental, such as to render the contract void.

The *commentary* specifies that a party cannot burden the other with the risk deriving from the consequences of the first party's negligence and that the a party must not bear the burden of checking if the other party has committed any mistakes due to its negligence.[42]

The fundamental concept of the Italian Civil Code of 1942 changes the former solution provided by the Italian Civil Code of 1865, tailored on the Code Napoléon, and as opposed to the actual will of the parties, and there-

[41] Cass (1987) n 6362. [42] *Principles* 241 ff.

fore on the so-called theory of reliance. Hence our law requires that a mistake, in order to render the contract invalid should be (not only fundamental, but also) recognizable. A mistake must be obvious, and it 'must be such as to appear evident to a person using normal diligence and without requiring greater inquiries than those which that person would normally carry out to ascertain the other party's will. It therefore follows that excusability changes its impact and is transferred from the subject making the vitiated representation or statement to the recipient of the same; the object also changes, because reference is no longer made to the formation of the mistake, but to the failure of its discovery'.[43] In our system, therefore, an excusable mistake of one party, by itself, is not relevant unless it is recognizable by the other party and the feature of excusability is absorbed by that of recognizability. However, as appears from the text of the Principles, the purpose is similar to that pursued by the Italian Civil Code, in the sense that it is not allowed to burden the other party with a negligent behaviour attributable to the party who is mistaken.

The Principles do not deal separately with contracts entered into under duress or in a state of need (or economic duress) which are features assumed in the Italian Civil Code to lead to the rescission of a contract (Articles 1447–1452). However, Article 4.109 refers to somewhat similar assumptions in rules dealing with 'excessive benefit' ('*a profit excessif*') and unfair advantage ('*avantage déloyal*'). The circumstances referred to in Article 4.109 regard a state of dependency, a relationship of trust with the other party, economic distress, a state of need ('urgent needs'), of improvident behaviour, ignorance, inexperience or absence of bargaining skills by one party *vis-à-vis* the other party. For these circumstances to render a contract voidable, they must have been known to the other party, or the other party ought to have known of them, and must have taken advantage of the situation in a way that was grossly unfair or reaped an excessive benefit.

The Italian Civil Code requires that, in a contract entered into under duress, the contract conditions must be unfair; in the event of '*laesio enormis*', it requires the other party to have taken advantage of the situation. In any case these conditions are far more restrictive.

The consequences are, however, quite different. Under the Principles a court may—upon the request of the party entitled to avoidance—proceed to adapt the contract and to amend it, so as to bring it into accordance '*ab origine*' with the requirements of good faith and fair dealing. It may intervene upon the request of the party receiving the unfair advantage if the latter offers to amend the contract and the party entitled to avoidance has not yet acted upon its entitlement.

[43] Relazione al Re, n 119.

In the Italian Civil Code some of these assumptions give rise to the possibility of rescission. As regards a contract under duress, however, no contractual amendment is allowed. The contract is rescinded, and the party receiving an unfair advantage may receive fair compensation for its performance. As regards a state of necessity or economic duress, adaptation of the contract in accordance with notions of fairness may only be effected upon the request of the party receiving an unfair advantage.

A totally innovative concept is expressed in Article 4.110, which brings into the fold of the general rules the regulation of unfair terms contained in consumer contract. Here it is envisaged that a term which has not been individually negotiated, which is contrary to the requirements of good faith and fair dealing, may cause a significant imbalance in the rights and obligations of the parties arising under the contract. In this event the term (and that term alone) may be avoided.

However, the *commentary* to this provision underlined that the authors have chosen not to provide a list of unfair terms and that judicial control may extend to query the '*iustum pretium*'. It is further noted that this particular section, though similar to the previous section dealing with excessive benefit or unfair advantage, differs because the former concerns an unfair advantage which was obtained as a result of the personal situation of the party entitled to avoidance, whilst the latter merely concerns the drafting of a contract prepared by the party receiving the unfair advantage.

From our point of view, we believe the provisions of Article 4.115, which concern the effect of avoidance or, in other words restitution, is quite useful. I use the term 'useful' because the Italian Civil Code does not specifically deal with this issue. This issue falls within the scope of actions for money had and received and of unjustified enrichment, which are regulated under quite general provisions (Articles 2033 and ff, Articles 2041, and 2042). In addition to the remedy of avoidance, the Principles envisage bringing about restitution through damages. Even this provision (Article 4.117) appears quite useful, because the application of our Article 1338 is not always self-evident.

It is not, in any case, an alternative remedy, but an integrating remedy, while alternative remedies to those envisaged for avoidance of a contract are those afforded to a party for non-performance by the other party (Article 4.119). This rule too appears useful. It is not envisaged in our own Code, which distinctly separates the two types of remedies, the former concerning only the circumstances which influence the formation of contract and the latter the circumstances which influence the performance of the same. It is obvious that in litigation, a party may pursue either of these remedies, but these are alternatives, therefore the latter must (logically) be subordinate to the former.

5.2.4. *Interpretation, contents, effects*

There are no particular problems posed by the provisions of chapter 5 of the principles on the interpretation of contracts (Article 5.101 et seq, which are substantially similar or akin to those of our own legal system (Article 1362 et seq), nor any problems with the rules governing contracts for the benefit of third parties (Article 6.110, Article 1411, Italian Civil Code). Nevertheless, three principles contained in chapter 6 on the contents and effects of contracts bear interesting innovations: Article 6.102 on implied obligations or terms ('implied terms', '*obligations implicites*'); Article 6.103 on 'simulation'; Article 6.111 on the 'change of circumstances' ('*changement des circonstances*').

Article 6.102—without defining 'implied' terms—lists the sources from which they stem, that is, the intention of the parties, the nature and purpose of the contract, good faith, and fair dealing.

These are sources of gap-filling of a contract which, in our own Code, are listed as the law, usages and '*aequitas*'. Whilst good faith and fair dealing, as per Article 6.102, may be comprised within the scope of the 'law', the nature and purpose of the contract may—by extension—be comprised within usages. The distinction between 'contract' and contractual terms is as a whole and contractual terms as single provisions included in the contract conceptually alien to the principles, but the distinction may be clarified taking in account the other rules of the principles.

In the *commentary*,[44] one is given to understand that the purpose of Article 6.102 is to fill in the 'gaps' of the contract which cannot be resolved by means of interpretation or by means of other principles, such as those relating to price (Article 6.104), to the quality of performance (Article 6. 108), to the fixing of a term by a third party, by a court (Articles 6.105, 6.106, 6.107) or by means of usages and practices (Article 1.105). When the other integrating sources are not sufficient, a court may 'fill in the gaps in an appropriate manner'. In order to limit any abuse on the part of the interpreter, Article 6.102 recalls three specific sources, that is the intention of the parties, the nature and purpose of the contract, good faith and fair dealing. In the view of the author, this provision should satisfy both the English lawyers, who reason on the basis of the distinction between terms implied by fact and terms implied by law and the French lawyers, who distinguish between '*obligations de résultat*' and '*obligations de moyens*'.

By comparison with the Italian experience, the integrating sources would be considerably extended. However, we should recall in this respect, the very extensive court rulings which have derived from the principle of good

[44] *Principles* 302 ff.

faith obligations of protection and obligations of other kinds complementary to those expressly envisaged by the parties.

Article 6.103 very succinctly provides that the 'covert act' or 'true agreement' shall prevail over the 'apparent contract'.

The *commentary*[45] is far more explanatory, indicating that the adopted formula brings together both absolute and relative simulations and identifies the secret contract with the counter-declaration ('*contre-lettre*'), as well as the false heading, which in turn recalls the regulation of misrepresentation as regards authority (Article 3.301). The secret act must satisfy the requirements of validity, and it is admitted as an expression of the free will of the parties. Moreover, the ostensible contract is not by and of itself considered void, unless it is illegal or pursues a fraudulent purpose. One party cannot use the ostensible contract as a defence to its obligations under the true or covert contract. The effects of ostensible contracts *vis-à-vis* third parties are left to the individual national regulations.

Article 6.111 deals with change of circumstances. The assumptions dealt with here come close to a form of supervening unconscionability which, in accordance with our own system is cause for termination of a contract (Article 1467 et seq It Civ Code). However, the consequences envisaged by the Italian legal system are different: the Italian courts have no power to interfere with the allocation of risks or with the advantages and disadvantages stipulated in the contract, since only the party to whom notice of termination has been served can avoid the termination by offering to amend in fair way the terms of the contract (Article 1467 c. 3).

Under the Principles, however, two devices are designed to bring the contract back within the realm of '*aequitas*' without necessarily resorting to termination: first, an obligation to re-negotiate the terms (Article 6.111 (2)) and failing which, secondly, an intervention by the court which, at its own choice, may terminate the contract or amend it in a just and reasonable manner to distribute losses and gains caused by the change of circumstances (6.111 (3) (a) (b)).

If either party refuses to negotiate or breaks off negotiations contrary to good faith, the court may award damages against that party.

Renegotiation by the parties and judicial amendment of the contract may take place upon three conditions: that the change of circumstances occurred after the conclusion of the contract, that the change of circumstances could not reasonably have been taken into account at the time of conclusion of the contract or that the party affected was not required to bear the risk of the change of circumstances (Article 6.111 (2) (a) (b) (c)).

These operating conditions do not diverge from the provisions of the Italian Civil Code, but the courts have allowed in the theory of pre-

[45] Principles 306.

supposition (deriving it from the German '*Geschaeftsgrundlage*'). According to the theory of pre-supposition, as interpreted, reference is made to objective good faith and to the type of contract employed by the parties. If it is ascertained that the parties at the time of formation took into account (even without any express reference in the text) a certain situation in fact or at law and considered the same as a requirement of the contract, then the disappearance of this essential element would assume relevance for the contract itself, provided the requirement is objective, external, common to both parties, and does not depend upon their wills.[46] It is possible that the failure of pre-supposition was '*ab origine*', and not only supervening, but in that case under Italian law we would be back in the domain of lack of '*causa*'.

The obligation to renegotiate is often provided for in the wording of the contract and such clauses are common practice in the drafting of international commercial contracts. The judicial adaptation of the contract to changed circumstances is advocated by the most recent scholarship, but the idea is still resisted by the courts and the more traditional authors.

Another rule which is in contrast with our own system concerns early performance ('*execution anticipée*') (Article 7.103). The Principles provide that a party may decline a tender of performance made before it is due, except where acceptance of the tender would not unreasonably prejudice its interest. Such prejudice being absent, a refusal to accept early performance would be in effect, abusive.

Execution, non-performance, and compensation for damages set forth rules which are not in contrast with the Code's regulations and we will be able to devote greater attention to the same in the subsequent analyses.

5.2.5. *Conclusions*

In brief, what is the significance of the Principles?

In addition to the more obvious models, which we find both in the Vienna Convention on the Sale of Goods of 1980 and in Unidroit Principles on International Commercial Contracts of 1994, we can easily see in many of the provisions the consolidated or recent trends of the different areas which make up the varied range of the continental systems and that of English common law.

Though frequent reference is made to the intention of the parties, a contract is considered objectively. It is obvious that the authors seek to save the economic transaction through the intervention of the courts. Furthermore it is self-evident, that there is the intent to 'clean up' contractual behaviour through frequent references to good faith and fair dealing

[46] Cass (1995) n 5460.

and with remedies aimed at suppressing the abuse of bargaining power. The contract's function prevails on the will of the parties. The contractual balance is not intangible, when extraordinary and unforeseeable external circumstances or serious imbalances '*ab origine*' place the parties in a substantially different position. The court's intervention, aimed at 're-writing' the contract in lieu of the parties signals the inexorable decline of the 'sanctity of contract'.

Certain devices and aspects which are found in the Italian Civil Code have not been included in the Principles. The omissions cover not only all the general regulation of obligations, which the Steering Committee may in part rectify in future drafting, but also the regulation of '*causa*', although in part covered in the regulation of the subject matter of the contract and contractual remedies, the 'purpose of the contract', the problems relating to the type of contract (often referred to under the 'nature of the contract'), preliminary contracts, conditions, withdrawal and repudiation, the regulation of contracts for the transfer of property and of real contracts, assignment of contracts, and consumer contracts (even if left to the enforcement of EC Directives on the subject matter).

For the aspects—and there are many—which are inspired by the Vienna Convention and the Unidroit Principles, we may envisage that the application of the Principles will be met with the same favour that greeted these two texts.

But what is worth noticing, is that many of the principles accepted in international commercial contracts, adequate for economic transactions between parties having the same status and operating in a business environment, may be activated also in the sector of relationships between parties who do not carry out a professional economic activity. The Principles are devoid of any social inspiration but reasonableness, good faith and fair dealing and, where these are appealed to, the amendment by way of '*aequitas*' of the contractual terms may replace, at least in part, the 'neutral' concept of contract accepted here.

5.3. THE CONSTRUCTION OF A EUROPEAN SUBSTANTIVE LAW AND THE EDUCATION OF JUDGES

5.3.1. Some preliminary remarks

I would like to express some simple thoughts about the education of the Italian jurist, then about the formation of the Italian judge, and open a short discussion on how the present situation could afford a useful contribution to the achievement of a European legal culture as the necessary basis for the foundation of a European unified substantive law. But the time has already come for thinking of a European and interactive adjudication.[47] For the time being we still need the use of different technical words, while common law scholars try to bridge legal cultures[48] and continental scholars go in quest of a common legal language.[49]

So, in talking about the education of judges in the Italian legal system, it is useful to express some preliminary remarks concerning the words we use. For example, the word 'judge' immediately evokes, from a continental perspective, a *civil servant*, a functionary. Owing to the needs of the administration of justice (or as now we are invited to say, following the EU terminology, the administration of judicial services) in Italy there are persons who actually work *as judges* solving cases of lower economic value (*giudici di pace*) lawyers who work as *honorary judges* (*giudici onorari*), or lawyers who are appointed to become judges of the Supreme Court of Cassazione. Currently speaking, a judge in a proper and ordinary way, is a person who has been admitted to the judiciary trough a nationwide examination.

A judicial career is one of the several possibilities open to a student graduating from a university law school. One of the most appreciated American teachers of comparative law, John Merryman, comparing the different judicial worlds of continental Europe, the UK, and the USA, looked at this situation saying:

> shortly after graduation, if he (the person who want to become judge) wishes to follow a judicial career, he will take a state examination for aspirants to the judiciary and, if successful, will be appointed as a junior judge . . . Before very long, he will actually be sitting as a judge somewhere low in the hierarchy of courts. In time, he will rise in the judiciary at a rate dependent on some combination of demonstrated ability and seniority. He will receive salary increases according to preestablished schedules and will belong to an organization of judges that has improvement of judicial salaries, working conditions, and tenure as a principal objective.[50]

Thus, the education of persons who want to have access to a judicial career begins in law school. History explains the reasons of this postulate. Coping with the needs of centralization of administration services and the needs of public administration of justice, the French Revolution and then the Napoleonic Empire draw a sharp separation from the past, created law schools and the basis of the legal education, common to lawyers, judges,

[47] Joerges 'Interactive adjudication in the Eurpeanisation process? A demanding perspective and a modest example' in 8 (2000) Eur Rev of Priv Law, 1 and Feiden, '*Europeanisation of European law adjudication—a comment*', ivi, 17.

[48] Markesinis 'Bridging legal cultures' in *Foreign Law and Comparative Methodology* (Oxford 1997) 194.

[49] Markesinis '*Learning from and learning in Europe*', ivi, 169; Campana '*Vers un langage juridique commun en Europe?*', in (2000) Eur Rev of Priv L, 8, 33; Urban '*On legal language and the maintenance of cultural and linguistic diversity?*', ivi, 51.

[50] *The Civil Law Tradition* (2nd edn Stanford 1985) 35.

and notaries.[51] The French model has been expanded in European continental countries and is still in force. So the legal education of continental judges still begins with law school. Different historical factors have influenced the legal education of common lawyers in the UK and the USA.[52]

At the time being, our situation is under a process of reforming the education provided by Universities (L 19 November 1990, n 341, L 15 May 1997, n 127, L 14 January 1999, n 4). The educational career is divided into three levels: the first level, concerning basic education, lasting three years with a certificate (DL, *diploma di laurea*); the second level, lasting two and ending with a certificate (DD, *diploma di dottorato*); a further two levels are considered (DS, *diploma di specializzazione* and DR, *diploma di dottorato di ricerca*); DS will be commented on below; DR concerns only those who want to pursue an academic career.

But for the exceptions mentioned before, in order to participate in the state examination, a person who wants to have access to the judiciary must have a DD certificate, and since 2001, must have taken a DS or other legally recognized professional certificate. Each state law school is requested to apply these rules, so in a short period of time (since 2001), teaching programmes will be divided in two levels (DL plus DD).

Until the 1990s the educational system was governed by statutes affording a centralized order: the state approved each programme submitted by faculties and a certain uniformity was the basis of legal education; after the enactment of new rules (L 19 November 1990, n 341, Article 11) each university was given an autonomous power to draft its own regulation, under the approval of the Minister for the University and Scientific Research, and the opinion of the Nation University Council (CUN). Notwithstanding the wide autonomy given to each university (and than to each law school, which is a *facoltà* belonging to a university) the programmes are very similar because a common cultural basis is considered the only way to assure a professional skill for all the students.

In the first triennium students are requested to learn the main subjects related to civil and public law. This means that they will study elements of 'legal techniques', such as private law, civil law, commercial law, civil procedure law; for the public section, constitutional, administrative, international, criminal law, and criminal procedure.

Here we find one of the main differences between the continental and the common law world: in continental Europe law schools are not only set up

[51] Carbonneau (ed) *The French Legal Studies Curriculum: Its History and Relevance as a Model for Reform*, in *Civil Law* (Rogowski Dartmouth 1996) 139 ff.

[52] Atiyah and Summers *Form and Substance in Anglo-American Law* (Oxford 1987) 384; Wilson, 'A survey of legal education in the United Kingdom' (1966) IX Journal of the SPTL 1.

for students/graduates who want to become *professionals*. The degrees 'grant access to jobs that are steppingstones to executive positions in industry and to the higher reaches of the civil service'.[53] Then, this first triennium is not shaped to educate only those who (taken the DD) will have access to legal professions: the new DL is the minimum required to become civil servants, consultants, private employees in banks and insurance companies, corporations, and so on. So classes concern also subject matters which have a different aim, eminently a cultural and formative one: the achievement of a method of reasoning, through classes on general theory of law and jurisprudence; the achievement of a historical background to understand the roots of our legal system and public institutions, through classes on Roman and Medieval Law; the connections between law and economics, sociology, anthropology, and so on.

A special focus is now given to EC law and comparative law, because to become a true European citizen one has to understand and know the European legal system and topics of the different legal systems still in force in Member States. English 'common law' is one of the preferred subjects of our comparative law classes, and we teach to our students mainly substantial law (contracts, torts, 'property'), the theory of precedent, inductive reasoning, and so on.

Also if programmes are devoted to shape the existing law and to discuss programmes of reform and of adjusting our system to the needs of a European common market (and may be, of a European unified or federated political entity), the method of teaching is the traditional one, coping technicalities with the element of the *science of law*. As to the way of teaching and learning, 'examinations are based on assigned textbooks . . . The texts and lectures are concerned largely with the explanation and classification of definitions and concepts': legal education means 'the inculcation of fundamental concepts and principles . . .; law is taught as a science'.[54]

In other (and simple) words, our method of learning and teaching law is highly theoretical. The basic notions—reviewed and adapted to the present needs—are still coming from the legal science rooted in Italy at the end of last century, in which the exegetical way of commenting written texts (the codes and the statutes) has been combined with the geometric structure of logic applied by German Pandectists. For example, we still use the notion of *juristic act* (*negozio giuridico*), of *legal capacity*, the institutes inherited by the Roman law mainly in the fields of property and successions and so on. But the prominent needs of the corporate economy lead to a more practical and efficient perspective: 'private law' actually means a body of rules devoted to business. We are so open to the foreign practice of contracts that

[53] Cappelletti, Merryman and Perillo *The Italian Legal System* (Stanford 1967) 90.
[54] Ibid 89.

we use the original English terms of 'new contracts', such as leasing, engineering, joint venture, merchandising, etc; we set great store by the most important reforms enacted in more developed countries concerning financial services, insurance and banking law, and even international commercial practice.

Case law has a special consideration in all classes: case law is now considered one of the most important sources of law, and the commentary of 'precedents', introducing judicial rules to fill the *lacunae* of the Civil Code, or introducing more detailed and specified rules of the Civil Code, is part of every programme of teaching. Many new legal positions (rights and protected interests) are created by judge-made law, mainly in the fields of privacy and tort law.[55]

Looking at the EC law, at the international principles of commercial law, at the needs of international exchanges, we assist at the foundation of 'a common core' of contract law, and even of tort law.[56]

At the second level we find the most technical subjects which are treated in the same way for all who will have access to legal professions. At this level the legal education is more detailed and is particularly devoted to deep understanding of substantial and procedural law. The use of informatics and informatics applied to law are now new, expanding methods of learning and teaching. Case law concerning the decisions of our supreme courts (Corte Costituzionale, Corte di Cassazione, Consiglio di Stato, Corte dei Conti) are all collected by databanks, available to students, teachers, practitioners. Many of the most important decisions of lower courts are collected as well. The use of databanks is so wide that it seems that also the style of writing papers, defences, and even decisions is affected by the new technologies, either in the content or in the literary form.

5.3.2. The schools of education for the legal professions and the State examination

Until today, the postgraduate education was left to personal free choices: a law graduate who wanted to become a judge had to study at home, or in a library provided with books of law and prepare the subject matters of the state examination; the same applied to a person who wanted to become a lawyer (who was requested to practice for two years in a legal firm) or a notary (who was requested to practice for two years in a firm of notaries). Better than an individual self-education, the Parliament and the legal community has chosen a compelling state education in order to follow the

55 Alpa 'The protection of privacy in Italian law', in Markesinis (ed) *Protecting Privacy* (Oxford 1999) 105.

56 Ibid 'The accordance and unification of contract law', in *Italian National Reports to the XVth International Congress of Comparative Law* (Bristol 1998) II.A.2., 360.

cultural proceeding from the beginning and control the attitudes to understand, to reason, to write, to behave, and to work as a legal professional.

(a) New statutes (L 19 November 1990, n 341; L 15 May 1997, n. 127; L 14 January 1999, n 44 and subs decrees) have enacted rules concerning the education needed for the access to legal professions after graduation (after level 2, DD). Two different kinds of 'schools' are envisaged:
   (i) the so called 'schools for the common legal education' (*scuole di specializzazione per le professioni legali*), which are reserved to those who want to become lawyers, judges and notaries; and are runned by Law Faculties, and require an exam to be admitted in a close number; and
   (ii) the so-called 'professional schools' (*scuole professionali*), which are parallel schools organized by the professional bodies of lawyers and notaries (dpr 10 April 1990, n 101) and open to those who did not choose the first rute or were not admitted.

   As to the first schools, the legal education is organized by public universities; the attendance is not open, because the access is limited in number (up to 3000 students, more or less) and an exam has to be taken prior to becoming enrolled; as to the others, they will be organized by professional bodies; lawyers are educated and trained by schools in which university teachers and lawyers are part of the teaching body. The number of students approximately will be 27,000.

   Both programmes last two years, but the first will be mainly rooted on a theoretical basis, the second being rooted on a practical basis.

   The state exams to become a judge or to be allowed to practice are different: the first is based on a closed number, the second on an open number.

   Both schools will afford classes on the main subjects of private and public law, with a special focus on case law and writing legal documents and papers.

   Universities play a relevant role in both type of schools and professors are appointed as teachers along with judges, lawyers, notaries.

(b) In order to acquire the first level of the judicial career (*uditore giudiziario*), and to be admitted to the state examination, according to the statute concerning the judiciary (rd 30 January 1941, n 12 and subs modifications) a person provided by a DD and a certificate given by a '*scuola di formazione comune*' has to pass many examinations:
   (i) a preliminary proof, concerning cultural legal subjects; questions are organized through forms where several answers are offered to the applicant, who has to choose from among them the right one;

(ii) according to the results of the preliminary proof, applicants are ordered in a list, whose number is five times the number of the tenures offered;

(iii) those who are admitted, have to pass a written proof concerning the writing of three papers on civil law, criminal law and administrative law;

(iv) those who acquire a good evaluation (not less than 12/20 grades for each paper) can be admitted to the oral proof, concerning, beside the subject matters already quoted, Roman law, civil and criminal procedure, constitutional law, tax law, labour law, EC law, international law, and informatics applied to law. Only those who have passed the oral proof acquiring not less than 6/10 are appointed as '*uditore giudiziario*'.

The role of universities and of teachers has not been forgotten even at this moment, because applicants are free to work as assistants to teachers, to attend classes, and to do personal research. Teachers are appointed as members of the examining commission.

5.3.3. The continuing teaching and formative programmes for judges

The training of the '*uditori giudiziari*' is governed by a decree (dpr 17 July 1998) which gives this competence to the constitutional body assuring the autonomy of magistrates (*Consiglio superiore della magistratura*, CSM). In every court the training must not last less than 18 months; 13 months are devoted to the ordinary training (*tirocinio ordinario*), and five to the specialized training (*tirocinio mirato*). The first one is devoted to the amelioration of the cultural legal basis and to the introduction into the art of judging, procedural rules, and questions of method; six months concern civil matters, seven months criminal matters. The use of informatics is requested.

The *uditore giudiziario* is evaluated not only as to his or her cultural and technical skill, but also according to his or her personal attitudes (will, good behaviour, independence of judgement) and according to the behaviour towards others (colleagues, lawyers, citizens).

During the last period of apprenticeship the *uditore* begins to learn his or her own task acting as a lateral assistant judge.

During the period of *tirocinio*, the *uditori* are requested to attend special classes of legal education organized by the CSM. But these classes are offered also to those who are already judges and want to update their knowledge.

So, culture and skill in practice, fair and reasonable behaviour, and independent judgment are the main objects of the judicial education:

the principle of separation of powers is pushed toward its logical conclusion: the judiciary is not only a separate but also an autonomous branch of government. Judges are appointed, promoted, and supervised by judges. Moreover, the judicial function is deemed to be fundamentally distinct from advocacy; consequently a judgeship is not the culmination of an advocate's career [but for the exceptions mentioned before] but a post to be earned by apprenticeship within the judiciary.[57]

5.3.4. European law and European common values as the basis of a common legal culture

Coming to the most intriguing question, can we say that domestic programmes regarding legal education of jurists, lawyers, and judges promote the harmonization and unification of European substantive law?

The interpretation and application of EC regulations, EC directives and recommendations, of the decisions rendered by the Court of Justice imply a common core of values, a common understanding of terms, concepts, and ways of reasoning. The fields of law affected by the competence of the EC Treaty are now 'a common law' for Europe. Exchanges made for educational and professional programmes help in building a European legal culture. Most of all, the project of drafting a European set of legal principles tries to 'bridge' the continents and the Member States.[58]

The study of comparative law opens another great door to the circulation of models[59] and assists in building a system in which common and civil law institutes can merge without detriment to the original systems.[60]

A 'Europeanization' of legal culture is not the only means to achieve a common language and common values: freedom of movement, combined with practicing law and with economic exchanges has opened the frontiers of the States and of our cultures. The consitutionalization of human rights common to every Member State has built a general and strong frame of protection for each European citizen.[61] Judges of each Member State are requested to use many rules common to other judges and—in the future—may be they will be asked to apply uniform rules in every field of law.

[57] Cappelletti, Merryman and Perillo, op cit, 102.

[58] Lando 'Optional or mandatory Europeanisation of contract law' in (2000) 8 *Eur Rev of Priv L* 59; see Bar, *The Common European Law of Torts* (Oxford 1998); Hondius, *Towards a European Civil Code* (Nijmegen 1998), 3; Alpa, 'European Community resolutions and the codification of "private law" , in 2 (2000) *Eur Rev of Priv L*, .

[59] Sacco and Gambaro, *Sistemi giuridici comparati*, Torino, 1996.

[60] Markesinis, 'Our Debt to Europe: Past, Present and Future', in Clifford Chance Millennium Lectures, ed by Markesinis (Oxford 2000) *The Coming Together of the Common Law and the Civil Law* 37; see Bar, *A New Jus Commune Europaeum and the Importance of the Common Law*, ivi, 67.

[61] Mirabelli, *Preliminary Reflections on Fundamental Rights as the Basis of a Common European Law*, ivi, 225.

5.3.5. Postscript

The education of those who want to have access to legal professions (judges, lawyers, notaries) is keeping the past, the present, and the future of law: the past, because is saves the roots of the legal knowledge; the present because it improves the acquirement of the technical aspects of the legal science and of legal practice; and the future because is it projected toward the harmonization of substantive and procedural law, through EC law and through the efforts of those who want to realize the dream of a unified Europe under a unified legal system. University professors are requested to work side by side with judges, lawyers, and notaries. The hope is to create a good legal system and a judiciary which is involved in legal education both at academic and professional level. Even differences in recruiting judges, in using different procedural systems, and in writing decisions according to different styles[62] are not insurmountable obstacles. All these aims seem to lead towards a common objective: the construction of a European substantive law, and possibly, a European judiciary.

The path is difficult, and warning against simplistic conclusions is mandatory. I will borrow the words of Lord Bingham, the Senior Law Lord, to conclude this book: 'We are right to continue to worry away at the unnecessary divergences which continue to divide us. But the things which unite us are greater than the things which divide us'.[63]

[62] *Juges et jugements: l'Europe plurielle. L'élabouration de la décision de justice en droit comparé* (Paris 1998).

[63] *A New Common Law for Europe*, ivi, 27.